St. Louis Landmarks and Historic Districts

Wainwright Building

Gary R. Tetley, 1989

i

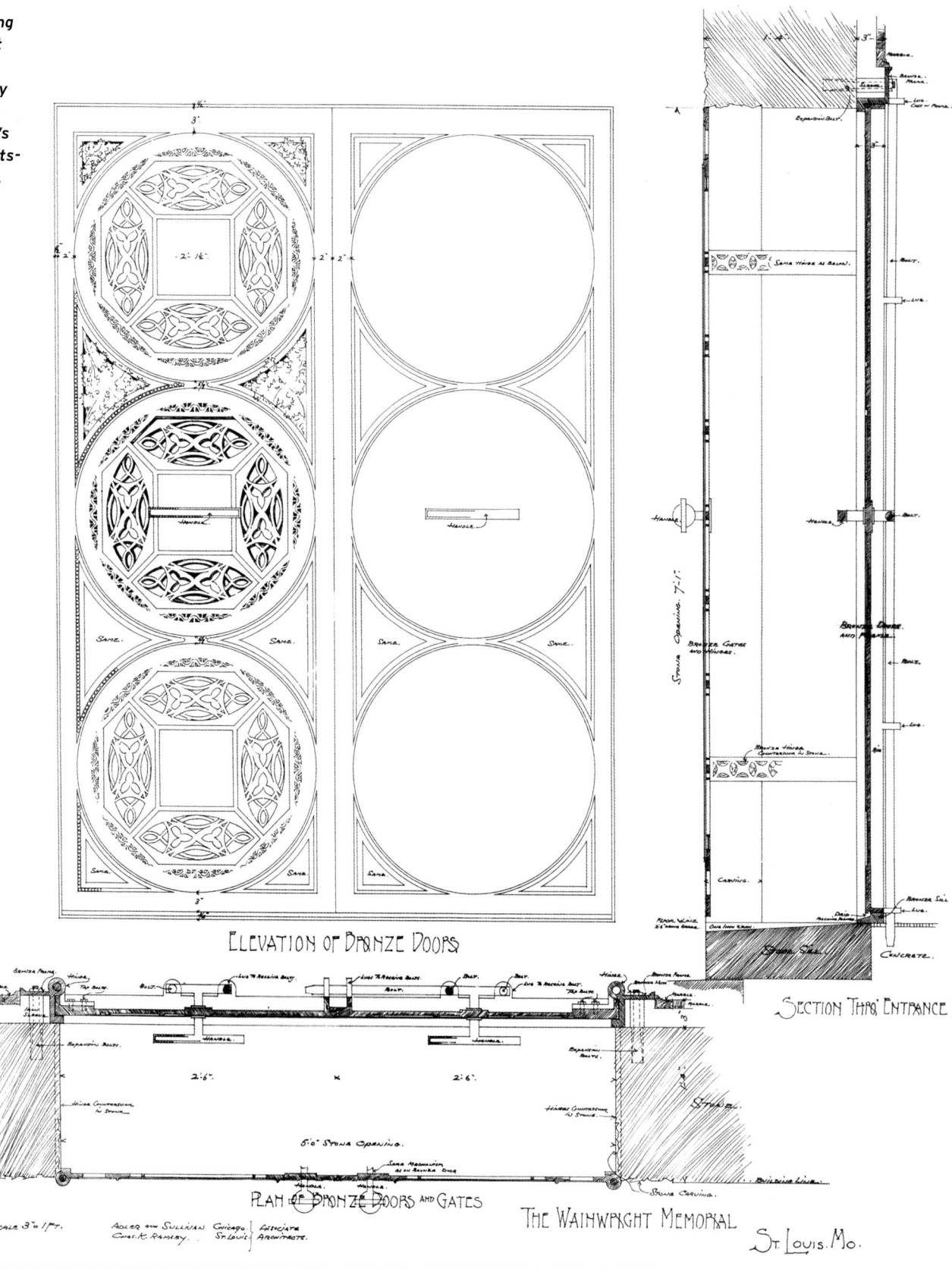

Original drawing for Wainwright Tomb bronze doors, probably executed from Louis Sullivan's design by draftsman Gustav P. Wuest

Landmarks Collection

St. Louis: Landmarks & Historic Districts

by Carolyn Hewes Toft
with Lynn Josse

Lead gifts from
Meade Summers, Jr. Foundation
The Regional Arts Commission

Financial assistance provided by

Anonymous
Jamie and Mary Jo Cannon
Tony and Melanie Fathman
Gary and Gloria Sextro
Dr. Donald M. Suggs
H. Meade Summers, III and Jerome E. Glick
Bill and Gina Wischmeyer
Bricklayer's Union Local No. 1 of Missouri
Commerce Bancshares Foundation
Community Program Development Corporation
Heartland Bank
McCormack Baron & Associates
Donald and Ruth V. Malvern Foundation
Mason Contractors Association (St. Louis)
Masonry Institute St. Louis
Mays-Maune & Associates
Jeffery E. Smith Co.

Book design by
Paradowski Graphic Design

Copyright © 2002
(second printing 2002)
Landmarks Association of St. Louis, Inc.

ISBN: 0-9721131-1-8

This is a guidebook to sites, buildings and districts officially designated by the City of St. Louis or the National Register of Historic Places. Each chapter opens with a map and list of contents by the original name of the property. (Later or current names can be located in the Index.) Where historic districts exist, entries located within district boundaries are arranged alphabetically for the ease of armchair, auto or pedestrian touring.

St. Louis is a city characterized by outstanding historic architecture. Although our guidebook offers an introduction to the topic, many interesting buildings and worthy districts await research and designation. We are greatly indebted to those whose financial assistance has helped make this edition a reality and look forward an expanded publication in the near future.

Acknowledgements

Although this book has drawn on multiple sources, nominations to the National Register of Historic Places prepared by present and former members of Landmarks' staff have been invaluable. Special credit is due Mimi Stiritz, Jane Porter, Cindi Longwisch and Stacy Sone. (Both the authors, especially Lynn Josse, have also written nominations.) Excellent nominations by Karen Bode-Baxter with Tim Maloney, Esley Hamilton, Jan Cameron, Laura Johnson, Bill Seibert and Bonnie Stepenoff have also been consulted. Others who contributed important research during Landmarks' twenty-seven years of National Register work include Jill Johnson, Pat Baer, Marion Piper, Katie Kurtz, Laura Aldenderfer, Deborah Wafer, Maureen Jones, Ilana Feitlowitz, Donna Laidlaw, Janice Broderick, John McClatchey Saunders, Emesee Wood, Duane Sneddeker, Tim Hagen, Aimee Pellet, David Alan Meyer, Nancy Kaiser, Barbara Lang and Bill Neuendorf.

More than one hundred years of guidebooks, planning documents and histories were reviewed. Particularly helpful were *The Building Art in St. Louis: Two Centuries* (1981) by George McCue, McCue's 1988 *Sculpture City: St. Louis* as well as McCue and Frank Peters' 1989 *A Guide to the Architecture of St. Louis*. Also essential to provide breadth were *Lion in the Valley* (1981 and later editions) by James Neal Primm, *Missouri's Black History* published by the University of Missouri Press in 1980 and 1993 and Norbury Wayman's series of neighborhood studies (1978-80) for the Community Development Agency. Publications by the St. Louis City Plan Commission from 1916 into the 1970s provided valuable insight into the changing visions for the city, as did the 1907 plan by the Civic League.

Information about the more prominent architects came from James Cox's *Old and New St. Louis* (1894), Ernest D. Kargau's *Mercantile, Industrial and Professional St. Louis* (c. 1902), John W. Leonard's 1906 and 1912 editions of *The Book of St. Louisans*, John A. Bryan's *Missouri's Contribution to American Architecture* (1928), the 1955 edition of the *American Architects Directory* and the Witheys' 1956 *Biographical Dictionary of American Architects* (Deceased).

Also consulted were exhibition catalogues of the St. Louis Architectural Club and the American Institute of Architects, *The Brickbuilder, The American Architect & Building News, The Inland Architect and News Record, Pencil Points, Northwestern Architect, Architecture & Decoration, The [St. Louis] Realty Record and Builder* and *The Western Architect*. Other information came from newspaper accounts and obituaries in the *St. Louis Globe-Democrat,* the *St. Louis Post-Dispatch,* the *St. Louis Star-Times, The St. Louis American* and the *St. Louis Republic*. Building permits and the *St. Louis Daily Record* were the major sources for dates assigned to buildings. In most cases, dates reflect the year of design rather than completion.

The lexicon of architectural styles is in perpetual revision. A free interpretation of National Register guidelines and Marcus Whiffen's *American Architecture Since 1780: a Guide to the Styles* (1969) has been augmented by more specialized regional studies in the attribution of architectural styles. Contemporary photographs attributed to Landmarks Association were taken by an assortment of staff members; historic photographs in Landmarks' collection have been gleaned from a variety of sources. Most maps and recent line drawings are by Pat Hays Baer.

Gratitude is owed many archival sources and professional photographers whose work enlivens these pages, but it is the images (both black and white and in color) by Sam Fentress, Ken Konchel, Robert C. Pettus, Gary R. Tetley and Jack Zehrt that evoke real-life interactions with St. Louis architecture. Bill Seibert read the manuscript in 2001 and contributed many insights. To John Knoll and Pat Smith, the authors give special thanks for their last minute, keen-eyed reading just before publication. We look forward to a third edition of *St. Louis: Landmarks & Historic Districts* wherein any remaining lapses will be amended.

— *Carolyn Hewes Toft*

Contents

Chapter

1 Central Riverfront 1
2 Central Business District: East 13
3 Central Business District: West 51
4 Midtown 75
5 West End 95
6 Northeast 145
7 Northwest 163
8 Southeast 179
9 Carondelet 201
10 Southwest 213
11 In Memoriam 245
Index 262

Gateway Arch and Busch Stadium under construction, August 1965

Preston Raymond Papin
Landmarks Collection

CHAPTER 1　Central Riverfront

Old Courthouse Dome
Jack Zehrt, 1976

Chapter 1

Central Riverfront

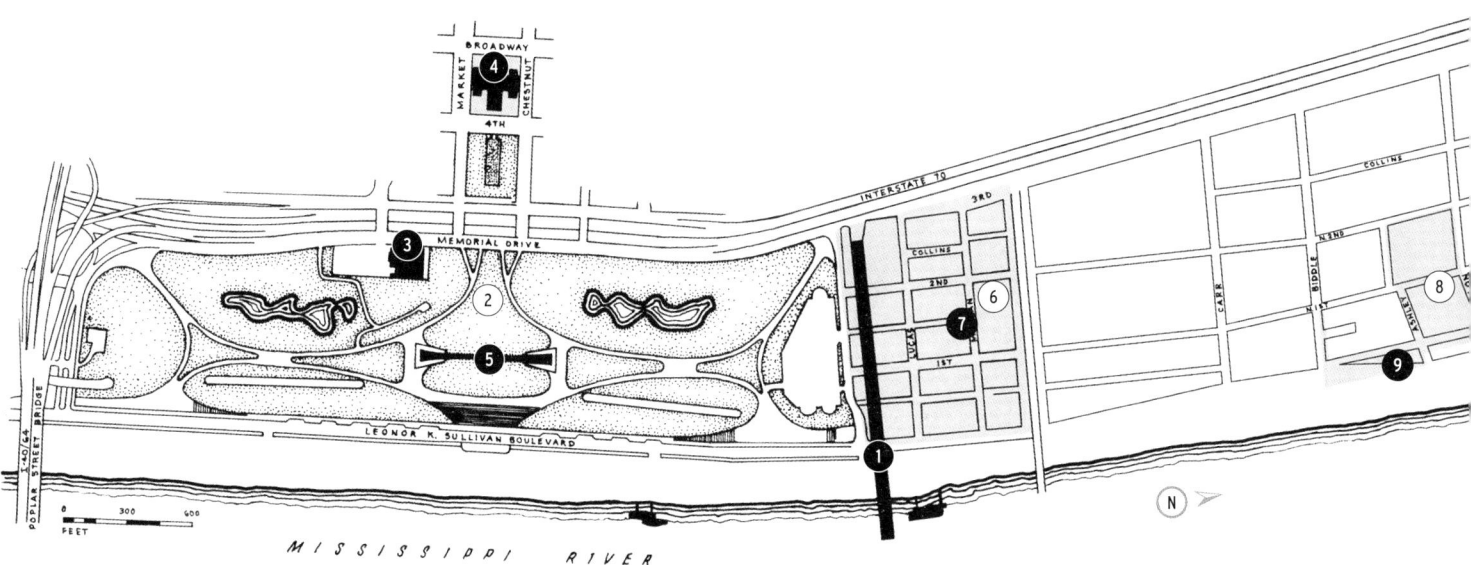

● Single Site ○ District

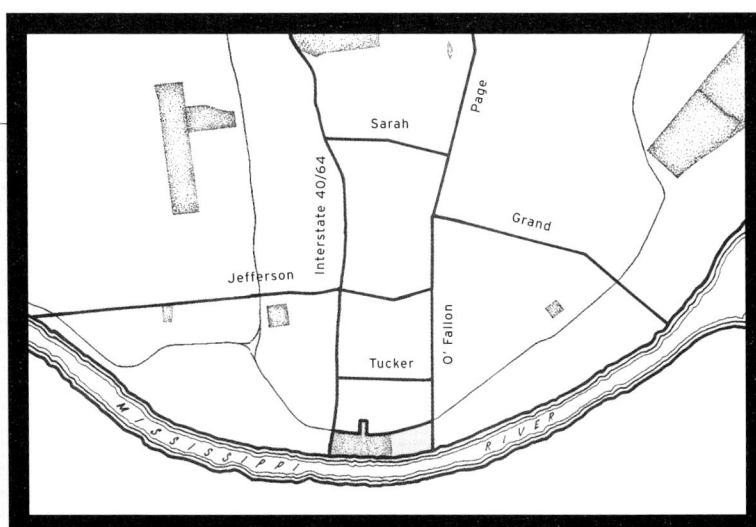

1 Eads Bridge
2 Jefferson National Expansion Site
3 Old Cathedral
4 Old Courthouse
5 Gateway Arch
6 Laclede's Landing District
7 Raeder Place
8 North Riverfront Industrial District
9 Ashley Street Powerhouse

Eads Bridge
Ken Konchel, 1998

1
Eads Bridge
City Landmark: June 1966
National Historic Landmark: October 15, 1966

One of the stars in a heroic age of engineering, Eads Bridge was designed in 1867 by James B. Eads and completed in 1874. Eads, a man of extraordinary enterprise and inventive talent, possessed a thorough knowledge of the river from salvage work. His brilliant solution for the bridge called for three enormous tubular arches carried down to bedrock on massive, granite-faced limestone piers. Working with mathematician William Chauvenet (Chancellor of Washington University) to test stress, Eads substituted chrome steel for traditional cast iron in the tubular arches—an innovation of great importance for later engineering. Colonel Henry Flad of St. Louis provided valuable technical assistance during the construction phase.

Eads was not the first to propose a bridge across the Mississippi at St. Louis; he was, however, the first to gain essential financial support over the entrenched opposition of steamboat and ferry interests. Meanwhile,

Chapter 1   Central Riverfront

Eads Bridge MetroLink Station
Gary R. Tetley, 1993

the Rock Island Line spanned the river at its Illinois namesake in 1855. By 1868, three additional railroad bridges connected Chicago with rich hinterlands to the west. Competition with the aggressive Windy City was all but over. The total cost of Eads Bridge and tunnel approached $12 million, almost 50% over 1867 estimates. One year after the celebratory opening, both the bridge and tunnel corporations were in default. Design changes, inflated land costs, increased wages, escalating bond interest and agents' commissions all contributed to cost escalations. So did "the bends," a tragic effect of long underwater confinement.

Although the bridge was not a financial success, its completion caused a dramatic shift in the physical form of downtown. Passenger and freight transfer operations moved from linear facilities along the levee to new concentrations located near the mouth of the Eads Bridge tunnel at 7th and Clark Streets (see **Cupples Station,** *page 22).* Property values along the river dropped. The almost-deserted levee was ignored as city planners of the 1920s developed visionary schemes to accommodate the automobile. The Depression put an end to any systematic implementation of those dreams; instead, the concept of a national monument took shape. By the time the great Saarinen Arch pictured below got underway in 1963, Eads Bridge was obsolete. Newer (and fewer) trains were too long to complete the curve in the tunnel. In 1974, 100 years after opening day, the last train rumbled across the span.

A swap of Eads Bridge and tunnel for the city-owned MacArthur Bridge downstream was first considered during ambitious transit planning in the late 1920s. Eventually, the germinated idea became part of an ingenious formula providing both route and local match for the MetroLink light rail system. Eads Bridge railroad deck opened to MetroLink transit vehicles in July 1993. After years of delay, the upper deck was scheduled to reopen to pedestrian and auto traffic in 2003.

2
Jefferson National Expansion Site
National Historic Site: October 15, 1966

Early 20th century plans to invigorate the central riverfront focused on attempts to regain lost river trade or create a futuristic system of roadways built over multi-

Model of Jefferson National Expansion Site
Date unknown

decked parking. All envisioned razing existing buildings and the often-seedy businesses they housed. In late 1933, attorney Luther Ely Smith persuaded Mayor Bernard Dickmann to form a committee to lobby for a national memorial to the pioneer settlers of the West and the Louisiana Purchase. The resulting Jefferson National Expansion Memorial Association, organized in St. Louis in 1934, persuaded President Roosevelt to create a federal commission later that year. In 1935, the city passed a $7.5 million bond issue (challenged unsuccessfully as a fraudulent election before the ballots were burned) which in combination with $9 million in federal funds would allow for the acquisition and clearance of everything in 40 city blocks except the **Old Cathedral, Courthouse** (page 6) and Rock House.

By the time Siegfried Giedion's important history of modern architecture was published in 1941, the cast iron structures on St. Louis' riverfront admired by Giedion as equal in quality and quantity to those in New York City had been razed for a vast parking lot. Elements salvaged from particularly significant buildings were put aside for a Museum of American Architecture slated for construction within the project site. It did not materialize. Without the perseverance of Luther Ely Smith, the entire Jefferson Memorial might well have been dead. In 1945, Smith and James L. Ford raised $225,000 for an international architectural competition. A panel of seven jurors was selected in 1947. The initial phase of the competition attracted 172 entries; a short list reduced the field to five. Harris Armstrong (1889-1973) was the only St. Louisan to make the cut.

Eero Saarinen's scheme was the jury's unanimous choice. His team included an architectural associate, Saarinen's first wife (a sculptor), an artist and landscape architect Dan Kiley. Their site plan from the competition's final phase is fascinating. Far from the passive park that evolved and is now defended as sacrosanct by the National Park Service, the winning scheme included museums, dense forests, a tea pavilion, a frontier village, a reconstructed historic ensemble designed to complement the **Old Cathedral** (described on page 6) and the Old Rock House adapted as an entrance to the Arch.

Although President Truman dedicated the site in 1950, the project stalled during prolonged negotiations with the Missouri Pacific and Terminal railroads. Saarinen vetoed a solution that would have sent track through the site at grade, designing instead a system of tunnels and cuts based on the catenary arch form. In the end the decision was made to reduce tunnel length and move the Old Rock House to another location on the grounds, a promise that the Park Service did not keep.

The Gateway Arch (page 9) was topped out in 1965. With the 1976 completion of the underground Museum of Westward Expansion designed by Aram Mardirosian, the federal government's total investment reached $42 million. The city had supplied $9.5 million. (Another $1.5 million came from the Bi-State Development

Agency, the Terminal Railroad Association and the Jefferson Expansion Memorial Association. More money would be spent on a 1,200-car garage in 1986.) Although the site quickly became one the most popular tourist attractions in the country, its separation from downtown by a formidable freeway is an expensive problem waiting for a feasible solution. Saarinen's original concept to bridge the freeway was developed by Harland Bartholomew & Associates (St. Louis) in 1973, but the overpass was omitted from the project.

Jefferson National Expansion Site, November 1, 1940; Old Rock House at left
Landmarks Collection

Site Demolition March 1, 1940
Landmarks Collection

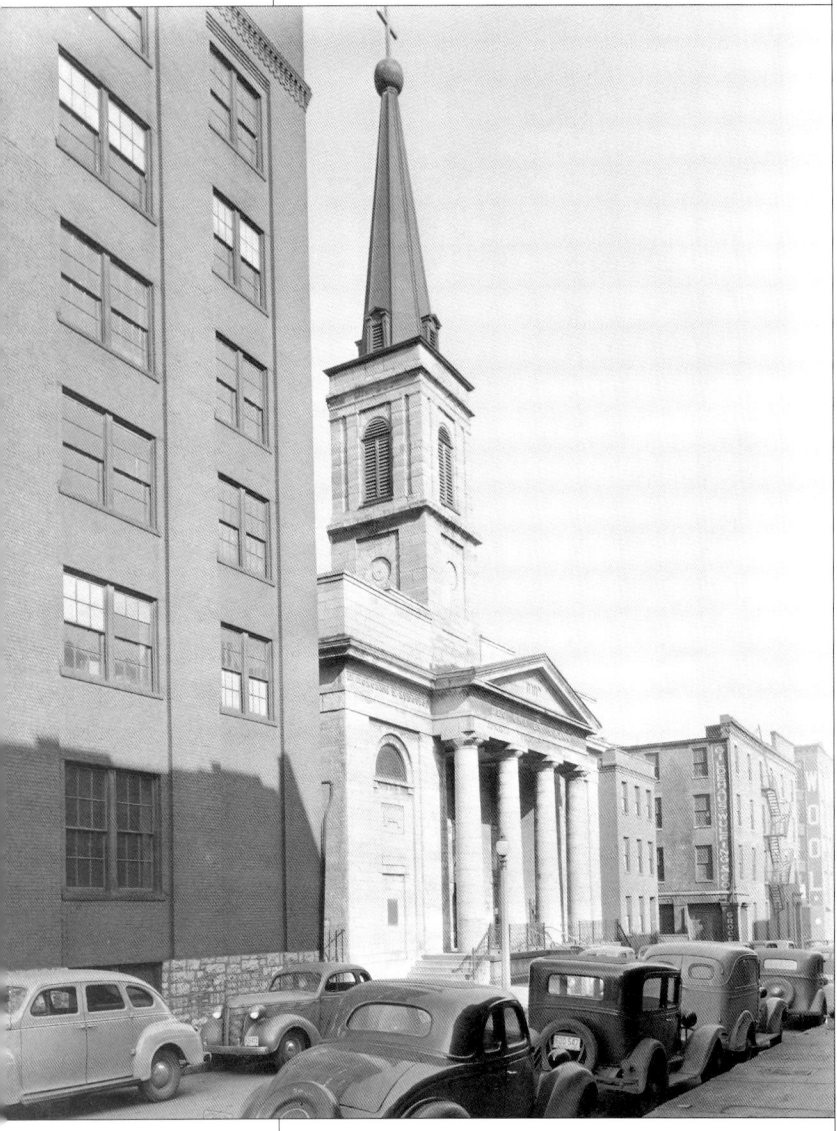

Old Cathedral from 3rd and Walnut Street, March 1, 1940

Landmarks Collection

in 1840 plunged the diocese into a $58,000 debt. Liquidation was left to an unhappy Bishop Peter Richard Kenrick who succeeded Rosati in 1843. Quickly, Kenrick constructed rental property on the southern portion of the church-owned block; rebuilding after the disastrous 1849 fire along the levee brought more mercantile buildings to the old town area. Meanwhile, new parishes had been organized to serve English, German and French-speaking Catholics in developing neighborhoods. The roster of parishioners within the cathedral's boundary began to shrink.

St. Louis' population had leapt from 16,469 in 1840 to almost 161,000 by 1860 when Kenrick acquired a new cathedral site at 23rd and Chestnut Streets. Architect Robert S. Mitchell was sent to Europe for design inspirations. But in April 1863 with a divisive civil war in progress, word was received in St. Louis that Mitchell had been lost at sea on his return voyage. Kenrick abandoned his vision of a new cathedral and moved instead to the recently completed **St. John the Apostle Church** at 16th and Chestnut *(page 65)*.

Sources credit parishioner Francis Fischer for twenty years of contributions that kept the Old Cathedral functioning during the late 19th century. Included in his generosity were funds for Victorian-era alterations, removed during restoration begun in 1959 under the supervision of Murphy & Mackey, St. Louis architects. In 1961, Pope John XXIII bestowed the title of basilica on the Old Cathedral. The bell and canopy symbolizing that status stand just inside the three main entrance doors above which are words from the Apocalypse in three (Latin, French and English) languages: "Behold the tabernacle of God with men and He will dwell with them." The most prominent inscription, however, is found on the pediment where gilded Hebrew characters spell out "the ineffable name of God."

3
**Old Cathedral
(Basilica of St. Louis, King of France)**
City Landmark: June 1966

The Old Cathedral is the fourth in a series of churches built on the block set aside for that purpose in 1764 by St. Louis founders Pierre Laclede Liguest and Auguste Chouteau. Consecrated October 26, 1834, the impressive Greek Revival structure was one of the finest churches to have been erected in the still-young Republic. Bishop Joseph Rosati, the first to hold that title in the new Diocese of the Upper Louisiana Territory, selected the St. Louis firm of George Morton (a native of Edinburgh, Scotland) and Pennsylvania-born Joseph Laveille to design his impressive stone cathedral.

Rosati's cost estimate was $30,000; the actual figure of $63,361 plus $5,000 worth of weather-related damages

4
Old Courthouse
City Landmark: June 1966

In 1839, architect Henry Singleton of St. Louis received a prize of $100 for his design for the new courthouse; it would be twenty-three years and $1,200,000 later before the building was pronounced complete. At least three other architects had a hand in its mid-century evolution: George I. Barnett (who drew the perspective for Singleton and designed the rotunda), Robert S. Mitchell and finally William Rumbold whose bold cast iron dome of 1859 predates the one on the Capital in Washington D.C. by two years.

Opened on Washington's Birthday in 1845, the elegant forum hosted rallies for relief of victims of the Irish famine, diatribes against immigration, calls to raise

Old Courthouse in 1989
Landmarks Collection

Chapter 1 Central Riverfront

Gateway Arch Underground Museum in 1993
National Park Service

and thus eligible to vote. The fate of her petition, denied first by the state and then the U.S. Supreme Court, redirected the suffrage movement from federal litigation toward changing state constitutions.

With the separation of the city and county in 1876, the courthouse lost the protection of its supervising architect. Judges were now free to remodel their space at will; mechanical systems were no longer maintained. Refurbishing the deteriorating courthouse was on the list of things to do before the 1904 World's Fair. It was not accomplished for reasons that soon became apparent. The 1907 Civic League plan for St. Louis drawn up by the same leaders as the Fair proposed demolition of all the old buildings along the riverfront except the Merchants Exchange. The Old Courthouse was passé, to be replaced by a formal new civic center near City Hall. The massive bond issue of 1923, the largest passed to date by any city, assured that a version of the public buildings grouping would be built. In June 1930, the civil courts moved west to a striking new building kitty corner from City Hall.

troops for the Mexican War and orator Thomas Hart Benton's "Westward the Course of the Empire"—a powerful appeal to link East and West by rail. Periodically, slaves were sold from the courthouse steps to settle debts or unpaid taxes; meetings to debate slavery were held as early as the 1840s. The lengthy Dred and Harriett Scott Case began in this courthouse in 1846. By the time the Supreme Court ruled against their bid for freedom, it was 1857. A far less well-known case dealing with basic civil rights started at the same courthouse in 1873 when Mrs. Virginia Louisa Minor filed suit (through her husband, since married women could not sue in Missouri courts until after 1889) contending that women were U.S. citizens under the 14th Amendment

A direct threat to the Old Courthouse site appeared next. Heirs of Auguste Chouteau and J.B. Lucas brought suit in an attempt to recover the courthouse block donated to the city in 1816. After the Missouri Supreme Court ruled against the heirs in 1933, the out-of-work construction industry was persuaded by architect John Albury Bryan to undertake a comprehensive study of the forlorn structure. The completed report from an eighteen-member team (comprised equally of architects and members of the building trades) was delivered to Mayor Bernard F. Dickmann in September of 1933 along with a persuasive letter urging his support for an immediate appropriation of $150,000. The Mayor, however, was preoccupied by a more expansive proposal—**The Jefferson Memorial Expansion Site** (page 4).

Laclede's Landing District framed by the Eads and Martin Luther King, Jr. Bridges
Robert C. Pettus, 1989

Title to the Old Courthouse passed as a gift from the city to the National Park Service on May 1, 1940. Architect Bryan, now employed by the Park Service, spent the war years sorting through court records, reading old newspapers and locating books from the 1850s in preparation for restoration of the Old Courthouse. By 1957, renovation (ironically financed with parking revenues from cleared blocks of the original town) in collaboration with Charles E. Peterson, Walter J. Nitkiewicz and Ralph Emerson neared completion. Today, National Park Service personnel provide tours through the landmark building and its exhibits of early St. Louis. The site of swearing-in ceremonies for new citizens and judges, the exquisitely proportioned rotunda also hosts a moving observance of Martin Luther King Day.

5
Gateway Arch
National Historic Landmark: May 28, 1987

"From the moment of the announcement that Eero Saarinen's design had won the competition, the Gateway Arch was analyzed, criticized, eulogized, scrutinized, diagrammed, photographed, painted and described as few other objects in history," stated E. F. Porter, Jr. in the *Post-Dispatch* 25th anniversary tribute. The American Institute of Architects in bestowing its Twenty-Five Year Award in 1990 stated that the Arch "embodies the boundless optimism of a growing nation…a symbolic bridge between East and West, past and future, engineering and art."

Saarinen (1910-61) did not live to see the completion of his 1948 design. Built under the supervision of his office between 1958-65, the shimmering 630 foot high catenary curve faced with 886 tons of stainless steel became St. Louis' most easily recognized icon—replacing the heroic statue of "St. Louis the Crusader" from the 1904 World's Fair. Key to the remarkable achievement were Hannskarl Bandel, (a structural engineer retained early by Saarinen), his partner John Dinkeloo and general contractor Robert E. MacDonald who remarked that he'd never been on a job that required so much math. A dramatic construction film "Monument to the Dream" by Charles Guggenheim is shown at regular hours in the underground museum where tickets can be purchased to ride one of 16, five-passenger cable cabs to an observation room holding 240 people at the top of the great arch.

6
Laclede's Landing District
National Register: August 25, 1976

Laclede's Landing, a recent appellation, is the only surviving portion of the natural levee topography and street pattern from the original 1780 survey for the French village that grew up by the trading post established in 1764 by Pierre Laclede Ligueste and Auguste Chouteau. Surviving buildings in the Landing, some of which predate the Civil War, were used for the production and warehousing of tobacco, hides, stoves, stamping and metal engraving, paints and oils, saws and engines, hardware, coffee, licorice, tents, boxes and labels, wholesale grocery, machines and other unglamorous but essential activities until the growing city with an economy based on rail and truck shipping left the Mississippi River and narrow cobblestone streets behind.

Considered "ragged" and seedy by the early 20th century, the riverfront was subjected to a series of high-minded but unfunded plans until the federal

Chapter 1 Central Riverfront

government helped clear a 40-block area for the **Jefferson National Expansion Site.** The massive barrier of **Eads Bridge** (page 3) kept demolition to the south of the Landing; construction of an elevated expressway to the west and the approach to the Martin Luther King Bridge to the north sealed the three-square block district in a time capsule awaiting redevelopment. Several proposals for the Landing were advanced in the 1960s,

Raeder Place
Robert C. Pettus, 1977

including one calling for total demolition, but it was not until 1974 that a group of businessmen led by the late William Maritz helped create the Laclede's Landing Redevelopment Corporation. The Board of Aldermen approved this plan, allowing interested owners to retain and improve their property, in late 1975.

National Register listing in 1976, marking the first St. Louis commercial district to be so designated, poised the Landing to take advantage of soon-passed changes in federal tax policy providing incentives for historic rehabilitation. A number of architectural firms have contributed to the renovation of the Landing under the watchful eyes of Thomas Purcell, the resilient president of the redevelopment corporation, who has worked tirelessly since 1975 to attract new investment into a mixed-use project with almost one million square feet of leasable space in historic buildings. In 2000, the Landing's foundation received a generous grant from the Whitaker Foundation to develop a comprehensive strategy for placing permanent and temporary works of art along the riverfront. "Footnote," a prominent permanent piece funded by the Regional Arts Commission, was installed in 2002 at the entry to Eads Bridge.

7
Christian Peper Building (Raeder Place)
City Landmark: March 1971
721-27 North 1st Street

Raeder Place is St. Louis' finest surviving cast-iron front building. Built 1873-74 for the Christian Peper Tobacco Company from plans by Frederick W. Raeder (a German-born and trained architect who worked on the Crystal Palace in New York before coming to St. Louis circa 1867), Raeder Place led the way to the rebirth of Laclede's Landing with an adaptive reuse from 1976-77 by Cohn/Thomson Associates (St. Louis). That project was also one of the first in Missouri to take advantage of the newly created federal tax incentives for historic rehabilitation.

Introduced to the United States in 1846, cast-iron buildings revolutionized American construction techniques. Curtain wall installations boasted larger windows than traditional masonry construction; designs showcased in catalogues ranged from elegantly refined to eccentrically ornamental. Cast-iron buildings could be fabricated, shipped anywhere, quickly erected and, if necessary, disassembled and rebuilt at another location. Offering the best-known protection from the frequent conflagrations plaguing 19th century cities, cast iron was essential to rebuilding the St. Louis levee district after the 1849 fire. It continued to be popular for building fronts into the 1880s.

8
North Riverfront Industrial District
National Register: pending
Bounded roughly by Biddle, Second, and O'Fallon Streets and Flood Wall

In 1874, Camille N. Dry and Richard J. Compton printed a specimen page to garner support for their publication of an outsized topographical book of St. Louis in bird's-eye views. Titled "Manufacturing Portion of the City,"

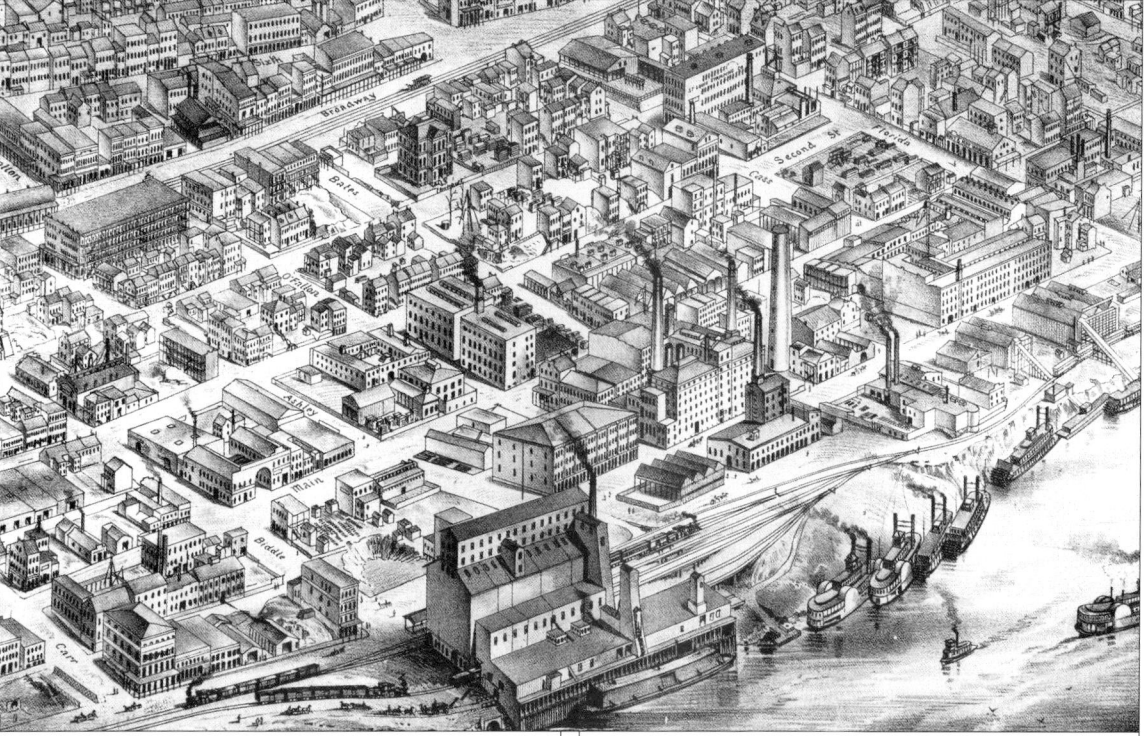

Specimen page used to raise printing funds for Pictorial St. Louis: 1875 by Compton & Dry

the page (depicting the riverfront immediately north of the new bridge) was selected to solicit subscriptions for a 150-page volume, dedicated to James B. Eads, "elegantly bound in muslin and gilt" and offered for the then-handsome price of $25. The chosen scene centered on the bustling St. Louis Elevator and the four-block Belcher Sugar factory complex. Traces of earlier eras—mounds, diminutive row houses and the former mansion of Governor Ashley—are also visible along with a city market, the Edward Bates public school, the St. Louis Shot Tower (176 feet tall) from 1847, the Biddle sewer (completed in 1854 and still in use today) and a massive tenement built to house cheap labor employed by the many industrial concerns located in close proximity to the railroads and steamboats.

The seven-block area of the North Riverfront Industrial District is carved out of a decidedly depopulated stretch of this once-prime acreage. Most of the land within the boundaries was part of the Belcher Sugar Refinery empire during its heyday as the nation's largest producer. Its signature twelve-story refinery (later known as the Fresh Building, razed in 2001) from 1881 featured heavy timber construction with each floor supported by twenty-four oak posts having an average dimension of twenty-two inches. Although the refinery's property was sold to various new owners starting in the 1890s, the company name lived on. The Belcher Bath Company privatized the locally famous sulfurous well, supplying free "Belcher Water" for the medicinal needs of the city. Its 1894 bathhouse at 1301 Lewis is the oldest building in the district.

Blessed with superb rail lines and docking facilities, the old Belcher plant was perfectly sited for the emerging refrigerated warehouse industry dominated by the pioneering McPheeters St. Louis Cold Storage Company. Even more significant, however, was the rapidly expanding electric business. The Laclede Power Company built the first district plant at 1240 Lewis beginning in 1900 from plans by Mauran, Russell & Garden of St. Louis. In 1902, the newly formed Union Electric Light and Power Company began work on its enormous **Ashley Street Powerhouse** *(see next page)* on the site of the great elevator destroyed in the 1896 tornado. Other district buildings include a small machine shop associated with the electric plant, a warehouse for the Beck & Corbitt Iron Company and a bonded warehouse for the J. Kennard & Sons Carpet Company designed by Isaac Taylor (St. Louis) in 1904-06.

In recent years the partly moribund district's immediate neighborhood has experienced heart-breaking demolition and an invasion by the once-proud Admiral, now reduced to a grotesque gambling boat complete with land-based eyesores. A bright future still seems possible. Trailnet, a regional land trust formed in 1988, has acquired the handsome brick and terra cotta Laclede Gas powerhouse for conversion to a multi-use trailhead facility for the Riverfront Trail—part of a forty-mile linear park (Confluence Greenway) on both sides of the Mississippi River. The St. Louis firm of TAO + LEE Associates was selected to design the powerhouse adaptive reuse.

Chapter 1 Central Business District: East

Ashley Street Powerhouse

Gary Tetley, 1994

9
Ashley Street Powerhouse
City Landmark: November 1971
Foot of Ashley Street at 1200-24 Lewis Street

This Classical Revival powerhouse of brick with terra cotta trim, designed by Charles H. Ledlie in 1903, is one of the skyline's most prominent landmarks north of downtown. The name of the client, the newly consolidated Union Electric Light & Power Company, is spelled out in terra cotta across and below two pediments on the southern elevation. Both south and west elevations are organized with colossal fluted Ionic pilasters carrying enormous arches.

The plant opened in time for the 1904 World's Fair with a 12,000-kilowatt capacity as St. Louis' first large central station. In 1922, a twenty-two mile downtown steam loop was established, harnessing the recaptured steam used to drive the massive turbines. The Dome, Busch Stadium, the Arch and more than 100 other business and offices buy steam power from the Ashley plant, which was rededicated in 1999 as a "forward-looking, efficient source of steam and electricity" by the Trigen Energy Corporation of White Plains, N.Y.

CHAPTER 2 | Central Business District: East

Hadley-Dean Glass Building
Sam Fentress, 1985

Chapter 2

Central Business District: East

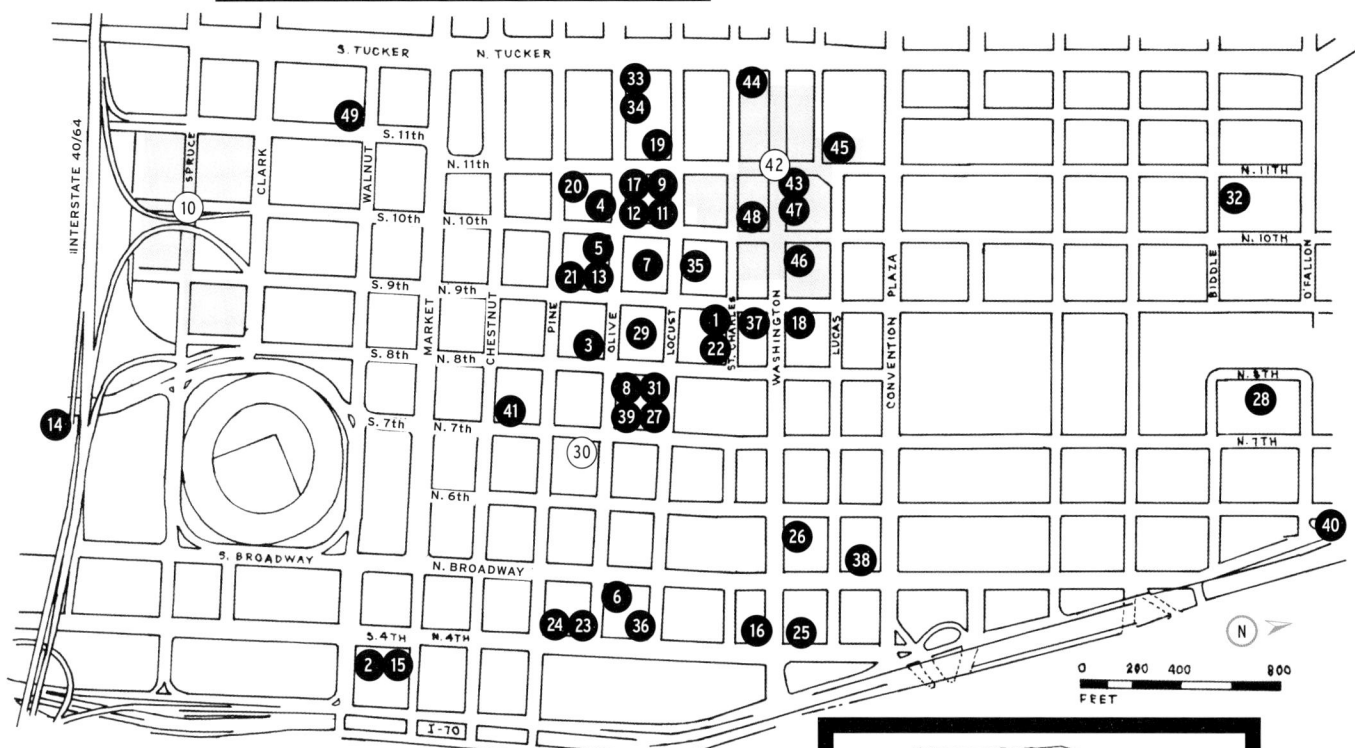

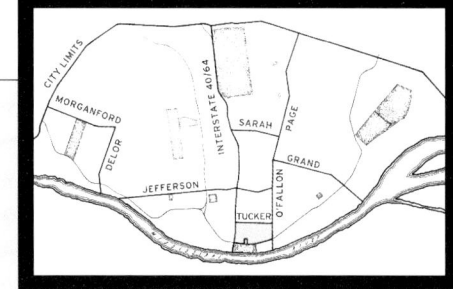

- Single Site
- ○ District

1. American Theatre
2. American Zinc, Lead and Smelting Company Building
3. Arcade/Wright Building
4. Balmer & Weber Music Company Building
5. Bell Telephone Building (S. G. Adams)
6. Boatmen's Bank
7. Century/Syndicate Trust Building
8. Chemical Building
9. City Club
10. Cupples Station Warehouse District
11. Delany Building
12. Eastman-Kodak Building
13. Frisco Building
14. Fulton Bag Company Buildings
15. International Fur Exchange Building
16. J. Kennard and Sons Carpet Company Building
17. Laclede Gas Company Building
18. Lennox Hotel
19. Louderman Building
20. Majestic Hotel
21. Maryland Hotel
22. Mayfair Hotel
23. Merchants'-Laclede Building
24. Mississippi Valley Trust Building
25. Missouri Athletic Club
26. Old May Company Department Store Complex
27. Mutual Bank Building
28. Neighborhood Gardens Apartments
29. Old Post Office and Custom House
30. Olive Street Terra Cotta District
31. Phipps-Wallace Store Building
32. St. Joseph's Catholic Church
33. *St. Louis Post-Dispatch* Building
34. *St. Louis Post-Dispatch* Printing Building
35. Scruggs-Vandervoort-Barney Warehouse
36. Security Building
37. Statler Hotel
38. Union Market
39. Union Trust Company
40. Vess Bottle
41. Wainwright Building
42. Washington Avenue/East of Tucker Historic District
43. Bee Hat Building
44. A. D. Brown Building
45. Hadley-Dean Glass Building
46. Lammert Building
47. Lindell Real Estate Company Building
48. Rice-Stix Building
49. Winkelmeyer Building

St. Louis Landmarks and Historic Districts

1
American Theatre Building
City Landmark: September 1978
National Register: March 18, 1985
416 North 9th Street

When the Orpheum (now American) Theatre opened on Labor Day 1917, St. Louis' newest vaudeville house joined more than two dozen theaters in the nationwide Orpheum circuit. The dominant force behind the local $500,000 "Parisian" Beaux-Arts delight was Louis A. Cella, a self-made St. Louis millionaire. Cella acquired the parcel at 9th Street and St. Charles in 1905. Ten years later he signed a lease with Martin Beck (President of the Orpheum Theater Co.) wherein Cella would retain financial interest in the new building and reserve rights to inspect all materials, plans and specifications. The architect chosen was G. Albert Lansburgh who had opened an office in San Francisco after graduation from l'École des Beaux Arts in 1906. Lansburgh had already designed seven theaters for the Orpheum circuit including one (now demolished) in Kansas City, Missouri and one in New Orleans now adapted for symphony concerts. For the St. Louis building, Lansburgh collaborated with Italian-born sculptor Leo Lentelli in the design of a

American Theatre circa 1917
Landmarks Collection

Chapter 2   Central Business District: East

American Theatre Terra Cotta
Landmarks Collection

lavish, slightly risqué program of terra cotta ornament executed by the Winkle Terra Cotta Company. Renamed the American in 1960, the theater (now a rock concert venue) is still owned by descendants of its original promoter, Louis Cella. It remains one of the most delightful, pedestrian-scaled buildings downtown thanks in large part to Lentelli's sensuous figures.

2
American Zinc, Lead and Smelting Company Building
Landmarks, 2001

American Zinc, Lead and Smelting Company Building
National Register: May 4, 1998
20 South 4th Street

The American Zinc Building is a rare example of a property recognized by the National Register to have such exceptional significance that it was listed long before the usual 50-year threshold. Completed in 1967, Hellmuth, Obata & Kassabaum's Zinc Building exemplifies the Modernist aesthetic of honest expression of structure. In this case the seldom-used Vierendeel truss system creates a rigid steel frame expressed in a stainless steel grid on the south elevation and 52-foot spans at the east and west, all joints rounding somewhat to express the thickening of the members where they connect. The flawless marriage of form and function is one of the most unusual and creative modern buildings in the region. Given an eleventh-hour reprieve from demolition in 1997, the American Zinc Building has found new life as part of the Drury Plaza Hotel in the **International Fur Exchange Building** *(page 26)*.

3
Arcade/Wright Building
City Landmark: December 1979
800-14 Olive Street; 801-15 Pine Street

Built on the site of Louis H. Benoist's Greek Revival mansion, the eighteen-story Wright Building was designed by Eames & Young of St. Louis in 1906. Plans a decade later for the adjoining Arcade Building were revised by Tom P. Barnett and engineer Fred C. Taxis after the discovery of quicksand at the troublesome site required additional floors to provide income offsetting foundation costs. This is the same bed of quicksand unearthed forty years earlier during excavations for the **Old Post Office** *(page 35)*. Redesigned, both the basement and sub-basement (with columns supported on caissons driven eighty feet into bedrock) of the Arcade Building had access into the Eads Bridge railroad tunnel just in case it was converted to subway use. On the first two floors above, the grand interior arcade space with 200 shops was extended through the Wright Building to a new entrance on Pine. The two buildings essentially became one.

The government cut off civilian steel supply during World War I, necessitating the use of a reinforced concrete frame—at that point a relatively new technology. One of the few local projects underway during the war, the $3.5 million Arcade Building (opened in August 1919) quickly became a premiere attraction in downtown. Located at downtown's busiest corner, the "Muny"

Arcade/Wright Building
Robert C. Pettus, 1979

Chapter 2 Central Business District: East

**Detail:
Arcade/Wright
Building**
*Gary R. Tetley,
1992*

(Municipal Opera) ticket office in the lobby drew crowds as did the fine specialty shops. Even into the early 1970s, cab drivers needed nothing more than the name of the building to whisk passengers to the offices of Pet, Inc. (one of St. Louis' largest corporations), the Cardinal baseball ticket office or the headquarters of the Building Owners & Managers Association of St. Louis. Then, everything changed.

Pet and other major tenants moved out at about the same time the emerging downtown in Clayton seriously began to challenge downtown St. Louis. One by one the astonishing collection of jewelry stores and ticket offices left the mezzanine arcade. With elevators determined unsafe, the Arcade Building was condemned for occupancy above the first floor in the late 1970s. Since then downtown's finest example of Gothic Revival architecture (determined eligible for listing in the National Register) has been the subject of endless litigation. Seemingly rescued in 2000 with the purchase of the full city block by a developer committed to rehabilitation, the Arcade/Wright building still faces an uncertain future due to the complexities of financing the multi-million dollar redevelopment.

terra cotta were twelve small parlors for merchandise display, each given a different decorative scheme featuring wall hangings of silk damask and tapestries. Before embarking on the building project, the company had secured an exclusive contract with the prestigious Aeolian company. Its featured product, the Pianola, was the most popular mechanical piano in the world. Aeolian bought out Balmer & Weber in 1907 and renamed 1004 Olive "Aeolian Hall" after their headquarters in New York.

Maritz & Young (St. Louis) remodeled the storefront and interior following a fire in 1928. Their elegant first-floor hall (much of it still intact) was a powerful advertisement for the high-end products sold within. Basement concerts and events brought additional patrons through the building. In 1970, the Aeolian franchise was purchased by the Ludwig Music House. Ludwig-Aeolian remained in its downtown headquarters until 1989. New owners hope to recycle the building as housing.

5
Bell Telephone Building (S.G. Adams)
City Landmark: January 1980
National Register: August 5, 1999
920 Olive Street

This important Richardsonian Romanesque building of brick and sandstone was designed in 1888 by Shepley, Rutan & Coolidge (successors to H. H. Richardson, originator of the style) for the Bell Telephone Company of Missouri. George Shepley, a St. Louis native, was Richardson's chief assistant as well as his son-in-law. After Shepley's sister married into the Lionberger family, Richardson's office designed three houses (two since razed) for various Lionbergers in St. Louis. Upon Richardson's death in 1886, Shepley, Rutan & Coolidge completed his unfinished commissions including the **Isaac Lionberger House** *(page 84)*.

**Balmer & Weber
circa 1928**
*Landmarks
Collection*

4
**Balmer & Weber Music Company Building
(Ludwig-Aeolian)**
National Register: August 31, 2000
1004 Olive Street

Constructed in 1905 in downtown's small music district, the Balmer & Weber Music Company Building was designed by Henry William Kirchner for one of the oldest music houses in St. Louis. Newspaper accounts described the new emporium as "something new and rather a radical departure from the usual downtown buildings." Inside an ornate facade of red

When the telephone building opened in 1891, all calls from the 2,900 subscribers were routed through the sixth-floor switchboard. An alliance with three other companies in 1913 created Southwestern Bell headquartered in St. Louis. A seventh floor was added in 1919; most of the non-technical offices had already moved out for lack of space. With a rapidly growing system, Bell embarked on the construction of a grand new headquarters to replace the obsolete 920 Olive. At thirty-one stories the splendid new Art Deco building (on the next block southwest) was said to be the tallest in Missouri when it was built in 1926. The old building was left to a variety of uses over the years; in its new 21st century life, loft apartments are anticipated over lower floor restaurant or commercial space.

6
Boatmen's Bank (Marquette Building)
National Register: October 22, 1998
300 North Broadway

Eames & Young's nineteen-story office tower was completed at the end of 1913, just a few months before a fire destroyed the 1890 Boatmen's Bank Building at 4th and Washington. The new Monward Building (after the realty group which commissioned it) was swiftly rechristened in honor of Boatmen's Bank. The bank, and the name, would remain for 62 years; from the 1970s onward the building was known as the Marquette.

This would be the last skyscraper designed by Eames & Young, a partnership that began in 1885 doing mostly residential work. After winning national acclaim for their early designs at **Cupples Station** (page 22), the firm gained a secure place in St. Louis' niche market for bank architecture. The Boatmen's Building is one of their best surviving commercial works, an expressive and well-organized building with unusually fine terra cotta. A projected slender tower of ten additional stories was never built.

In 1915, Eames & Young designed a six-story annex for the quarter-block immediately north; four more stories were added in 1920. One of downtown's few entirely terra-cotta clad buildings, the annex was surprisingly non-historical in inspiration. As part of a plan to redevelop the original Boatmen's Building into residential units, the City Treasurer's office demolished the annex and replaced it with a parking garage opened in 1999. In 2001, the New York owner scrapped its plan for rehab and put the building back on the market (its value greatly increased by the availability of adjacent parking). The downtown YMCA retains two floors in the building; the rest is vacant, awaiting redevelopment.

7
Century Building & Syndicate Trust Building
National Register: October 16, 2002
Bounded by 9th, Locust, 10th and Olive Streets

Few buildings downtown can match the tumultuous history of the Century/Syndicate Trust complex. The Century, constructed in 1896 from plans by the Chicago firm of Raeder, Coffin & Crocker, was an enormous undertaking for its time: the half-block complex included a large theater and countless small offices, all wrapped in a stylish neoclassical exterior boasting three shades (including amethyst) of Georgia marble. Despite its location at the western fringe of the business district, the new building attracted a number of high-profile tenants, only to be sold in a sheriff's sale a few years later. The new owners, the Syndicate Trust Company, announced plans for a lavish sixteen-story "annex" by St. Louis architect Harry Roach. The Syndicate Trust Building, as it became known, was to be the new home of Scruggs-Vandervoort-Barney— St. Louis' most prestigious department store.

Century Building
Robert C. Pettus, 1979

Chapter 2   Central Business District: East

Syndicate Trust Building
Gary R. Tetley, 1988

Chemical Building
Robert C. Pettus, 1979

Although skeptics predicted failure because the retailer located so far from other major stores, Scruggs prospered. The Syndicate Trust Building opened in 1907: by 1912, the store took over most of the Century Building as well. Truly a marvel of early 20th century consumerism, Scruggs catered to every need: clothing, dry goods, furnishings for everything from homes to banks, and no fewer than five separate millinery departments (including a special shop for the large-headed woman). Office tenants included forces of social unrest and reform: the Equal Suffrage League of St. Louis made its first home in the Syndicate Trust. By the time the 19th Amendment gave women the right to vote, the organization had moved over to the Century Building. From this office the organization hosted the National American Woman Suffrage Association's Golden Jubilee Convention in 1919 (based at the nearby **Statler Hotel**, *page 40*) where the group voted to organize the League of Women Voters. A generation later in 1944, the Citizens Civil Rights Commission led a series of sit-ins in Scruggs' basement cafeteria, one of the city's first successful actions of its kind. For many years this remained the only downtown establishment where black St. Louisans could sit down for lunch.

Architecturally, the two halves of the block provide a succinct lesson on the contrasts between turn-of-the-century Classical and Renaissance Revival styles as employed in large commercial buildings. The ten-story Century responds elegantly to the **Old Post Office** to its east (*page 35*) with a formal but complex organization. Projecting volumes define the corners of each elevation; bays that vary in width reinforce the pattern. Ornament is restrained, often integrated into the massing. At the taller Syndicate Trust, however, the organization is extremely simple while the exuberant ornamental program rejects style authenticity. Some of the terra cotta ornament consists of enlarged versions of the Century's wreath panels between the first two stories, but the imaginative sculpture also include shields, triglyphs oddly disembodied from any appropriate Doric order entablature, orderly rows of lions' heads and foliated modillions.

Although the two-building complex is nominated to the National Register as we go to press, the future has been in jeopardy since its purchase in 1993 by a would-be developer who evicted remaining tenants (save long-leased Walgreens) and then bailed out when a minor structural problem in the Century came to light. Assertions of calamitous public safety danger have been rewarded over the years by a city-installed fence in the street—impeding vehicular traffic, preventing pedestrian activity and removing at-curb parking around a full city block. Litigation has also proved useful for the owner. In the current scheme that can only be described as politically expedient and urbanistically disastrous, the city has placed its full support behind a heavily subsidized project that will pay the owner about $6.5 million (he paid 625,000 in 1993), raze the Century half of the historic asset for huge parking garage directly west of the **Old Post Office** (*page 35*).

Nuns of the Franciscan Missionary of Mary atop the Alverne (City Club) in 1963

St. Louis Mercantile Library

8
Chemical Building
City Landmark: September 1976
National Register: March 19, 1982
721 Olive Street

Toward the end of the 19th century, prominent architects first from the east and then Chicago were invited to design major office buildings, museums and mansions worthy of the city's growing prosperity and optimism. Downtown, the Turner Building, designed in 1883 by the eminent Boston firm of Peabody & Stearns, was followed by works from Shepley, Rutan & Coolidge (also Boston) and Adler & Sullivan, Chicago. The Chicago firm's 16-story **Union Trust Building** *(page 42)* already dominated a corner site at 7th and Olive Streets when fellow Chicagoan Henry Ives Cobb received the commission to design a neighboring skyscraper for the Chemical National Bank in 1893.

Almost complete at the time of the deadly 1896 tornado, the Chemical Building came through the storm unscathed. But the skyscraper was greeted a few months later with faint praise by local critics who deemed the palette of "very vivid red brick and terra cotta quite out of the ordinary in this day of lighter colors" and criticized the façade as broken up by "too many angular bays and numerous ornamented horizontal lines." (A matching addition to the north in 1903 by St. Louis architects Mauran, Russell & Garden replaced the twenty-year-old Turner Building.) Today, it is the undulating rhythm and rich color of Cobb's building that make it one of the most universally acclaimed structures downtown. The last office building in St. Louis to display highly decorative cast iron storefronts, the Chemical Building was also the last designed by a prominent architect from outside the city until after World War II.

9
City Club (Hotel Alverne)
National Register: pending
1012-24 Locust Street

Founded in 1910 as a populist offshoot of the elite Civic League's noontime discussions, the City Club quickly became "the community yeast cake"—a place where men came together to share ideas and learn about important issues without taking any stand on behalf of the organization. Membership was limited to 1500 because of space limitation. But within six months the popular new club with quarters (a lounge, office and

Hotel DeSoto (City Club) in postcard circa 1936
Landmarks Collection

Cupples Station Warehouse District Map
Pat Hays Baer

dining rooms) on the 7th floor of the Board of Education at 911 Locust had already attracted half that number. Initial planning for another site began before World War I. In 1922, architect Tom P. Barnett was elected to the Board of Directors; later that year, he received the commission (at 5% of construction costs) to design a new club. President Warren G. Harding laid the cornerstone in June 1923; the club moved to the unfinished building in a body that New Year's Eve with each member carrying something—from saltshaker to a stove—in a two-block parade up the street.

Membership briefly peaked at more than 3,500 after transfer to the new fifteen-story building where audiences were exposed to up to three stimulating speakers every week. Local issues such as "The Court House Site: 12th Street or 4th Street" and "Solving the Traffic Problem in St. Louis" were balanced by international themes including "Recent Political and Cultural Developments in China" and "Peace Through Political Action" along with the perennial query, "Is Civilization Decaying?" "Exotic" cultural programs (A. T. Freeman, full-blooded Sioux singing songs of his people) also found a forum at the City Club. But with little working capital and monthly operating losses of up to $9,000,

the board in 1926 required members to purchase at least one $50 share in a separate holding company. Many resigned. Next, the club negotiated an arrangement with an hotelier to invest $40,000 and lease floors two through ten as the Missouri Hotel (designed by Preston J. Bradshaw).

In February 1929, the floundering organization unsuccessfully attempted to sell the building; one month later the Missouri State Life Insurance Company began foreclosure proceedings. With new ownership the club consolidated functions to the two top floors—a move that could have saved it had it not been for the Depression. Doors closed February 1933. The DeSoto Hotel operated at this address for over twenty years. In 1956, the Archdiocese purchased the building and opened the Hotel Alverne, a residence for senior citizens. A chapel open to all finally closed in 1991, four years after the last resident had left. Today, the building remains a tantalizing candidate for adaptive reuse.

10
Cupples Station Warehouse District
City Landmark: March 1971
National Register: June 26, 1998
Bounded roughly by 8th, Clark, 11th and I-40

Constructed between 1894 and 1917, the nine remaining warehouses in the Cupples Station complex form an unparalleled grouping of national significance. All but one were designed by Eames & Young (St. Louis)

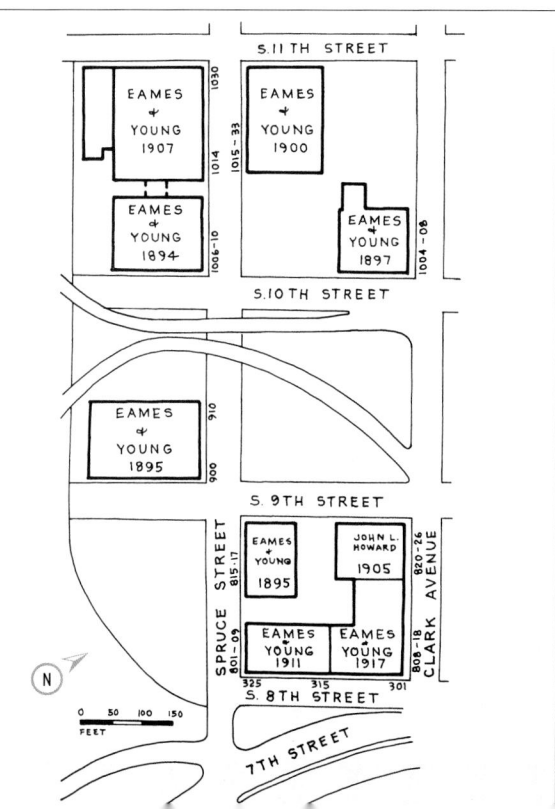

Eads Bridge Tunnel at Cupples Station, detail from stock certificate issued in 1872

who unified the complex by arcaded continuous pier and spandrel systems, fenestration patterns, materials and understated ornamentation. Developed and conceptualized by Robert Brookings (partner and Vice President of the Samuel Cupples Woodenware Company, the largest such company in the world), the unique complex was connected directly to railroads and **Eads Bridge** (page 3) by an intricate system of tunnels and spur lines.

The *Inland Architect* judged the complex as having "brought warehouse design to a point where little improvement is possible" while *Scientific American* remarked upon the technical prowess at a "scale of elaborateness with a perfection of detail unequaled by any similar institution in the world." In 1900, Samuel Cupples and Robert Brookings (President since 1895 of the Board of Directors of Washington University in St. Louis) endowed Washington University with all of their stock in the Cupples Station property. Their gift was valued at $3 million.

The university commissioned additional warehouses including the two still standing just west of Busch Stadium, but demolition in the 1960s for the stadium, the concurrent freeway construction and an unrelated fire brought down almost half of the total complex. By the 1970s, most of the remaining buildings were only marginally occupied. In 1985, Washington University exercised its right to object to listing the properties on the National Register. Thus the nomination, reviewed and approved at the state and federal levels, would sit in limbo for the next decade. Meanwhile ownership passed to Blue Cross and Blue Shield of Missouri.

Plans to demolish the block across from Busch Stadium to provide parking for a new hockey arena surfaced in 1989. Mayor Vincent C. Schoemehl's 1991 decision to oppose demolition was a critical factor in saving the buildings as was a 1994 predevelopment study funded in part by Landmarks Association of St. Louis and the National Trust for Historic Preservation. On March 2, 2001 the ribbon was cut at the stylish new Westin Hotel, a $75 million adaptive reuse of four of

Cupples Station
Robert C. Pettus, 1978

Chapter 2 Central Business District: East

the buildings by developer McCormack Baron & Associates from plans by Trivers Associates, St. Louis, with interior design by Anderson/Miller of Chicago. The second in a rapid-fire series of hotel adaptive reuse projects in St. Louis, the Cupples Station project demonstrated the value of federal and state historic rehabilitation credits and the importance of patience. The rest of the complex (minus a structurally unsound building razed in 2000) is slated for conversion to office use after completion of a 760-space parking garage in early 2002.

11
Delany Building
National Register: March 1, 2002
1000-06 Locust Street

Designed by Matthews & Clark (St. Louis) in 1899 as an investment property for Dr. John O'Fallon Delany, the five-story commercial building erected at the southwest corner of 10th and Locust replaced a three-story red brick house. The new building (estimated to cost $40,000) was clad with the latest fashion in local masonry—light-colored brick trimmed with glazed terra

Frisco Building
Robert C. Pettus, 1979

cotta. (This choice of brick color was selected partly in the vain hope it would withstand the pollutants from coal-burning furnaces.) The Delany Building also introduced a novel attempt to reflect additional light into the interior by trimming unique angled plate glass windows with white glazed bricks. Although Delany (a descendent of the prominent Mullanphy family) held a medical degree from Columbia University, he devoted his time to real estate rather than medicine. Disputes over the estate after his wife's death led to the sale of this building on the steps of the Civil Courts Building in 1953. The price was $226,000. Vacant for some years, the property has recently been purchased for adaptive reuse to include housing.

12
Eastman-Kodak Building
National Register: May 9, 2002
1009 Olive Street

This tiny 1928 store sits across the street from the **Balmer & Weber Music Company** *(page 18)* in one of the few blocks downtown with any remaining concentration of low-rise commercial buildings. The façade is almost pure Art Deco down to the half-covered original sign, a theme reflected in the front storeroom's plasterwork. Klipstein & Rathmann's design was one of the city's few downtown examples of the style, setting the stage for the same St. Louis firm's impeccable 15th Street Substation north of Washington Avenue just a few years later. Current plans envision a small loft development with a first floor tenant capable of capitalizing on the intact historic interior.

13
Frisco Building
National Register: March 29, 1983
900-06 Olive Street

The Frisco line originated in the compelling mid-19th century American dream of an Iron Horse starting from St. Louis on its "journey to the setting sun." Organized in 1876 from the South-West branch of the Pacific (later Missouri Pacific) Railroad, the St. Louis-San Francisco company under the leadership of Texas-born Benjamin F. Yoakum embarked in the late 19th century on a phenomenal period of growth. Between 1897 and 1904, the Frisco more than quadrupled its trackage. A new corporate headquarters was essential.

The Frisco Building Company organized in 1902 by Isaac T. Cook ("the Napoleon of office building construction in St. Louis") included the three men

International Fur Exchange Building
Gary R. Tetley, 1992

responsible for the design and construction of the building: architects William S. Eames, Thomas C. Young and contractor James W. Black. Only a year after the $750,000 building was completed, merger with the Rock Island (giving the line claim to the largest railroad in the country) precipitated a matching $250,000 addition to the west by Eames & Young. After consolidation with the Burlington Northern in 1980, Frisco left downtown. The building was sold to Burnham Development Company, Chicago, which hired St. Louis architects Hastings & Chivetta for a $14 million renovation completed in 1984. The Frisco Building changed hands several times before purchase in 2001 by Spinnaker of St. Louis.

14
Fulton Bag Company Buildings
National Register: September 5, 1991
612-18 South 7th Street

The four-story warehouse building at 612 South 7th was built by the Cupples Real Estate Company in 1899 to complement the company's nearby **Cupples Station** warehouse development *(page 22)*. Located near the mouth of the Eads Bridge Tunnel, the eastern end of the Mill Creek Valley became a shipping and rail hub for St. Louis. Twin buildings at 606-08 (demolished) and 612 South 7th were ideally sited immediately southeast of Cupples Station and adjacent to the Missouri Pacific and St. Louis & San Francisco freight houses. Both buildings were leased to the Fulton Bag & Cotton Mills Company, which later purchased the single-story former livery attached to the south. Eames & Young's design for the main building is reminiscent of their designs at Cupples Station, emphasizing a single round-arched bay with recessed spandrel panels and fine but simple brick detailing. The one-story building to the south (with an Arts & Crafts-inspired façade from the mid-1920s) was converted to a restaurant in 1993.

Chapter 2 | Central Business District: East

J. Kennard Building
Robert C. Pettus, 1989

Hellmuth to design a seven-story commercial warehouse. The prominent new building opened in 1920 with a spacious trading floor flooded with natural light where buyers could inspect pelts. The fur market collapsed almost immediately. Auctions, removed to smaller spaces from 1925 through 1934, stopped altogether in 1956. In 1934, the Carradine Hat Company leased space, then purchased the building in 1948 and added a ten-story addition to the south in 1959.

Demolition for a surface parking lot had already begun when the Fur Exchange, its addition (known as the Thomas Jefferson Building) and its neighboring **American Zinc Building** *(page 16)* caught the attention of hoteliers Charles and Shirley Drury. "We don't want to see those buildings shoved into the river," Drury said in a 1997 newspaper interview. Three years later the $26.5 million Drury Plaza Hotel opened to the public, a happy conclusion to a story that nearly ended very badly.

16
J. Kennard and Sons Carpet Company Building (WS on Washington)
National Register: May 5, 2000
400 Washington Avenue

In 1900, Isaac Taylor designed this handsome Italian Renaissance building as the headquarters of the J. Kennard & Sons Carpet Company. According to newspaper accounts, family patriarch John Kennard moved his company (and his stock of rugs) from Baltimore to Lexington to Pittsburgh, arriving in St. Louis in the mid-1850s. Within two decades the family business was heralded as one of the "most extensive dealers of carpets, foreign and domestic, oil cloths, curtain and lace goods, in the West." Under Kennard's sons Samuel and John, Jr., the company continued to prosper. Samuel Kennard in particular became one of the city's leading citizens, serving as president of the St. Louis Exposition Company, the Business Men's League and the Autumnal Festivities Association. His position as a vice president of the Louisiana Purchase Exposition (also serving as Vice Chairman of Buildings and Grounds) may have helped influence the selection of Taylor as Director of Works.

15
International Fur Exchange Building
National Register: April 13, 1998
14-22 South 4th Street

Although the day of the unwashed mountain man/trapper was long gone by the early 20th century, St. Louis remained an important market for raw furs. Bolstered by an exclusive government contract to sell pelts from Alaska's protected Pribilof seal herd, the International Fur Exchange commissioned local architect George W.

Located across the street from the **Missouri Athletic Club** *(page 31)* within easy walking distance of the Arch grounds, the former Kennard (later Edison Brothers) building underwent a $16 million adaptive reuse project in 2001. Both federal and state historic rehab credits were essential to finance the new use as an all suite, 78-unit boutique hotel (WS on Washington) from plans by Grewe Architectural & Engineering Services Inc.

17
Laclede Gas Company Building
National Register: November 26, 1980
1017 Olive Street

Designed in 1911 by Mauran, Russell & Crowell of St. Louis as a lavish new headquarters for the Laclede Gas Light Company, this architectural statement signified the utility's growing prosperity. Incorporated in 1857, Laclede (at first controlled by New York investors) struggled to compete with the hometown monopoly until locals led by politician/transit magnate Erastus Wells gained control of the company. Laclede left this ten-story Classical Revival building for a new office tower in 1970. In 1984, renovation as "LGL Centre" was completed from plans by Ross & Baruzzini, St. Louis.

18
Lennox Hotel
(Renaissance St. Louis Suites Hotel)
National Register: September 6, 1984
823-27 Washington Avenue

In March 1928, Preston J. Bradshaw (architect/investor with numerous hotels and apartment buildings to his credit in St. Louis, Louisville, Detroit, Kansas City and Dallas) announced plans for the city's tallest hostelry in partnership with owner/operator Charles Heiss. Estimated to cost $2.5 million, the Lennox opened September 2, 1929. Dinner receptions complete with orchestral concerts welcomed invited guests. Less than two months later, the stock market crashed. No new hotel would be built in downtown St. Louis until the Bel-Air East opened at 4th and Washington in 1963.

Designed as a 400-room "commercial hotel" with no ballroom and comparatively few private dining rooms, the Lennox was home to the well-known "Rathskeller," an atmospheric restaurant popular for decades. A twenty-third floor dining room perched overlooking Washington Avenue was added in 1957; later improvements included a rooftop swimming pool and fifteen-story garage. But in spite of promotion in 1977 as the "restored" Lennox, this hotel like the **Gateway Hotel** across the street *(page 40)* grew dependent upon bookings from trucking companies to stay open.

Conversion to apartments in 1986 by Mackey & Associates (St. Louis), with a *trompe l'oeil* on the east wall by Evergreene Painting Studios, New York, required a convoluted financial package predicated on loans and grants from local and federal agencies. After developer Pantheon Corporation defaulted in 1987, the Department of Housing and Urban Development (HUD-insurer of the first mortgage) paid the bank $6 million. Next, the city paid Pantheon $1.4 million for the garage, then razed it for the Convention Center expansion. Efforts by the

Above:

Laclede Gas Building
Gary R. Tetley, 1986

Left:

Detail: Laclede Gas Building
Gary R. Tetley, 1986

Chapter 2

Lennox Hotel circa 1929
Landmarks Collection

resuscitated developer to convert the Lennox into an all-suite hotel failed. HUD finally foreclosed in 1993 and turned the building over to the city for one dollar. The Lennox reopened in 2002 with 165 suites as the first part of the ambitious Headquarters Convention Hotel complex designed by RTKL.

19
Louderman Building
National Register: November 22, 2000
317 North 11th Street

William Louderman built this twelve-story office building as an investment from plans by LaBeaume & Klein, St. Louis. Constructed in 1925 just as New York-inspired setback styles were becoming locally popular, this would be one of the final downtown office buildings to use the traditional base-shaft-crown formula. It may be the most historically intact building downtown, with a well-preserved cornice, lobby and storefronts. Careful cleaning in 2001 prepared the way for anticipated $12 million mixed-use development, including upper floor residential, by Loftworks LLC.

20
Majestic Hotel
National Register: January 26, 1984
1019 Pine Street

Built in 1913-14, apparently from plans by Albert B. Groves in spite of a preliminary announcement that Harry F. Roach would be the architect, the $250,000 Majestic Hotel was located to attract out-of-town merchants and buyers who swarmed to St. Louis during its heyday as a regional commercial capital. Streetcar lines ran past the hotel west on Pine to **Union Station** *(page 69)*; only a block away was Olive Street, "the great east/west thoroughfare of St. Louis." With 204 rooms priced from $1.50 to $2.50 including full bath, the Majestic lived up to its motto, "Comfort without Extravagance." Lists of buyers registered at the Majestic between 1918-20 reveal a large percentage from states within St. Louis' primary sphere of trade: Arkansas, Mississippi, Tennessee, Kentucky, Kansas, Oklahoma, Nebraska, Texas and Colorado as well as out-state Missouri.

The hotel, later named the DeSoto, closed in 1979 amid rumors of potential demolition for surface parking. Purchased by new owners in 1983 including the real estate arm of Southwestern Bell Telephone Company (with headquarters directly across the street), the hotel (renamed the Majestic) opened in 1987 with 91 rooms as "St. Louis' Only European Concierge Hotel" after a $15 million historic tax credit renovation designed by Mackey & Associates (St. Louis).

Maryland Hotel circa 1910

Landmarks Collection

21
Maryland Hotel (Mark Twain Hotel)
National Register: February 16, 1996
205 North 9th Street

Albert B. Groves' specifications to the Winkle Terra Cotta Company for the decoration of the Maryland Hotel may have read like this: "please include some of everything." A full dictionary of motifs—Greek fretwork, arabesques, bead and reel, wave moldings, water leaves, cherubs, griffins, wreaths, garlands, shells, volutes and abundant others—decorate the projecting bays, center bays and bands between stories. Opened in fall 1908, the hotel offered special salesmen's suites combining large merchandise display rooms with attached bedrooms and baths.

By the end of the century, the hotel had become a run-down residential property known primarily for the assortment of illegal activities within. Amos Harris of the Mark Twain Hotel Partners engaged Trivers Associates to do a multimillion-dollar renovation, using historic and low-income tax credits to rehab the building into quality long- and short-term SRO (Single Room Occupancy) housing for downtown workers and others. The new Mark Twain was dedicated in 1999.

22
Mayfair Hotel
National Register: September 17, 1979
806 St. Charles Avenue

Designed in 1924 by St. Louis' preeminent hotel and apartment building architect Preston J. Bradshaw, the $2.5 million Mayfair was a tribute to the

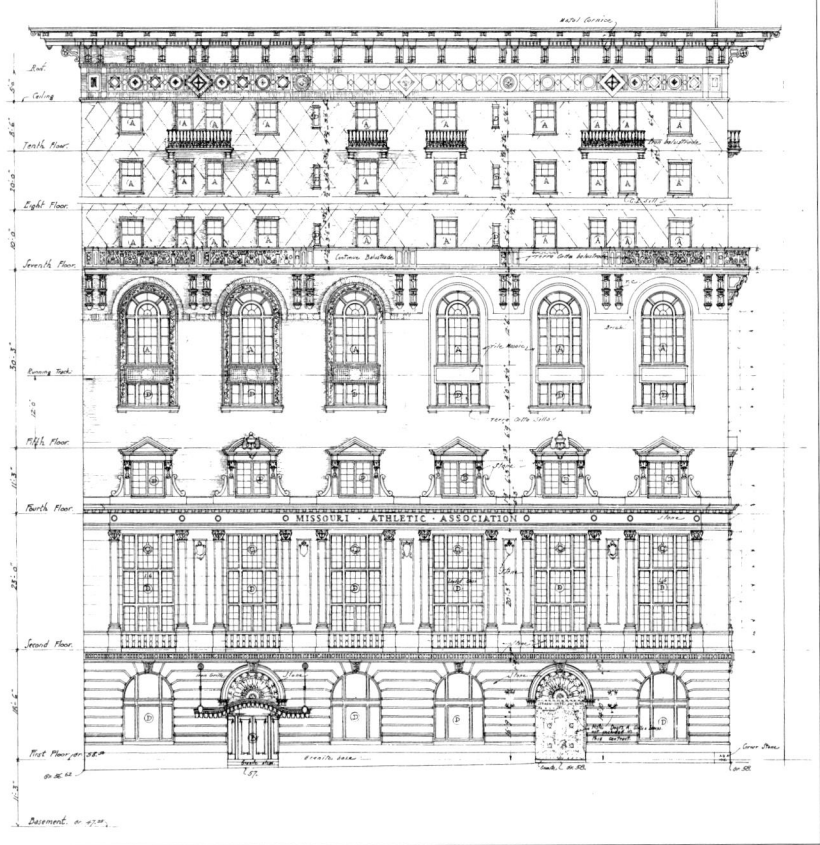

Missouri Athletic Club, original drawing, 1914

business acumen of owner Charles Heiss who began his career as a busboy at the Victoria Hotel in Heidelberg, Germany. Manager of the Tudor Hotel in London by age twenty-four, Heiss went to Detroit with the Statler chain before being sent to manage the new **Statler** in St. Louis *(page 40)* where he gained the experience and resources to open his own property.

The 400 room Mayfair, named for London's premiere hotel district, offered rooms from $3 to $6 a night above a mezzanine featuring noontime and dinner hour organ concerts. With a location in the heart of downtown's theater district next door to the Orpheum (**American Theatre** *page 15*), the Mayfair counted stars of stage and screen among its guests. The first KMOX radio studio occupied adjacent glass-windowed suites on the mezzanine; prohibition-era restaurants gained a reputation for fine dining. In 1934, the newly christened Hofbrau Restaurant offered a unique setting to celebrate repeal in a space graced by pedestrian-level stained glass windows from Jacoby Art Glass (St. Louis) with an old world theme.

Charles Heiss died in 1956 in his apartment at the Mayfair, but ownership remained in the family until 1970. Departure of the Bar Association of Metropolitan St. Louis from its headquarters on the top two floors in 1977 coincided with purchase of the hotel by a politically active St. Louis partnership with ties to Las Vegas. Their years of Runyonesque intrigue ended in 1985. Ownership passed through several hands before the hotel closed in 1987 for a $29 million transformation into 184 suites by Team Four Architects.

23
Merchants'-Laclede Building
City Landmark: July 1978
National Register: August 6, 1998
408 Olive Street

Regarded as a pioneer in the "lofty fire-proof buildings of St. Louis," the eight-story Merchants'-Laclede Building by Stephen D. Hatch (New York) and L. Cass Miller (his St. Louis representative) was completed in 1889. Standing at the threshold of steel frame construction, this early "skyscraper" adopted a transitional system of wrought iron frames supporting firewalls of hollow brick behind face brick. The exterior displays more than a hint of mischief in the nonacademic stone capitals above two-story stone pilasters and the naughty subject matter of at least one decorative terra cotta block placed high on the Olive Street elevation. Hotel magnate Charles Drury acquired the almost-vacant building in 2001 for yet another one of his important adaptive reuse projects.

24
Mississippi Valley Trust Building
City Landmark: July 1978
National Register: May 25, 2001
401 Pine Street

The Mississippi Valley Trust Company, formed in 1890, had the backers and the resources to become one of the city's most prosperous financial institutions. In 1896, it added to the success formula with an admired new building in the perfect location, a prominent corner in the heart of St. Louis' Fourth Street financial district (often referred to merely as "The Street"). Soon after the turn of the century, as it embarked on subscribing for capital stock for the Louisiana Purchase Exposition, the company recorded assets of more than $7 million. Mississippi Valley also played an important role financing transportation, utility and communication networks in St. Louis and the region.

Eames & Young's two-story building was sited to take full advantage of its corner location. The Classical Revival façade and the two-story banking hall within (still intact) "express the conservatism of a great

Trust Company and the security offered to its depositors and patrons." As the company continued to expand, it took over the five-story building to the north (now gravel-faced). A 1929 merger with the Merchants'-Laclede Bank and another institution prompted a further expansion into the Merchant's-Laclede Building at the north end of the block, so the lower floors of all three buildings on this side of the street operated as one large office. A year later, the new institution consolidated into a single building one block west. Its connection with its neighbors severed, the Trust building remained vacant through most of the 1930s. Since then, it has served as an aircraft company, a nightclub and a medical clinic (for which an unobtrusive third story addition was built). In 2001, new owner Plaza 44 LLC began the process of restoring the main banking hall and rehabilitating the rest of the building for offices from plans by The Lawrence Group Architects.

25
Missouri Athletic Club
City Landmark: October 1978
409 Washington Avenue

Designed in 1914 by a one-shot partnership between William B. Ittner and G. F. A. Brueggeman (both of St. Louis), this is the second home for the Missouri Athletic Club at this location. Clubhouse doors above Boatmen's Bank had first opened here in 1903, just in time for members to participate in events at the 1904 Olympics. Facilities included a swimming pool, gym, billiard room and bowling alley in addition to sleeping rooms. After a deadly fire destroyed the building March 8, 1914, the club elected to rebuild at the same site. The bank leased prime space in the just-completed, nineteen-story skyscraper at Olive and Broadway with the stipulation that the building's name be changed from Monward to **Boatmen's** *(page 19)*. A celebration on March 1, 1916, attended by 5,000,

Old May Company Department Store circa 1905
Landmarks Collection

marked the formal opening of the new ten-story club. Distinguished by intricate brickwork combined with brightly colored mosaic tiles, the $650,000 building was a gift to the street from August A. Busch and other prominent businessmen who bought the bonds necessary for construction. But only they, other gentlemen members and their guests could enjoy the fine interior finishes and artwork. Membership grew to nearly 3,500 in the early 1920s and the club built an addition in 1927 to the north along Broadway. (Another addition from 1950 is not as compatible.) In September of 1988, the Missouri Athletic Club finally voted to admit women as members. Offering reciprocity privileges with over 100 private clubs across the nation plus selected foreign countries, the club now actively solicits memberships from businesswomen.

26
Old May Company Department Store Complex
City Landmark: May 1978
National Register: June 23, 1983
555 Washington Avenue

The opening of **Eads Bridge** in 1874 *(page 3)* brought a surge of new construction to Washington Avenue including the Italianate-style Bradford-Martin Building designed in 1875 by Francis D. Lee with Thomas B. Annan. In 1876, the elegant cast-iron front Finney Building was constructed to the east. Both buildings were acquired by the D. Crawford Drygoods Company in 1898 for conversion into a "commercial palace." Architects Weber & Groves of St. Louis joined the buildings, reinforced the structural underpinnings and carved an ornate two-story glass-domed entrance into the Washington Avenue façade.

But in 1904, Crawford's was bought by David May—part owner of the largest retail company in the country. May greatly enlarged the complex by purchasing the Meyer-Bannerman Building (designed in 1888) at the southeast corner of 6th Street and Lucas Avenue, constructing an addition on Lucas and joining the disparate parts with an alley infill. The caption from a 1905 photo reads: "The up-to-date Department Store at Washington, Sixth and Lucas is one of the points of interest in St. Louis. A beautiful restaurant and fifty different stores are under this one roof."

The May Company moved a few blocks south to the new Railway Exchange Building in 1913. Gradually, history began to unravel as the Washington Avenue complex was subdivided for smaller tenants. By the 1970s, the "Dollar Store" was considered an eyesore on a street characterized by low-rent uses. Rancorous arguments about demolition dissipated after a partnership of James Dwyer and architect Kimble Cohn successfully acquired the bits and pieces of the complex held by separate owners. Restored for $22 million and reopened in 1987 as "555 Washington," the project reigned briefly as downtown's most alluring example of adaptive reuse. A depressed market for office space, inadequate cash flow and a bank unwilling to put more money in for tenant improvements combined to doom the partnership and close the building.

On an afternoon in December 1991, the shuttered property's saga entered the realm of the surreal: the Postal Service bought it for $12.5 million from a seller who paid the bank $4.1 million that same morning; the Postal Service spent $1.7 million more, then abandoned its plans and moved employees out at a cost of nearly $2 million; a federal judge fined the seller $250,000 for lying to the government; he, in turn, filed a $36 million suit against the Postal Service claiming emotional distress to which the Postal Service filed suit to void the sale. When the dust settled, the Postal Service still owned the building. A leasing agent brought in a local marketing company as the sole tenant in 1997; a handful of other firms moved there in 2000. The Postal Service reported in June 2000 that it had a contract on the property for an undisclosed amount; the asking price was $4.2 million.

27
**Mutual Bank Building
(Lashly & Baer Law Office)**
City Landmark: July 1978
716 Locust Street

Author Mary Powell recognized architecture as one of the arts in her 1925 *Public Art in St. Louis* in which this small bank received mention. A formal Classical Revival essay from architect Tom P. Barnett (St. Louis), the elegant limestone-faced cube is entered through a two-story quartet of finely sculpted Corinthian columns tucked inside the portico. Constructed for $125,000 in 1917 for the American Trust Company, the building is better known for its many years as the home of Mutual Bank.

The bank was in danger of demolition for surface parking in the 1970s. After a local Baptist college moved out, the projecting time and temperature sign advertising "Master Charge" remained the only sign of life. Inside, cheap paneling and tattered carpeting along with dropped ceilings made it difficult for the partners of attorney Charlie Valier to visualize any potential for law offices. But the Lashly & Baer firm made the leap; in 1979, it hired Mackey & Associates (St. Louis). The architects came up with an ingenious scheme utilizing almost every square foot inside the building. New doors by St. Louis sculptor Ernest Trova and a *trompe l'oeil* on the east wall by Pat Schuchard in 1987 completed the transformation.

Mutual Bank Building
*Robert C. Pettus
1979*

Chapter 2 Central Business District: East

Neighborhood Gardens Apartments looking west toward The Shrine of St. Joseph, circa 1936
Landmarks Collection

28
Neighborhood Gardens Apartments
City Landmark: February 1974
National Register: January 31, 1986
Bounded by O'Fallon, North 7th, Biddle and North 8th Streets

Completed in 1935 from plans by the St. Louis firm of Hoener, Baum & Froese, the nationally significant housing project was the culmination of over five years of unflagging efforts by the Board of Directors of Neighborhood Association and its Executive Director, J. A. Wolf. Wolf, a social worker, received a fellowship in 1931 to study low-cost housing in Europe. Upon his return, the Post-Dispatch published a long feature story: "Berlin and Vienna Did—Can St. Louis?" With $2,000 in hand for a study to determine the best site for a model project, Wolf embarked on an unsuccessful campaign to convince St. Louis businessmen to form limited dividend housing corporations. Instead, financing would have to come from ten Neighborhood Association Board members who put up $10,000 each plus a Public Works Administration loan of $640,000 maturing over a thirty-five year period.

Neighborhood Gardens offered rents from $19.50 to $33.00 a month. All apartments featured entrances directly off stairs rather than corridors, 12-foot ceilings, cross ventilation and balconies. Although it seems clear that the design was a collaboration between Wolf and the architects, Hoener, Baum & Froese brought multiple talents to the project. P. John Hoener was involved with the Depression housing crisis at the local, state and national levels. Albert H. Baum, Jr., as an engineer for William B. Ittner's precedent-setting school buildings (**Carr School,** page 54), had worked with the city's preeminent master of brickwork. Ewald R. Froese most likely was the lead designer for the firm whose Eden Publishing Company (Chouteau at Dolman) from 1932 is unabashedly Moderne. The enduring strength of that design and Neighborhood Gardens rests with the understanding of brick as a multiplane material into which ornament is integrated rather than applied.

It is still possible to learn and apply the lesson of Neighborhood Gardens even though its condition has become deplorable. In site plan, massing and materials, it is clearly one of the exceptional examples of American-designed and built housing projects. The choice of a brick exterior instead of the white stucco and glass of the avant International School was appropriate for a city known for its fine brickwork as well as its bituminous coal pollution. Sixty percent of the site was devoted to open space; not space left over between boxcar buildings, but designed, landscaped, defensible space. It is ironic that little attention was paid to the architectural accomplishments of Neighborhood Gardens when it opened and that nearby Pruitt Igoe first received national acclaim, then scorn.

29
Old Post Office and Custom House
City Landmark: July 1966
National Historic Landmark: November 22, 1968
Bounded by 8th, Olive, 9th and Locust Streets

Designed in a monumental French Second Empire style by Alfred Bult Mullett (the first Supervising Architect for the United States Treasury Department), the St. Louis Post Office and Custom House was plagued by acrimony and lawsuits from the 1872 selection of its site through the many slow years of construction. Business interests considered the location too far west of the linear downtown alongside the river; opposition was equally firm from neighborhood residents who correctly viewed the new building as a formidable encroachment in their snug community.

Preliminary investigation suggested that the site was well suited to support the large building projected for it, so the route of **Eads Bridge** tunnel *(page 3)* then under construction was adjusted to abut the east elevation of the soon-to-start post office. Excavation went smoothly to a depth of about thirty feet, at which point a rolling sea of quicksand was encountered. The solution, driving hundreds of Missouri yellow pine pilings thirty feet into the sand topped with a four-to-six foot limestone mat, shows no evidence of failure after well over a century.

The total project cost over $6 million by the time it was completed and fully occupied in March of 1884. A bulwark of Missouri red granite and gray granite from Hurricane Island in Maine, the building originally had a silhouette terminating with a cast iron cupola (removed in 1925) rising sixty feet above the dome. On the Olive Street elevation, "Peace & Vigilance" (modeled at half-scale in 1876-78 by Daniel Chester French and carved by William Struthers in 1881) was removed, restored and relocated inside the building in 1991. A replica of polymer reinforced concrete now presides from the crowning pediment of the central pavilion.

The last gavel fell in the Old Post Office courtrooms in 1935 when the new Federal Court Building at 12th and Market Streets opened. Gradually, other federal tenants departed. By 1961, only a branch post office remained and the building was threatened. A fifteen-year effort to save Mullett's building led by Landmarks Association's Old Post Office Committee culminated with the announcement in late 1977 that the General Services Administration would proceed with a mixed-use project to include federal offices. On May 5, 1978, Senator Thomas Eagleton announced that the design submitted by Patty, Berkebile, Nelson Associates (Kansas City) with Harry Weese Associates of Chicago had won the architectural competition.

Delays in the $16 million rehab project pushed the celebratory formal opening to October 13, 1982. But the much-vaunted public/private partnership was doomed. Wounds from the decade-long war of words did not heal easily; the development/marketing team could not agree among its members; competing projects **Union Station** *(page 69)* and St. Louis Centre moved forward with more vigor, more direction. As the failure of retail and food service at the Old Post Office became obvious, suggestions were made that the building now equipped with escalators to the old railroad tunnel level could be the perfect downtown central station for the MetroLink transit system still in the planning phase. They were rebuffed.

Webster University's announced interest in the Old Post Office as an education and cultural center galvanized the team of consultants and sponsors of the Downtown Now! Plan, an expensive epic begun in 1997 and concluded in 1999 with revitalization of the "Old Post Office Square District" called out as a top priority. At this writing it is not clear if a distorted implementation of that directive will result in replacing the historic **Century Building** *(page 19)* at the west face of the Old Post Office with a parking garage of behemoth proportions.

"Peace and Vigilance"
Old Post Office
Robert C. Pettus, 1979

30
Olive Street Terra Cotta District
National Register: January 2, 1986
622 Olive Street

Until the summer of 1988, the small-scale white terra cotta clad buildings in this district flanked both Olive Street elevations of the utilitarian Famous-Barr parking garage. With the demolition of the Boyd's complex and two adjoining buildings, the only remnant from the district is the earliest and most individually significant structure. Designed in 1910 by Louis Curtiss of Kansas City for jeweler William A. Gill, this structure (Curtiss' only known work in St. Louis) is closely related to his masterpiece in Kansas City, the 1908 Boley Building. Both were among the earliest in the United States to use rolled wide flange sections of steel for columns; their reinforced concrete floors reflect the architect's long interest in and experimentation with concrete structural systems.

31
**Phipps-Wallace Store Building
(United Missouri Bank)**
City Landmark: July 1978
National Register: November 22, 2000
312-16 North 8th Street

One of the few Richardsonian Romanesque buildings to survive in downtown St. Louis, Alfred Rosenheim's 1888 store building for the Phipps and Wallace families has three-story arcades with carved sandstone trim at spandrel panels and capitals. The original rusticated stone base was replaced in 1921 and 1925 by the Security National Bank (later United Missouri Bank), which hired Klipstein & Rathmann (St. Louis) to design a more classically styled entrance. Vacant for several years after United Missouri departed in the 1990s, the building is slated for conversion to luxury lofts and a new restaurant designed by Jeff Clark and Carlos Mindreau from Metropolitan Design & Building, St. Louis.

Opposite page:
Old Post Office circa 1894
Landmarks Collection

Below Left:
Detail: Shrine of St. Joseph's
Landmarks Collection

Phipps-Wallace Store Building

32
**St. Joseph's Catholic Church
(The Shrine of St. Joseph)**
City Landmark: August 1973
National Register: May 19, 1978
Biddle and North 11th Streets

The earliest portion (1844) of St. Joseph's was built by the Jesuits as a German-speaking parish for immigrants attending St. Louis University's Church a block north of Washington Avenue at 9th and Christy. Enlarged in 1866 after news of an 1864 cure (later declared one of two miracles essential for the canonization of Peter Claver) swelled the congregation, the church's Baroque façade and flanking towers designed by Adolphus Druiding (St. Louis-Cleveland) were added in 1881. (Tower cupolas were removed in 1954.)

By the opening of the 20th century, the view from the steps of St. Joseph's was becoming increasingly industrial and blighted. Clearance of a multi-block slum a few blocks east for the **Neighborhood Gardens Apartments**

St. Joseph's Catholic Church circa 1950

Landmarks Collection

ship meeting at the church and to engage architect Ted Wofford to study renovation costs. That report and the formation of the Friends of St. Joseph assured the future for the shrine and proved to be the stimulus for rebuilding the neighborhood. Twenty-five years later the Friends are still immersed in painstaking restoration. Rededicated at a festive concert on September 23, 2001, the rebuilt 112-year-old Pfeffer pipe organ can now be heard in a uniquely appropriate setting. The next phase will include major repairs to the stone south façade.

33
St. Louis Post-Dispatch Building
National Register: February 11, 2000
1139 Olive Street

Barnett, Haynes & Barnett's eight-story headquarters for the *St. Louis Post-Dispatch* (1917) is listed in the National Register for its significance in the history of publishing. The *Post-Dispatch* was founded in 1878 when young Joseph Pulitzer, new owner of the *Evening Dispatch*, merged it with the *Evening Post*. (Pulitzer's journalistic career had begun some ten years earlier writing for the German-language *Westliche Post*, where he quickly became editor and owner.) Using a maxim of high moral principle to address issues of prostitution, gambling, street paving, garbage disposal and other urban challenges generally unrecognized by the other papers, Pulitzer soon boosted the *Post*'s circulation. In 1883, he purchased the *New York World* and left St. Louis.

Under Joseph Pulitzer II, the St. Louis newspaper continued to grow. Recognizing the need for larger headquarters, Pulitzer spent a year studying state-of-the-art facilities worldwide before hiring Barnett, Haynes & Barnett of St. Louis to design the combined home of editorial, advertising and printing departments. On its opening, the new building was heralded in an editorial: "It is the physical and visible instrumentality of a finer spiritual structure, the great journal with heart and soul, wielding for civilization the force of publicity—the most potent moral force in the world. The meaning and purpose of the building are to expand the field and enhance the beneficent moral power of the newspaper."

Operating from this building, the newspaper became widely recognized as a forerunner of "crusading journalism," investigating the Pendergast machine in Kansas City, the Teapot Dome Scandal and St. Louis election fraud—a story that won the paper a Pulitzer Prize. In 1965, the fine Classical Revival façade was "modernized" by filling in windows and covering the building with a curtain wall. When the sheath was removed in 1999, new owners were delighted to find that most of the expensive limestone exterior remained intact and many alterations were reversible.

described above did not alleviate the general conditions. By 1944, only 20 families remained in the parish. Control of the church passed to the Archdiocese in 1965 in a time period when urban renewal projects razed two nearby 19th century churches. Persistent rumors that St. Joseph's was also doomed led to Landmarks Association's decision to hold its 1976 annual member-

St. Louis
Post-Dispatch
Printing Building
circa 1917
Post-Dispatch

34
St. Louis Post-Dispatch Printing Building
National Register: August 29, 1984
1111 Olive Street

Designed in 1941 by Mauran, Russell, Crowell & Mullgardt (St. Louis) using an architectural vocabulary sharply in contrast to the adjacent corporate headquarters *(page 38)*, the *Post-Dispatch* Printing Building was the first International Style building constructed in the Central Business District. (A number of quasi-International School slipcovers were unfortunately applied to existing historic buildings in the 1960s.) After the newspaper moved to the former *Globe-Democrat* building on 12th Street in 1962, the Olive Street property housed the Pulitzer Publishing Company's KSD radio and television stations from 1962 to 1982. A fourth floor was added in the mid 1980s as part of a renovation by new ownership.

35
Scruggs-Vandervoort-Barney Warehouse (Saint Louis Design Center)
National Register: February 21, 1985
917 Locust Street

The 1913 annual statement from the Merchants' Exchange reported signs of local prosperity with pride: "The aggregate volume in dry goods alone is estimated at $65,000,000. As a distributing point for dry goods, silks, notions and allied lines, St. Louis is easily holding her place in the front rank." Of the hundreds of dry goods merchants listed in the city directory, at least nine were major retailers. The crème de la crème was Scruggs-Vandervoort-Barney. Considered both a commercial establishment and a social institution, the company was praised in *The Western Architect* for the "skill, taste and promptness" it displayed in furnishing the interior decorations for the new **Missouri Athletic Club** *(page 31)*. That job was directed from the company's newly expanded full-block department store (now known as the **Century/Syndicate Trust Building,** *page 19*) between Locust and Olive, 9th and 10th.

Harry F. Roach (St. Louis), architect of the 1907 portion of the department store, was hired in 1913 to design a warehouse for Scruggs-Vandervoort-Barney reached by

St. Louis
Post-Dispatch
Printing Building
circa 1917
Post-Dispatch

Chapter 2 Central Business District: East

Joseph Pulitzer at cornerstone laying circa 1916
Post-Dispatch

tunnel under Locust Street. In use as warehouse space into the 1950s, the twelve-story structure was recycled in 1986 as The Saint Louis Design Center from plans by La Plante & Associates, St. Louis. Touted as a much-needed resource and greatly admired for its many creative showrooms and special events, the Design Center experiment attracted like-minded tenants including Landmarks Association. Unfortunately, the creative venture was not a financial success and the property at this writing is a run-of-the-mill office building.

36
Security Building
City Landmark: July 1978
National Register: February 10, 2000
319 North 4th Street

Designed in 1890, the Security Building is St. Louis' only extant commercial or institutional building from the office of Peabody, Stearns & Furber (Boston and St. Louis). Their Turner Building on 8th Street, the Museum of Fine Arts on Locust and the **(Unitarian) Church of the Messiah** (page 259) near Midtown have all been razed. From 1893 until 1964, the prestigious Noonday Club occupied the top two floors where sweeping views of the Mississippi River enhanced the courtly club interiors. Designed and under construction during the same years as Sullivan's **Wainwright Building** (page 43) a few blocks to the southwest, the Security Building can be read as St. Louis' last great work from an earlier aesthetic.

37
**Statler (later Gateway) Hotel
(Renaissance St. Louis Grand Hotel)**
National Register: March 19, 1982
822 Washington Avenue

Designed by George W. Post & Sons of New York with Mauran, Russell & Crowell of St. Louis, this top-of-the-line Statler won an award from the Saint Louis Art League as the best work of local architecture completed in 1917. It also attracted the attention of a reviewer for *The Architectural Forum*; seventeen pages devoted to the 650-room establishment

Statler Hotel
Gary R. Tetley, 1992

appeared in February 1918. The writer provided a brief essay on high-rise hotel design (an architectural newcomer), glowing appreciation of the massing, materials and palette of the Italian Renaissance structure along with an incredibly valuable set of floors plans, elevations and photographs.

The small site necessitated the tallest building city ordinance would allow: twenty-two stories, some 235 feet above the sidewalk. Patrons of the two-story colonnaded ballroom at the top enjoyed the panoramic view in an era when such rooms were lavish and well proportioned. The tripartite grouping of dining rooms on the first floor was centered on the glass-domed Palm Room, leading to the general dining room along Washington Avenue and the grill room/men's café along St. Charles. A vaulted lobby extending the entire 9th Street frontage acted as an arcaded passageway from Washington Avenue to the new Orpheum Theatre (**American Theatre** page 15). The mezzanine overlooking the lobby provided a "quiet, retired lounging place for the women guests, and for those delicately constituted personalities to whom the hurly-burly and intimate contact of the main floor are objectionable."

The new hotel also brought the remarkable Charles Heiss to town. Sent by the Statler chain to manage its fourth property, Heiss would create a tightly concentrated node of interrelated hostelries, (**Mayfair** page 29 and **Lennox** page 27). Dependent upon downtown's theater and shopping district as much as out of town guests, all would share the same misfortune as residents of the city moved west. By 1970, city population at 622,236 had been eclipsed by St. Louis County's 951,353 residents. Only a third of the rooms were in service at the Statler, by then Gateway, when it was purchased in 1981 for $3.2 million. The new partnership, with the same principals as the one that took over the Mayfair, did not accomplish its avowed plans for renovation.

Vacant with windows open to the elements, its interior damaged by a suspicious 1987 fire, the Statler was a likely candidate for demolition until a committee (with new members selected by Mayor Clarence Harmon) endorsed a scheme to combine the vacant Statler and Lennox Hotels with a new tower next to the Statler to form the convention center hotel complex. That decision in December 1997 was followed by several years of byzantine politics, negotiations, acquisition, lawsuits, design, redesign and reviews before financing was finally secure and the heavily subsidized $266 million project developed by HRI (New Orleans and St. Louis) in partnership with Kimberly-Clark broke ground. Opening date for the 916-room Statler is set for early 2003.

Union Market
Robert C. Pettus, 1989

38
Union Market
City Landmark: September 1978
National Register: January 16, 1984
Bounded by Broadway, North 6th, Lucas and Convention Plaza

At the turn of the 19th century, even though its haphazard growth made it a perennial subject for complaints, Union Market boasted the largest patronage of the seven municipal markets scattered throughout the city. No action was taken, however, until 1923 when an $87 million bond issue allocated one million for a new market building. At the cornerstone laying ceremonies in February 1925, Mayor Henry Kiel underscored the significance of rebuilding on a site used for market purposes since 1866: "We have made a mistake of jumping around too much. Property values have been constantly changing as the result."

The new market was designed by Mauran, Russell & Crowell with construction documents by E. E. Christopher, Architect for the Board of Public Service. A model of cleanliness and progressive functional design boasting indoor parking for 700 cars, Union Market (reported to be the second largest of its kind in the world) proved to be a commercial blunder. Some claimed that

Chapter 2   Central Business District: East

**Union Market
circa 1930**
*Missouri Historical
Society*

**Union Trust
Company
circa 1894**
*Landmarks
Collection*

burgeoning new chain stores or delivery service suited the new generation of housewives, commenting that only the "shawl" trade from the "old country" took pride in personally selecting family food. Criticism was also directed toward City Hall, which, in contrast to other large cities, did not share a percentage of gross receipts with vendors or promote group advertising.

A portion of the market was converted to a bus terminal in the mid-1930s; in 1967, the City, citing burdensome maintenance costs, announced its intention to sell the market. Opposition from merchants, customers and the Board of Aldermen forestalled the inevitable closing until 1982. A consortium with a 75-year lease tried to revamp the interior space and operate the building with funds from the garage. But even with the addition in 1990 of a two-story Drury Inn on the roof, the city received scant payment on its lease. Civic Entrepreneurs Organization studied the market as a possible permanent venue to traveling blockbuster art shows in 1997, but decided not to proceed.

39
**Union Trust Company
("705 Olive" Building)**
City Landmark: March 1971
National Register: June 17, 1982
705 Olive Street

"Ground costs money and air does not." In 1892, when James Cox aptly rephrased the obvious, ground at the corner of 7th and Olive Streets commanded $8,000 a front foot—the most expensive in town. The phenomenal rise in St. Louis real estate values did not deter investors from Chicago who saw opportunities for profit no longer available at home. One transplant remarked: "I find that same tendency here to laugh at the man who has the nerve to pay present prices for central property, but, mark the prediction, the history of Chicago's real estate market will be repeated here."

On July 9, 1889, St. Louisan John A. Scudder leased a lot about 128 x 84 feet to a group of Chicago investors at a yearly rent of $15,000 for 99 years with the stipulation that within six years the lessee construct a "good and substantial, absolutely fire-proof building" to cover the entire lot. Designed in 1892 by Dankmar Adler and Louis Sullivan (Chicago) with Charles K. Ramsey (St. Louis), the Union Trust was the tallest building yet constructed in St. Louis and the only Adler & Sullivan skyscraper to incorporate an exterior light court. The first two floors were embellished by one of Sullivan's most flamboyant installations of ornament centered on an expansive terra cotta-clad entrance flanked by large porthole windows and outsized high-relief griffins holding shields. Above, terra cotta "bear-cat" heads acted as sentries two stories below the intricate cavetto cornice with six bands of terra cotta. The roof, designed as an observatory, provided a unique site for a stratospheric beer garden.

A 1905 addition to the north along 7th Street by Eames & Young (St. Louis) faithfully adhered to the original Adler & Sullivan design above the two-story base. It is not known whether or not the St. Louis firm replicated the fanciful storefronts of the original building for the addition. But at some point early in the 20th century, the griffins were removed and windows squared-off. (An unadorned porthole window along the alley is the only hint of how stunning this display must have been to the passerby.) A later 20th century "update" substituted a weak "Sullivanesque" entrance for a Moderne one of stainless steel announcing "705 Olive" in large format.

40
Vess Bottle
North 6th & O'Fallon Streets
City Landmark: March 15, 1990

One of at least three giant Vess bottles installed around town in the early 1950s, this thirty-four foot tall work of pop art on a pole delighted (or perhaps infuriated) folks around Hampton & Gravois with over 600 feet of neon tubing gently rotating at three rpm. The beloved icon, designed by Treesh Neon Sign Co. of East St. Louis, was believed to be "the largest, revolving, lighted bottle in the world." Discovered in storage years after its decommissioning, the bottle was remounted in a tiny plot on the north side of downtown with the support of Vess.

41
Wainwright Building
City Landmark: July 1966
National Historic Landmark: May 23, 1968
101 North 7th Street

The Wainwright, St. Louis' most acclaimed historic building, was Adler & Sullivan's first St. Louis commission (1890-92) and the work Sullivan later described as the turning point in his career. Not the first steel-frame skeleton skyscraper or a completely logical outward expression of that structure, the Wainwright is nonetheless one of America's great monuments to the Art of Architecture. It appeared on the St. Louis scene in November 1890 with relatively little fanfare or reason for notice as a small sketch of a building for brewer Ellis Wainwright—most probably drawn by Charles K. Ramsey, the local associate of Adler & Sullivan credited with bringing them to town. Within a month his Chicago partners would assume project leadership and total redesign.

In contrast to Chicago architects who by 1890 had collectively made an impression on the Eastern establishment and its mouthpiece, *The American Architect & Building News*, St. Louis' relatively conservative designers were virtually unknown. But St. Louis offered fertile territory for the "foreign" firms that had begun reconnaissance of the local market in the 1880s. Dankmar Adler and Louis Sullivan had firsthand knowledge of the local building scene and architect Charles K. Ramsey through their mutual leadership in the upstart Western Association of Architects, a credible rival of the American Institute of Architects until merger. The 1885 meeting, held in St. Louis, was a triumph for the fledgling organization, its host city and the Chicago partnership. Alder was elected President; Sullivan delivered his virgin speech before an audience of peers. Prophetic thoughts about the profession's perennial desire to achieve an "American" architecture and his personal path to that architecture through commercial design, especially high-rise buildings, make this speech an exceptional source.

Today, it should not be forgotten that St. Louis and Chicago were among cities that allowed the destruction of works by Adler & Sullivan. The Wainwright Building could have been among them. Fortunately, the State of Missouri and Governor Kit Bond (with prodding by Landmarks Association's President Meade Summers, Jr. and financial assistance from the National Trust)

Vess Bottle
Ken Konchel, 1998

stepped in during the early 1970s when the building was threatened by demolition for a parking lot. But the Wainwright State Office Complex—an exemplar of intelligent architecture and urban design from Mitchell & Giurgola (Philadelphia) and Hastings & Chivetta (St. Louis)—is surrounded by an alien environment as the competition program developed by the state required demolition of all other buildings on the city block. The loss of the DeMenil Building (Isaac Taylor-1893) to the north started an erosion of the Wainwright's historic context that culminated with the demolition for the aborted Gateway Mall of the **Title Guaranty** (Eames & Young-1896, *page 251*) and Buder Buildings (Albert Swasey-1902).

Wainwright Building

Robert C. Pettus, 1989

42
Washington Avenue/East of Tucker District

National Register: March 24, 1987
Roughly bounded by Tucker, St. Charles, Ninth and Lucas Streets

When **Eads Bridge** opened in 1874 *(page 3)*, jobbers were already clustering in new buildings at the eastern edge of Washington Avenue. Heading west, the eighty-foot-wide boulevard passed by the Lindell Hotel, First Methodist and Trinity Episcopal churches, the campus of St. Louis University and well-appointed townhouses on the way to Washington University at 17th Street. The street would be transformed in little over a decade. Trade (once limited primarily to distribution) began to diversify; soon, St. Louis manufactured boots and shoes, millinery, notions, men's and women's clothing. Most of these burgeoning enterprises located on or near Washington Avenue as residents and mid 19th century institutions gave way to a remarkable corridor of multi-purpose buildings designed to include corporate headquarters, manufacturing and warehouse space.

Development would continue westward in a hopscotch pattern for the next two decades. *The Brickbuilder* noted in April 1899: "Washington Avenue has become a center of the wholesale and light manufacturing interests. When buildings were erected in the vicinity of 9th Street a few years ago they were considered quite a risk, but almost the entire property to 12th Street has been built up with large buildings." Throughout this boom an impressive assortment of local (and occasionally out of town) architects contributed to a robust streetscape of high art, signature buildings expressed in a variety of materials, styles and ornamentation. Common-wall construction triggering building restrictions affected height and mass to provide a coherent framework.

With few exceptions the Depression brought construction to a standstill. Growing concern in the 1940s about the dispersal of light manufacturing to outlying areas in Missouri and Illinois was offset by St. Louis' sudden fame as the national center for the "Junior Dress"—a brand new item in the fashion industry. Reporters from across the country flocked to St. Louis to see what chic trends the Washington Avenue houses were promoting. But by the 1960s, little manufacturing remained and clothing companies had lost their niche in the fickle high-style market place. Factors which had led to success—the large concentration of related industries, direct access to good public transportation for workers from all parts of the city, the proximity of a vital downtown—were becoming irrelevant in the age of sprawl and globalization. Underutilized and underappreciated, the loft area became a haven for artists, who found the cheap, well-lit spaces made perfect studios or live/work space. Remaining small businesses (many dating from the garment district period) coexisted with the newcomers, their galleries and the nightclubs that became common by the 1980s. Interest in the architecture also heightened as research established Washington Avenue's prominence in local and national history.

Many of the eighteen buildings in the district are City Landmarks and/or individually listed in the National Register *(see below)*. Other buildings of special interest include: 1) the self-important Mallinckrodt Building (later Bank of St. Louis) at the northwest corner of 9th and Washington where third-story panels carry the Medici family coat-of-arms and a corner escutcheon bears the monogram of Edward Mallinckrodt; 2) the building at 707-11 North 11th Street that was built as a black church circa 1875, purchased and converted to a firehouse

Wainwright Building Under Construction in 1891

Landmarks Collection

Chapter 2   Central Business District: East

(with a new front elevation) by the city in 1904 and later used as an annex by the Hadley-Dean Glass Company; 3) the Dorsa Building at 1009-13 Washington Avenue where Bessie Recht enjoyed success as exclusive designer for the Dorsa line of junior dresses while chairing the country's first four-year academic degree program of Fashion Design at Washington University.

43
Bee Hat Building
City Landmark: November 1979
1025 Washington Avenue

Designed in 1899 by St. Louis architect Isaac S. Taylor two years after Louis Sullivan's Bayard Building in New York City (which assuredly was its inspiration), Bee Hat enjoys a corner site where refined, elegantly vertical façades topped by a terra cotta frieze of sphinx-like, bosomy females linked by garlands can be viewed with appreciation.

44
A.D. Brown Building
National Register: March 28, 1980
1136 Washington Avenue

Designed in 1897 by St. Louis architects H. E. Roach & Son for the Hamilton-Brown Shoe Company as part of an unfulfilled City Beautiful scheme for 12th Street, this corporate headquarters is clearly influenced by the work of Louis Sullivan, especially the **Union Trust Building** of 1892 *(page 42)*. By 1912, Hamilton-Brown was the world leader in shoe production and sales.

Opposite page:

Washington Avenue west from 6th Street in 1906

Missouri Historical Society

Above:

Detail: Bee Hat Building

Robert C. Pettus, 1988

47

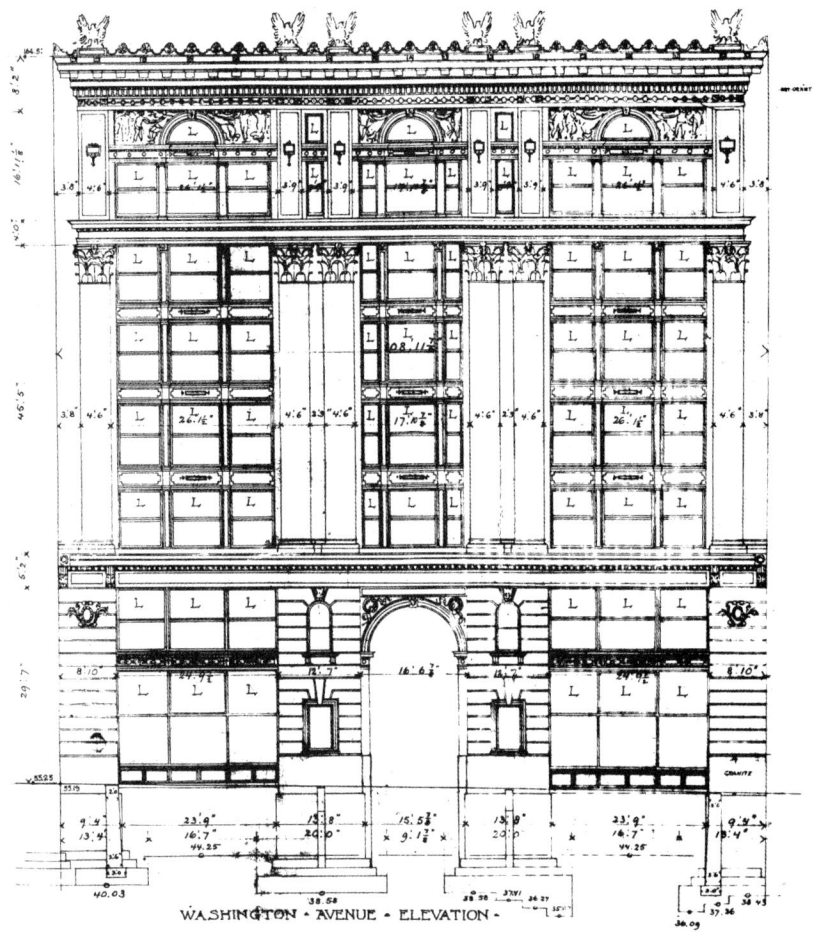

Lammert Building
Original drawing
1897

Detail: A. D. Brown Building
Gary R. Tetley, 1998

45
Hadley-Dean Glass Building
National Register: October 1, 1979
1101 Lucas Avenue

Prolific Isaac Taylor of St. Louis gained a sixth commission in the district in 1903, this for one of the first plate glass firms established west of the Mississippi. The lobby and flanking mezzanines were transformed in the 1930s by a vividly colored Art Deco world of Egyptian motifs in glass tiles. Some were removed and reinstalled at a new entrance to the building during a 1982 conversion to "Hadley Square" by Peckham, Guyton, Albers & Viets (St. Louis).

46
Lammert Building
City Landmark: November 1979
National Register: March 19, 1982
911 Washington Avenue

High relief, classically attired females grace the attic story of Eames & Young's Renaissance Revival building of 1897 for Commerce Realty Co. and Hargadine-McKittrick, the oldest dry goods company in St. Louis. Now identified with the furniture company which occupied the building from 1924 to 1981, the Lammert Building was adapted to office space in 1986 from plans by Mackey & Associates of St. Louis who removed storefront and entrance alterations from the 1920s and replaced them with a close replica of the original design in new materials.

47
Lindell Real Estate Company Building (1015 Washington Building)
National Register: March 19, 1982
1015 Washington Avenue

Built in 1901 from plans by the newly formed St. Louis firm of Mauran, Russell & Garden, 1015 Washington was one of the first buildings in St. Louis to be clad with rather than merely decorated by terra cotta. The successor firm (Mauran, Russell & Crowell) was responsible in 1912 for the city's largest installation of glazed terra cotta at the twenty-one-story Railway Exchange Building (Famous Barr, the May Department Stores).

Hadley-Dean Glass Building
Sam Fentress, 1985

Rice-Stix Building
Landmarks, 1999

48
Rice-Stix Building (Merchandise Mart)
City Landmark: November 1979
National Register: February 16, 1984
1000 Washington Avenue

Arguably one of the masterpieces of late 19th century commercial design, this imposing Romanesque Revival building was built in 1888-89 for local tobacco company magnates John E. Liggett and George S. Myers from plans by Isaac Taylor of St. Louis. Bold but disciplined, the block-long medley of materials includes polished and rough cut rose granite, pressed brick, terra cotta, sandstone, cast iron and copper. Original tenants included the Rice-Stix wholesale dry goods company, a relative newcomer to St. Louis that by 1907 had expanded to fill the entire building. In 1913, Mauran, Russell & Crowell (St. Louis) were called on to design an eleven-story addition to the south linked across St. Charles by an upper floor walkway.

Renamed the Merchandise Mart, the 500,000 square foot building continued in limited operation even after a local purchaser announced redevelopment plans in 1983. A different partnership, Ameritas of Atlanta, actually started on a major renovation a few years later.

The project ground to a halt soon after the firm placed a façade easement on the property with the statewide preservation organization. The giant of Washington Avenue sat empty, threatened with demolition until 2001 when a conversion into 213 apartments by Historic Restoration Inc. (St. Louis and New Orleans) was approved.

49
Winkelmeyer Building (Court Square)
National Register: July 11, 1985
107 South 11th Street

Designed in 1902 by German-trained St. Louis architect Otto J. Wilhelmi as investment property for his aunt, Christina Stifel Winkelmeyer, the building was purchased in 1985 by Atlanta-based Ameritas Inc. Trivers & Associates of St. Louis recycled the warehouse as Court Square, an office building designed to attract attorneys with business at the nearby courthouses. Threats of demolition in the late 1990s to construct a new Justice Center were averted by litigation receiving more press coverage per square foot than any other building in St. Louis history.

CHAPTER 3 | Central Business District: West

Former J. C. Penney Warehouse and MetroLink Station
Sam Fentress, 1993

Chapter 3

Central Business District: West

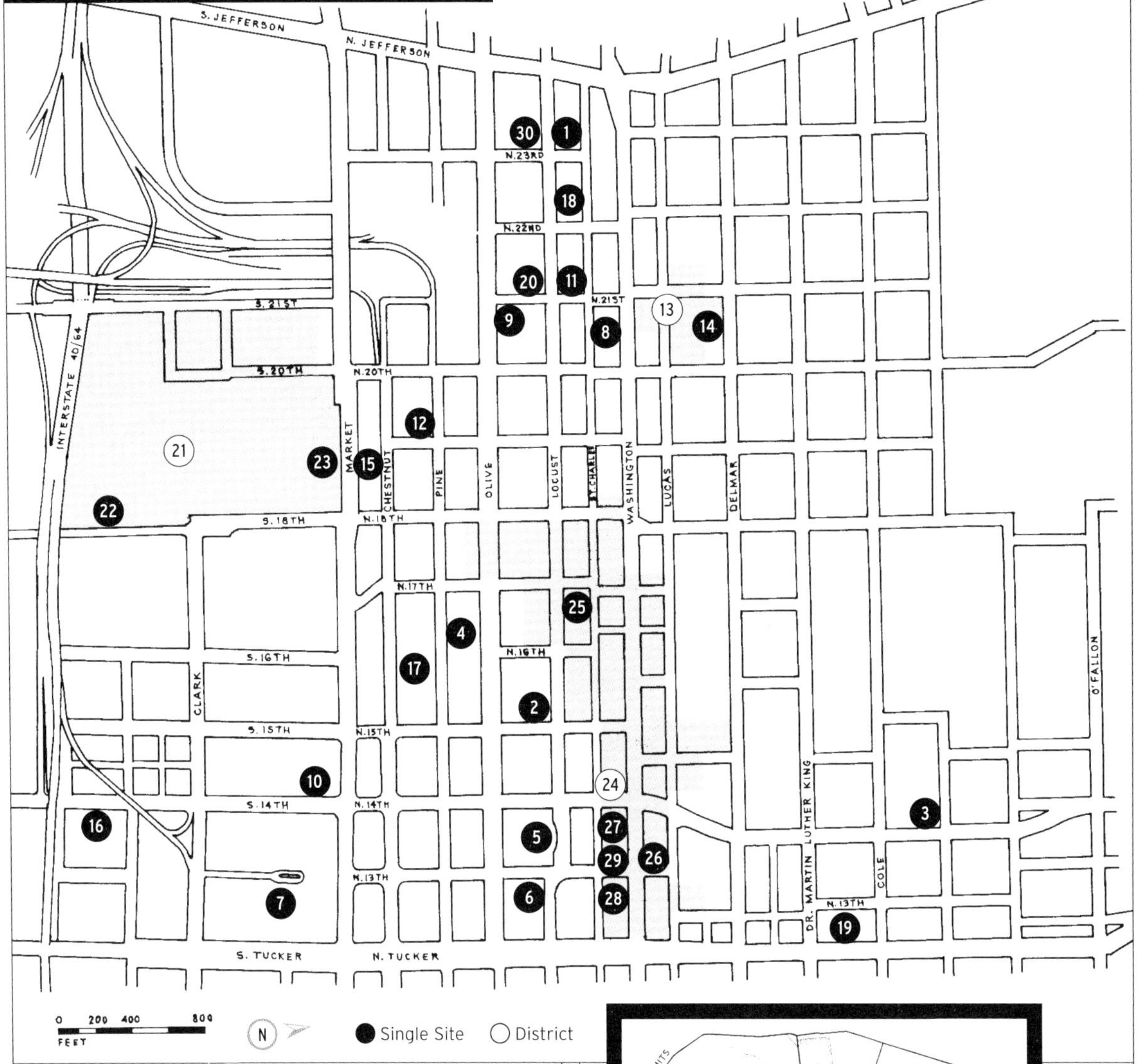

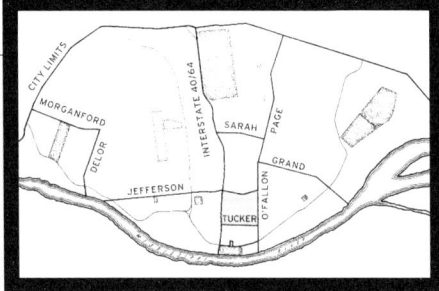

● Single Site   ○ District

1. Beethoven Conservatory
2. Campbell House
3. Carr School
4. Centenary Methodist Church
5. Public Library
6. Christ Church
7. City Hall
8. Emerson Electric
9. Hamilton-Brown Shoe
10. Kiel Opera House
11. Lambert Pharmaceutical
12. Liggett & Myers Tobacco
13. Lucas Avenue District
14. Majestic Manufacturing
15. "Meeting of the Waters"
16. J.C. Penney Warehouse
17. St. John the Apostle and Evangelist Church
18. St. Louis Provident Association
19. Sommer House
20. Swift Printing
21. Union Station District
22. Post Office Annex
23. Union Station
24. Washington Avenue District
25. Advertising Building
26. Fashion Square
27. Lesan-Gould
28. Peters Shoe
29. 1300 Washington Avenue
30. Willys-Overland

St. Louis Landmarks and Historic Districts

Beethoven Conservatory original drawing 1891

1
Beethoven Conservatory (Bruton Stroube Studios)
National Register: March 2, 1989
2301 Locust Street

The Beethoven Conservatory, established in 1871 by German-born violinist August Waldauer, moved in 1892 into a handsome new building at the western edge of Lucas Place. Its extensive faculty offered voice, violin, piano, organ, harp, cello, cornet, flute, guitar and mandolin along with harmony and composition, counterpoint, German and elocution. Waldauer founded many other musical organizations including the St. Louis Musical Union, a direct progenitor of the St. Louis Symphony Orchestra. But his conservatory designed by Beinke & Wees (St. Louis) was sited in a rapidly changing neighborhood. In less than two decades, Lucas Place would become Locust Street. Engulfed by warehouses and manufacturing facilities, the conservatory moved west.

The 1892 building was adapted first for Otis Elevator, then Cordes Printing Company. In early 2000, Bruton Stroube Studios (commercial photographers working primarily for art directors and designers) set about the task of recycling the resilient old conservatory into yet another use. Bill Wischmeyer of Christner, Inc. designed the space. Federal and State historic rehab credits were essential components of the $2.9 million project.

2
Robert G. Campbell House
City Landmark: July 1966
National Register: April 21, 1977
1508 Locust Street

Recognized today as a particularly fine house museum, the 1851 three-story townhouse with side garden and carriage house is the only residential survivor from once elite Lucas Place. Robert G. Campbell, the house's third owner, made his fortune as a partner in the Rocky Mountain Fur Trading Company. After his death in 1879, the house and furnishings remained in the family until the late 1930s. In 1941, Stix, Baer & Fuller bought the house and presented it to the new Campbell House Foundation as part of the department store's 50th anniversary celebration.

A series of St. Louis architects beginning with John Albury Bryan through Gerhardt Kramer provided the limited restoration work the foundation could afford. In 1997, Kimble A. Cohn & Associates spent nearly a year directing an in-depth analysis of the building. Findings including major structural problems (bulging walls) and inadequate wiring meant that the museum would need to close down for restoration. With report in hand, the foundation set off on a capital campaign. Work on the carriage house was completed in 1998 before furnishings from the townhouse were carefully packed and moved into storage. Then contractors and restoration specialists took over. Scaffolding encased the exterior while it was peeled back to the bare

Chapter 3 Central Business District: West

Carr School
Gary R. Tetley, 1991

Architect
William B. Ittner
Landmarks
Collection

bones; inside, layers of paint, wallpaper and upholstery were removed to discover original stencils and fabrics. The empty, structurally sound house was opened for a brief period during summer 2001 to celebrate the completion of Phase I (costing over $2 million) before work resumed in the fall.

3
**Carr School
(Part of the William B. Ittner MPS)**
National Register: December 13, 2000
1419 Carr Street

Carr School is one of eight schools listed in the National Register under the umbrella of the "St. Louis, Missouri Public Schools of William B. Ittner" multiple property submission. Ittner, associated with St. Louis' Board of Education from 1897 until 1914, revolutionized school architecture in the United States with his development of the "open plan" which emphasized light and air in both halls and classrooms. His earliest school designs are adaptations of the more boxy buildings already common in the St. Louis Public Schools. After years of experimentation and review of concepts from Europe and elsewhere in America, Ittner settled on an E-shaped plan with classrooms on only one side of the corridor.

He eventually boiled his ideas down to a near science, determining the ideal proportions for classrooms to the inch (24 feet by 32.5 feet) and fixing standards for lighting and ventilation. Although all of his St. Louis schools after about 1902 met similar standards, variations of siting and the imaginative use of exterior ornament result in a distinct style and identity for each. Ittner wrote extensively about his theories, helping to spread the fame of the St. Louis Public Schools nationwide. Forty-seven of Ittner's schools for the St. Louis district are still standing. Many are included within the boundaries of historic districts. Eleven are individually listed on the National Register: **Carr, Clark, Eliot, Emerson, Field, Jackson, Mann, Soldan, Sumner, Rock Spring** and **Wyman Schools** *(see Index)*.

One of the smallest but most impressive schools designed by Ittner during his career with the St. Louis Board of Education, Carr School is perhaps the clearest example of the open plan's adaptability to different sites and conditions. In its unique L-shaped design from 1908, two arms of equal length open from a single-story kindergarten at their intersection. Craftsman style brackets and vivid tile mosaics by Michael Lippman enhance the concrete-framed building. The school served the district from 1909 until the 1980s. Vacant for over ten years, it is currently owned by the Carr Square Tenant Management Corporation.

4
**Centenary United Methodist
Episcopal Church, South
(Centenary United Methodist Church)**
City Landmark: March 1971
National Register: January 16, 1997 North 16th and Pine Streets (55 Plaza Square)

Constructed of St. Louis limestone with De Soto, Missouri limestone trim under the supervision of Jerome B. Legg (St. Louis), the imposing Gothic Revival church with a towering 200-foot steeple was built in 1869 from plans by Thomas Dixon of Baltimore. Centenary's sanctuary designed "so as to bring the preacher as near as possible to his audience" underscored the Methodist emphasis on preaching rather than liturgy. A showcase of fine wood craftsmanship (mostly in black walnut), the intact auditorium-style sanctuary with exposed wood ceiling is surrounded on three sides by a narrow balcony.

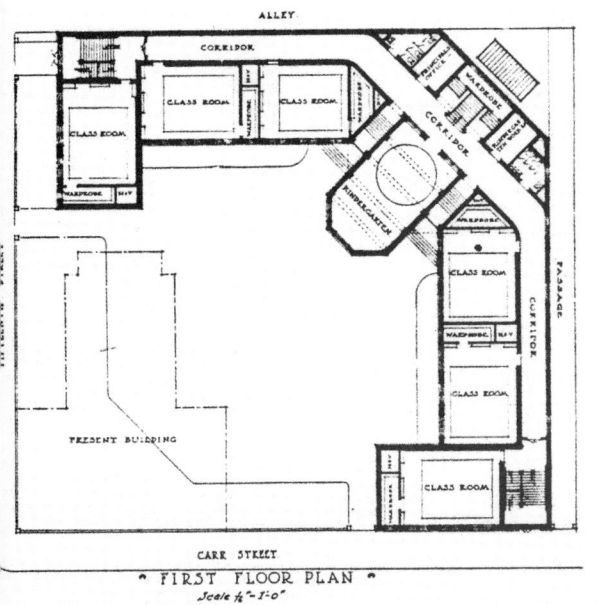

Left:

**Carr School
first floor plan**

Organized in 1839 as the second oldest Methodist congregation in the city, Centenary made a long-term commitment in 1900 to remain at this location at a time when almost all the nearby congregations moved west. Improvements from that date included new art glass windows; another building project in 1924 brought construction of the three-story limestone addition (Mauran, Russell & Garden, St. Louis) along Pine. Membership peaked at 3,601 in 1930, but decline was inevitable as the neighborhood continued to change. Clearance for the Plaza Square Apartments in the 1950s isolated Centenary and its Catholic neighbor, **St. John the Apostle** *(page 65)*. Renovated in 1964 by P. John Hoener & Associates, the church became Centenary United Methodist in 1968 when Methodists merged with Evangelical United Brethren. Today, Centenary, the seat of the Eastern Missouri Episcopacy, benefits from a nucleus of Plaza Square residents as it reaches out once again to attract members from throughout the region.

Below:

**Centenary
Methodist**
W.C. Runder, 1955

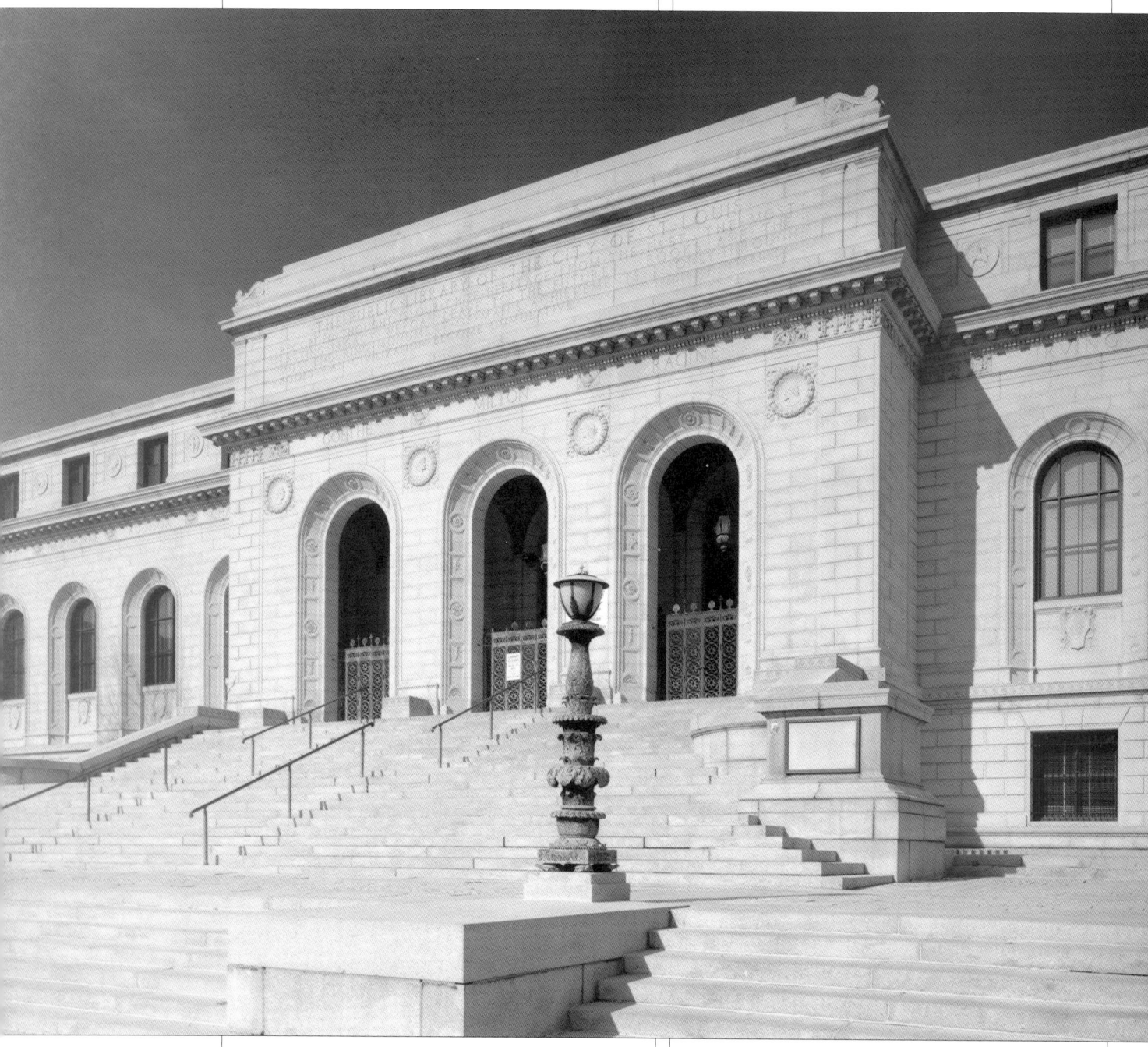

Central Public Library
Robert C. Pettus, 1986

5
Central Public Library
City Landmark: September 1966
Bounded by Olive, 13th, Locust and 14th Streets

Cass Gilbert of New York City won the competition for the St. Louis Public Library from a field of nine invited firms in 1907. Five were local: Barnett, Haynes & Barnett, Eames & Young, William B. Ittner (who placed second), Theodore C. Link and Mauran, Russell & Garden. All had been paid $1,000 to enter; the winner was to receive a $60,000 commission. Local press reported that a commitment to stay within the $1 million budget was a factor in the selection of Gilbert's scheme. A few years later that same press reported grumbling from tradesmen about the New York firm's slow production of working drawings. When the stately Renaissance Revival building opened in 1912, $1.5 million had been spent including the $500,000 gift from Andrew Carnegie. Land for the building, donated by the city, was worth another million.

The library's exterior walls and terraces are Maine granite. A monumental staircase leads to the main entrance on Olive Street with ornate bronze grilles cast by the Gorham Company of Providence, Rhode Island. Fine finishes, including intricate ceilings based on models from Renaissance Florence, are featured in most public spaces. The jewel of the interior may well be the two-story central hall covered by a gilded coffered ceiling touched with green and red. Happily, an advanced mechanical system designed by Gilbert allowed air conditioning to be installed at a later date without disfiguring the interior.

A monograph about the new building published in 1912 concludes with the following: "...in addition to the education obtained from books is that which comes from surroundings of quietude and refined good taste. A love of beauty is an element of good citizenship and to inculcate this lesson is a proper part of the general educational function of the library."

6
Christ Church Cathedral
City Landmark: July 1966
National Historic Landmark: October 12, 1994
13th and Locust Streets

After an 1857 contract with Buffalo, New York architect Calvin N. Otis was rescinded, the Vestry of Christ Church Episcopal selected Leopold Eidlitz of New York to design their new building. Work began in 1859 under the supervision of St. Louis architect William John Beattie, but financial problems and the Civil War delayed the project and altered its design. The chaste, Gothic Revival sandstone church was dedicated in 1867, becoming a cathedral in 1888 upon its selection as the seat of Bishop S. Tuttle's Episcopal Chair. The Mary E. Bofinger Chapel designed by James B. Legg (St. Louis) replaced an original chapel in 1893. By the time work began in 1911 on the church's carved limestone porch and tower by Tully & Clark (St. Louis), the neighborhood was in transition. Cass Gilbert's library across the street was nearing completion; just to the west, even the name of once-exclusive Lucas Place disappeared as Locust Street cut through Missouri Park north of the library. Christ Church stood fast.

Demolition in 1928 of the Schuyler Memorial House from 1892 by Shepley, Rutan & Coolidge (Boston) allowed for construction of the six-story Bishop Tuttle Memorial by Jamieson & Spearl (St. Louis) housing parish and diocesan offices, meeting rooms, gymnasium and swimming pool. Sixteen light fixtures designed by Nagel & Dunn (St. Louis) in 1939 incor-

Left:
Christ Church Cathedral
W. Philip Cotton, Jr., 1989

Below:
Christ Church Cathedral
Robert C. Pettus, 1989

Chapter 3   Central Business District: West

porated symbols of crown, miter, fish and fleur-de-lis. Frederick Dunn also redid the chapel interior in 1960; in 1969, Burks & Landberg (St. Louis) reworked the nave, removing pews to accommodate secular concerts and plays. Retiring Senator John C. Danforth's 1994 donation of a dramatic painting by American artist Steven Hawley (hanging in the Bofinger Chapel) is only one of the latest examples of the fine works of art located within the complex now serving the community through programs ranging from social services to the distinguished Shepley Program of Music and Art.

7
City Hall
City Landmark: March 1971
Tucker Boulevard at Market

Whenever a new municipal or other public building is to be erected in this country, intelligent people have learned to expect that officers elected and appointed to care for its erection will distinguish themselves by the adroit way in which they will delay its completion, entangle its construction and increase its cost regardless of all legal restrictions. The new City Hall at St. Louis... now stands as an empty skeleton, the sport of the elements while a 'thorough investigation' is conducted by city officials.

City Hall
Robert C. Pettus, 1988

Thus did *The American Architect and Building News* in 1895 proclaim St. Louis among the worst managed cities in the country. City Hall, the most obvious physical evidence of an inept government, was impossible to conceal from the multitudes gathered for the opening of **Union Station** in September of the previous year *(page 69)*. Architect George G. Mann and draftsman Harvey Ellis (who may have contributed to the design) had moved to St. Louis from St. Joseph, Missouri in 1891 to push toward the completion date of 1892 set out in the 1890 City Hall competition. Instead, construction limped along on yearly doles from the Board of Aldermen's General Revenue fund. Even with an agreed-upon fee for the final design and superintending, Mann had been subjected to appalling countermands, constant political inference and "downright insolence" from his multi-headed client.

Loosely modeled on the Hotel de Ville in Paris, City Hall was occupied (still only partially finished) by the late 1890s but not completed until Albert Groves of St. Louis was brought in to design the marble rotunda and grand staircase in time for the 1904 World's Fair. A central tower and two flanking spires on 12th Street, now Tucker Boulevard, were removed in 1936. Efforts to clean and restore the exterior during Mayor Clarence Harmon's term at the end of the 20th century did not receive sufficient public support or funding.

8
**Emerson Electric Company Building
(Sporting News)**
National Register: November 6, 1986
2012 Washington Avenue

Today a giant in the worldwide market, Emerson Electric Company was founded in 1890 as a three-man operation named after Judge John Wesley Emerson, its first president. Research and development of new electrical products in this country quickly turned an industry producing novelties into one providing the necessities of life. Emerson experienced spectacular success. In 1920, at the brink of a long period of expansion and product innovation, the company commissioned Albert B. Groves (St. Louis) to augment its manufacturing capacity with the design of "Building D." An eight-story reinforced concrete skeleton with brick-clad façade,

Building D is credited with the first progressive assembly line in St. Louis. It was also the 1937 scene of the longest sit-down strike in national history to date (53 days) when Emerson's President refused to negotiate unionizing with the Congress of Industrial Organizations (CIO).

After Emerson moved to St. Louis County in 1938, the building was headquarters for the "Bible of Baseball" run by the Spink family. Founded in 1886, *The Sporting News* remained on Washington Avenue for twenty-five years before a move to St. Louis County; it was sold in 1977 to the *Times-Mirror* of Los Angeles. Ownership of Emerson's Building D (the sole survivor of its early empire downtown) fell first to the city for back taxes, then to a developer who acquired the property for $5,000 with as yet unrealized plans to convert it to loft housing.

Selling electric fans (one of Emerson's most profitable items) in the off-season was a challenge met by bold marketing.

Advertisements from Emerson Electric Company: a Century of Manufacturing 1890-1990

From left to right:

Renovation begins at Hamilton-Brown Shoe
Landmarks, 1999

The former Lambert-Deacon-Hull Building (now the Tap Room) in the foreground; Hamilton-Brown Shoe at the left
Landmarks, 1999

9
Hamilton-Brown Shoe Factory
National Register: May 5, 2000
2031 Olive Street

This seven-story factory produced Security School Shoes and other lines for the Hamilton-Brown Shoe Company between 1902 and 1924. It was built as an adjunct to the company's larger American Gentleman factory across the alley to the north (now best remembered for the spectacular firestorm which destroyed it in 1976). At the time of its construction, Hamilton-Brown was the largest shoe manufacturer in the world. Although Isaac Taylor is credited with the design, it is one of many commissions which probably fell under the supervision of chief draftsman Oscar Enders while Taylor was occupied as Director of Works of the Louisiana Purchase Exposition. In 2000, the factory and its single-story 1955 annex were converted into elegant offices for owners Welsch, Flatness & Lutz from designs by the Lawrence Group (St. Louis).

10
Kiel Opera House
National Register: February 11, 2000
1400 Market Street

While Union Station was under construction in the 1890s, St. Louisans voiced growing concern about the "decrepit sin-soaked area" (as the *Post-Dispatch* later called it) greeting visitors outside the city's new front door. Over the next several decades, public groups and planners advanced schemes to clear entire blocks between Union Station and 12th Street (now Tucker) and create a parkway, public buildings and/or park blocks in varying combinations. In 1919, the City Plan Commission reviewed the 1904 Public Building Commission's report and found a statement that could be applied to numerous such planning documents in the more than eight decades since: "This commission presented an admirable report, but their suggestions were not followed."

A 1923 bond issue, the largest in the United States ever passed to that point, included measures funding large-scale clearance and the construction of parks, a new courthouse (the Civil Courts), War Memorial and a "Municipal Auditorium." This updated version of a town hall was to "provide suitable meeting places for educational, moral, musical, industrial, labor and other purposes." Land acquisition for the $5 million project continued through 1932; ground was finally broken in August of that year.

Designing for the publicly appointed Plaza Commission, the firm of LaBeaume & Klein (St. Louis) submitted an ambitious program which included a 3,500-seat opera house, an auditorium with a capacity of over 12,000, four "small" assembly rooms (seating up to 800) and an exposition hall running beneath the entire complex. Mayor Bernard Dickmann suggested that employers declare a half-day holiday on April 14, 1934, so all citizens could attend the dedication. Those who could not, however, would still have two solid weeks of opening festivities to satisfy their curiosity. Renamed after Mayor Henry Kiel in the 1940s, the complex regularly hosted sports events, exhibitions and conventions. It was the home of the St. Louis Symphony Orchestra from 1934 until 1968 (see **St. Louis Theatre,** page 87) and was the site of a G. I. Service Center during World War II.

In 1991, the complex was closed in a plan to demolish the auditorium side of the building for a new sports arena and to renovate the Opera House. The St. Louis Blues began playing in the new Kiel (now Savvis) Center in 1994. As late as 1995, the lease-holding Kiel Partners maintained that renovation of the Opera House would proceed, but by 1996 they determined that the $2.5 million already spent satisfied all legal obligations. At press time the splendid Art Deco interior of the Opera House, grand lobby and auxiliary spaces are closed to the public. Dreams of creating a downtown arts and cultural center await the rare combination of vision and cash which could make them come true.

Above:
Newly completed civic center in postcard circa 1935
Landmarks Collection

Below:
Kiel Opera House with Savvis Center
Sam Fentress, 1994

Chapter 3 Central Business District: West

Lambert Building

Pen & Sunlight Sketches of St. Louis, *1892*

11
Lambert Pharmaceutical Building
National Register: February 24, 1983
2001-07 Locust Street

Attributed to architect Thomas B. Annan of St. Louis, the 1891 Lambert Building is one of St. Louis' best remaining examples in the Richardsonian Romanesque tradition. A superb addition to the west from 1902 (designed by Samuel L. Sherer, businessman, art critic, architect and later Director of the St. Louis Art Museum) doubled the factory and added a suite of corporate offices facing the street on the first floor. Founder Jordan W. Lambert developed Listerine (the company's best-known product) at this address. Only when the immense popularity of Listerine plummeted during World War I was an aggressive new marketing campaign adopted. Featuring potent images such as dejected women wondering why they were always the bridesmaids, never the bride, the successful strategy was adopted at the urging of the "Father of Halitosis," Gerard Lambert—one of the founder's five sons who eventually became involved in the company. (Brother Albert Lambert, a pioneer aviation enthusiast, purchased and improved the first portion of what is now Lambert-St. Louis International Airport in 1920.)

The building was sold to the T. M. Sayman Company in 1938, which incised its name in the sandstone above the entrance and added a stuffed horse to the lobby as a ghoulish reminder of its soap products. Sayman left the building in 1975; the following year a dramatic fire almost consumed this building and the former Lambert-Deacon-Hull printing company property across the street (**Swift Printing Company** *page 67*). The Lambert Building was purchased by Chase Development which opened twelve loft condominiums in 1991.

12
Liggett & Myers Tobacco Co. Building
National Register: February 10, 1983
1900 Pine Street

Probably designed by Henry E. Roach (St. Louis), the six-story red brick building is among St. Louis' best-preserved examples of 1880s industrial architecture. It was built in 1889 as a tobacco-drying house for Liggett & Myers, the largest manufacturer of plug tobacco in the world. Liggett & Myers supplied half of Missouri's total output—about 20% of the national total—until acquisition in the early 20th century by tobacco tycoon James Buchanan Duke of North Carolina. The leaf-drying house was sold in 1901 to a real estate company, then leased to a succession of light manufacturing and business firms. Clearance in the 1930s of city blocks including the adjacent Liggett & Myers warehouse to the south for Aloe Plaza opened an impressive view of Union Station and later the Carl Milles Fountain, **"Meeting of the Waters,"** described below. The building was recycled for offices in 1983 from plans by Henderson/Gantz of St. Louis.

13
Lucas Avenue Industrial District
National Register: August 31, 2000
Roughly bounded by Washington, Delmar, 20th and 21st Streets.

From eighth largest in 1860 to the nation's fourth in both population and gross value of manufactured products by 1900, St. Louis at the turn of the century enjoyed a final period of dramatic growth. Along with an expanded and diversified economic base came a rapid change in land use as business interests pushed west from downtown to acquire property originally built up as residential. The first new owner to break ground within district boundaries was John E. Liggett, whose extraordinary success in tobacco manufacturing *(see above)* left profits for speculative real estate investments. In March 1889, Liggett began construction of a two-story brick building at 2030 Delmar for tenant August Gast & Co., German-trained engravers and lithographers whose nationally recognized St. Louis firm dated back to at least 1852. (Gast remained at this location until 1926.)

Next came Jacob B. Ulrich's short-lived Woolen Mills at 2019-15 Lucas followed by a new building for the Majestic Manufacturing Company *(next page)*. Construction in 1899 of the Desnoyers Shoe Co. factory at 2031 Lucas brought one of the city's fastest growing industries. That plant, designed by the ubiquitous Isaac Taylor, was the seed for what became the dominant industry in the nine-building district. Desnoyers' descendant, the McElroy-Sloan Shoe

Company famed for its Billiken children's line, erected buildings in 1919 and 1920 from another favored St. Louis architect of the period, Albert B. Groves. The district is currently the subject of an ambitious adaptive reuse scheme based on housing.

14
Majestic Manufacturing Company Buildings
National Register: December 31, 1998
2014 Delmar and 2011-17 Lucas Avenue

The September, 1904 *World's Fair Bulletin* boldly asserted that the best display in the Palace of Manufactures, or possibly any exhibit building, was the steamship "Majestic" fitted up with the company's top-of-the line ranges. Founded in 1891 by Lucius Lewellyn Culver, then reorganized a year later with Robert Henry Stockton as Vice President, the company was the first manufacturer of long lasting, malleable iron ranges in the nation. After Culver's death in 1899, Stockton became President of the fast-growing corporation. Stockton, who remained at the helm until his death in 1912, just happened to be chairman of the World's Fair Publicity Committee.

Barnett, Haynes & Barnett (St. Louis) received the commission for the company's 1895 building at 2018 Delmar next to the original facility, now demolished. (The same firm was responsible for Stockton's 1890

Advertisement for Majestic Manufacturing
World's Fair Bulletin
July, 1901

family home in **Midtown**; Chapter 4.) By 1901, increased business necessitated erection of a one-story plant across the alley at 2015-17 Lucas. Four floors were added in 1913 along with an overhead bridge connecting to the 1895 factory. Among the five local stove companies still active after World War II, only Majestic and Magic Chef expanded into gas ranges in response to consumer desires. Production continued at the Delmar plant until 1951.

15
"Meeting of the Waters"
City Landmark: September 1966
Aloe Plaza between 18th and 20th Streets

The best-loved piece of public art in the city and one of the most engaging fountains in the country, the bronze nudes and their fanciful water sprite attendants were originally entitled "The Wedding of the Waters" by Swedish-born sculptor Carl Milles. Installed in 1940 with an altered name after howls of public prudery reminiscent of an earlier flap over **"Naked Truth"** in Reservoir Park (page 219), the wedding parties led by the male Mississippi figure welcoming his Missouri bride remained unclothed.

Revealing a tantalizing hint of the widespread polemics, George McCue in Sculpture City: St. Louis (1988) playfully tallies a four-day St. Louis Star-Times reader's ballot with 96 for and 377 against "the Milles nudes for Aloe Plaza."

Milles had become intrigued by the site across Market Street from Union Station after a chance meeting in 1931 with the widow of Louis Aloe, former President of the Board of Aldermen for whom the two-block plaza was named. By the time the commission was actually extended five years later, Milles had already developed working models. Both Mrs. Aloe, the patron, and the artist remained steadfast during what now seems a most provincial controversy.

16
**J. C. Penney Co. Warehouse
(Sheraton St. Louis City Center)**
National Register: December 31, 1998
400 South 14th Street

In the twenty-five years between 1902 and 1927, James Cash Penney rose from manager of a small dry goods store to owner of a chain with nearly 900 locations. His company consolidated its distribution activities in New York beginning in 1919, but growing demand and the high concentration of western stores demanded a second warehouse center. St. Louis was already the chain's national employment center (although there were as yet no stores in town); the city's central location, proximity to transport routes and position as a jobbing and manufacturing center led the company to establish the second office/warehouse building here in 1929. Construction and design of the massive utilitarian building were by engineer John F. Miller and contractor Starrett Brothers (best known for constructing the Empire State Building) of New York with architect Tom P. Barnett and engineer Taxis & Becker of St. Louis—the local team involved a decade earlier with the structurally challenging **Arcade Building** (page 16).

The St. Louis facility was used only until 1954, when Penney abandoned its multi-story warehouses in favor of more modern distribution methods. Over time the connection with Penney was all but forgotten. Later known as the Edison Brothers Warehouse (after its owner from 1967 to 1994), it is now beloved for the 1984 trompe l'oeil murals by New York artist Richard Haas who covered three sides of the thirteen-story building with over three acres of flamboyant architecture and references to the Louisiana Purchase Exposition. Threats to this highly visible public art inspired tremendous outcry in 1997 when demolition of the building for surface parking was proposed. In

"Meeting of the Waters" circa 1950
Landmarks Collection

Former J.C. Penney Company
Westrich Photography, 1998

2001, the Sheraton City Center Hotel with 144 suites and an eight-story atrium the length of a football field opened to great acclaim. Artist Richard Haas was in attendance as were architect Dick Henmi and developer/owner Don Breckenridge. Up to seventy-two condominium units are slated for completion by 2003.

17
St. John the Apostle & Evangelist Catholic Church
City Landmark: March 1971
16th and Chestnut Street

The twin-towered Lombard Romanesque Revival brick church designed in 1859 by Patrick Walsh (St. Louis) was completed by architect Thomas Mitchell after construction problems forced Walsh's resignation. Founded in 1848 as the eighth Catholic parish in the city, the church was affiliated with the Archbasilica of St. John Lateran in Rome and could thus hold ordination and consecration services. In 1876, St. John's became the Pro-Cathedral—the residence and administrative center for Archbishop Kenrick and his staff.

Kenrick had left the **Old Cathedral** (page 6) to escape the grime and noise of the mercantile city. Yet within two generations, factories, budget hotels and saloons surrounded St. John's; by the 1930s, the church ministered exclusively to transients and travelers from nearby **Union Station** (page 69). The federal government passed legislation creating the far-reaching urban renewal program in 1949. A 54-block area including St. John's

St. John the Apostle Church circa 1900
Mercantile Library

Chapter 3   Central Business District: West

Union Station District: Train shed before renovation
Robert C. Pettus, 1975

and **Centenary Methodist**, described on page 54, was chosen by the city to be the first local project. The Archdiocese renovated St. John's in 1961 at the conclusion of the Plaza Square project, selecting Murphy & Mackey (St. Louis) as architects.

18
St. Louis Provident Association Building
National Register: June 20, 2001
2221 Locust Street

Founded in 1860 by William Greenleaf Eliot, the St. Louis Provident Association (originally Society) was among the city's leading providers of social services until merger with the Children's Aid Society in the 1930s. Its programs were wide-ranging including job training, day care, in-home health services, free meals and emergency housing. The association even operated a lumberyard and laundry to provide employment for low-skilled men and women. In 1910, many of the departments were consolidated into the new Locust Street building designed by J. H. Lynch (St. Louis). By the 1920s, the building became known as the "Social Service Building" as the Provident Association leased space to groups such as the Girl Scouts, Urban League, YWCA and the Pure Milk Council.

Underutilized through the Depression, the building was transformed in 1944 as the new home of People's Hospital. The 75-bed facility was among the few hospitals where African-American patients were treated regardless of their ability to pay. Founded in 1894, People's Hospital had begun a training program for nurses in 1898—one of the city's only opportunities for black women to receive any kind of professional medical training for many years. The hospital remained at this location until 1966. It closed due to financial problems in 1978.

19
Sommer House Restaurant
City Landmark: November 1978
911 North Tucker Boulevard

The sole survivor of a once-dense 19th century neighborhood, the former Sommer House Restaurant is a

Aloe Plaza in 1934 before construction of "Meeting of the Waters" fountain
Landmarks Collection

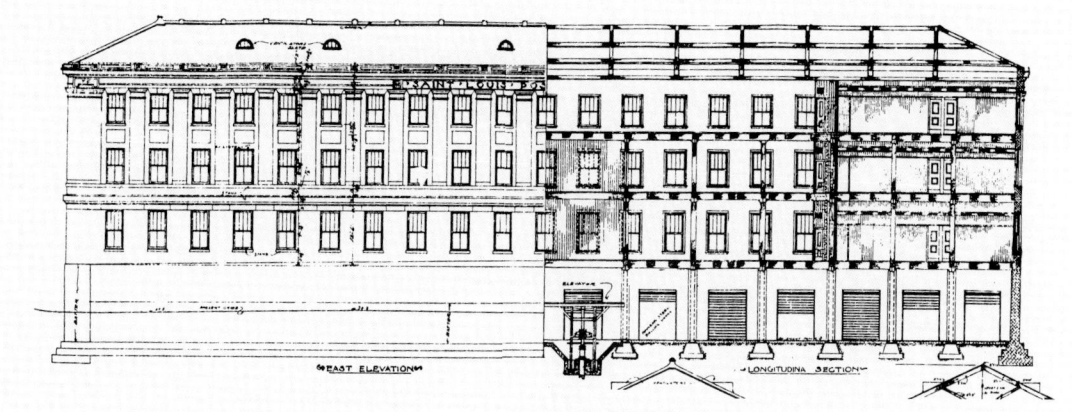

Post Office Annex
Original drawing, 1902

microcosm of immigration patterns in St. Louis: first the Germans, next an upwardly mobile family of Polish Jews, then a resourceful southern Italian couple who operated a speakeasy and boardinghouse. Alderman Bruce Sommer purchased the 1840s townhouse in 1979 and turned it into a restaurant briefly popular with politicians and newspaper employees. The next owner closed the building. Vacant for ten years, it was donated to the Downtown St. Louis Foundation in 1997 for conversion to a downtown headquarters for the mounted patrol, but was determined not suitable for this purpose after work was completed.

20
**Swift, originally Lambert-Deacon-Hull, Printing Company Building
(The Saint Louis Brewery and Tap Room)**
National Register: October 20, 1980
2100 Locust Street

Designed in 1901 by Samuel L. Sherer, this building for a small, quality press blended restrained Jacobethan motifs with an exceptional understanding of brickwork to create an important example of Arts & Crafts "Free Style." The only architect in St. Louis history to have been widely read as an architectural critic and greatly respected as the director of the Saint Louis Art Museum, Sherer believed that a knowledge of architecture should be the common property of all and argued vigorously for the "awakening of the public to the realization that a great city should be something more than a place to make money." The breadth of his career and the quality of his buildings are even more remarkable given the fact that he was not formally trained as an architect or artist.

The printing building (after 1939 the John S. Swift Co.) maintained its original function for over 75 years. On May 1, 1976 one of the worst fires in recent St. Louis history raged out of control across the street to the east. Sherer's building, though damaged, was spared to begin a new life as a microbrewery in 1991. First, majority owner Tom Schlafly had to overturn state laws favoring giants in the industry. Architect Tom Cohen (St. Louis) designed the adaptive reuse.

21
Union Station District
City District: April 18, 1979
Bounded roughly by Market, 18th, I-40 and 20th Streets

One of the first proposals to revive the under-used Union Station complex came in 1960 when a committee headed by Judge Anton Sestric suggested converting it into a downtown motel, office building and supermarket with extra tracks covered by a new concrete roof for adjacent parking. In 1962, consultants for the Illinois Department of Transportation promoted the station as a downtown terminal for a new regional airport proposed for the Columbia-Waterloo area. Two years later Donald Gunn, President of the Board of Aldermen, called for converting the site into a St. Louis Cultural Center. In 1966, owner Terminal Railroad Association presented a plan for a massive Convention Center that could cost up to $100 million. And so it went until the almost irrepressible Wally Wright appeared on the scene in 1974.

Wright, successful developer of Salt Lake City's Trolley Square, organized Union Center Venture and set off in search of financial support for a "phantasmagoria of activity." Although his concept for the 56-acre site was approved by the Board of Aldermen, financial commitments were vague. When Amtrak decided to depart, Wright's only small source of monthly income at the station was lost. Creditors' threats of a foreclosure sale on the courthouse steps galvanized support

Chapter 3 Central Business District: West

Union Station
Robert C. Pettus,
1988

for a hastily prepared historic district designation. Heavy political pressure from Missouri's congressional delegation stopped Amtrak from building a new permanent station; instead, a temporary (now in its 26th year) station dubbed "Amshack" was built a few blocks east of the project area.

Union Center Venture ended in bankruptcy in 1979. In the settlement Oppenheimer Properties of New York emerged as a central player for the next phase of planning. In 1980, Oppenheimer announced the joint participation of the Rouse Company of Columbia, Maryland with Omni International Hotels, Inc. in a $135 million festival marketplace/hotel complex. St. Louis Union Station reopened August 29, 1985, as the largest historic rehabilitation tax credit project in the country.

22
Post Office Annex: Union Station
National Register: September 26, 1985
329 South 18th Street

Designed by Eames & Young (St. Louis) in 1903 as part of a challenging plan to more than double the station's capacity to handle passengers and freight arriving for the 1904 World's Fair, the red brick Renaissance Revival building was adapted to office use in 1984 from plans by Mackey & Associates, St. Louis.

23
St. Louis Union Station
City Landmark: September 1966
National Historic Landmark: June 15, 1970
Market between 18th and 20th Streets

In early 1891, twelve architectural firms received a detailed monograph from the Terminal Railroad Association describing a competition for the design of St. Louis' new Union Station. Four of the firms (S. S. Beman of Chicago, Eames & Young of St. Louis, Shepley, Rutan & Coolidge and Peabody, Stearns & Furber of Boston) immediately notified the Terminal that they would not compete due to inadequate compensation. On July 1, 1891, drawings from Grable & Weber, James Stewart & Company, Link & Cameron, George R. Mann (all of St. Louis); H. Wolters and F. W. Mowbray (Louisville); Bruce Price (New York) and Van Brunt & Howe (Kansas City) were in hand.

Complete credit for the winning design submitted by Theodore C. Link and Edward A. Cameron of St. Louis may never be properly assigned. Cameron was well versed in the Richardsonian Romanesque style so eloquently expressed in the Station, having superintended Richardson's Marshall Field Warehouse and Glessner House projects in Chicago. But the partnership

Above and below left:

Union Station interiors
Balthazar Korab, 1985

Washington Avenue: Northwest corner of 12th and Washington circa 1905

Missouri Historical Society

was dissolved before the cornerstone incised with only Link's name was laid in 1893. (Cameron left St. Louis in 1898 and died in Philadelphia one year later at age 38.) John Willard Adams, talented chief assistant architect in Link's office at the time of the competition, was brought in to share possible design authorship with the publication of Osmund Overby's seminal contribution to a 1994 publication on Union Station for the St. Louis Mercantile Library.

The station opened with tumultuous celebrations on September 1, 1894. Local scribes praised the allegorical window, gilded Grand Hall, Gothic corridor, tasty dining rooms and massive train shed by George H. Pegram:

"If Chicago had such a structure, the world would long ago have been wearied of the iteration of its merits." That author would surely be satisfied with the publicity the station received almost one hundred years later as the largest rehabilitation project in the country. Plans were by Hellmuth, Obata & Kassabaum, St. Louis; the Conrad Schmitt Studios of New Berlin, Wisconsin crafted the exquisite restoration of the Grand Hall.

24
Washington Avenue: West of Tucker District
National Register: February 12, 1987
Bounded roughly by 18th, Lucas, Tucker
and Olive Streets

In the waning years of the 19th century, speculation was rampant along Washington Avenue west of 12th (Tucker) as realtors (and occasionally Washington University) scrambled to collect large parcels of land for future development. Although the first new buildings appeared on two corners of Washington and 13th in 1899, the dream of an orderly progression west was replaced by the realities of a marketplace that produced an erratic pattern of construction for 30 years.

Monumental designs from Shepley, Rutan & Coolidge (succeeded in 1900 by Mauran, Russell & Garden), Eames & Young and Albert B. Groves dominated the first decade. Three buildings started in 1906 document the diversity of architectural expression within the post-Fair expansiveness of St. Louis' economy: The White House (razed in 1975 for a surface parking lot between 16th and 17th Streets) for Brown Shoe Company by Groves was an eight-story *pièce de résistance* city block covered in glazed white terra cotta from the Winkle Terra Cotta Company. The Butler Brothers Building, still extant, also covers a city block. Designed by Mauran, Russell & Garden in 1906, the "largest structure in America occupied by a single wholesale concern" was built as a branch of a Chicago firm. Renamed the Plaza Square Building, this giant of the wholesale district is located between 17th and 18th, Olive and Locust Streets. The architects' subtle mastery of ornamental brickwork for Butler stands in sharp contrast to their bold expression of concrete structure at the small **Lesan-Gould Building** *(page 73)* completed the next year. For the Ely & Walker Dry Goods Company at 1514-46 Washington, Eames & Young designed one of their most deliberately artful mercantile buildings with brown brick walls decorated with reddish-orange and black terra cotta Mannerist details over a steel frame skeleton. By 1914, Ely & Walker carried more open stock than any other dry goods firm; as late as 1947, the company was the country's largest wholesale house with such prominent clients as Macy's, Marshall Field & Co., Jordan Marsh and Famous-Barr.

But the post-war years did not see continued prosperity along Washington Avenue. Cheap land at the fringe of the metropolitan area and cheap labor in other states (or countries) offered irresistible competition. Underutilized and under-appreciated, the loft area became a haven for artists who found the cheap, well-lit spaces made perfect studios or live/work space. Remaining small businesses (many dating from the garment district period) coexisted with the newcomers, their galleries and the nightclubs that became common by the 1990s. Interest in architecture also heightened. In 1987, research for historic districts

Above and below left:
International Shoe Company Interior and detail
Gary R. Tetley, 1992

Chapter 3 | Central Business District: West

International Shoe Company
Robert C. Pettus, 1988

encompassing Washington Avenue from 9th to 18th Street documented the corridor's prominence in local and national history. Although a few buildings were successfully developed as housing, it took one stunning achievement at the end of the 20th century to spotlight the dormant opportunities. In 1997, Gail and Bob Cassilly's captivating conversion of the vast International Shoe Company warehouse (701 North 15th Street) into City Museum changed the reality of what a museum could be and the perception of what was possible through adaptive reuse.

Other district buildings of special interest in addition to those described below include: Albert B. Groves' 1909 building at 1509-11 Washington for the White Branch-Shelton Hat Company—a nicely proportioned smaller structure with an encompassing Baroque storefront; the 1909 Robert, Johnson & Rand Shoe building at 1501-07 Washington by Theodore C. Link—a recapitulation of the Wainwright expressed in a late Art Nouveau vocabulary; the slender Gothic Revival building at 1214 Washington designed in 1918 by Tom P. Barnett for the Erker Optical Company and the 15th Street Union Electric substation—an Art Deco delight built in 1930-31 from plans by Klipstein & Rathmann.

25
Advertising Building (Mary Muffet Lofts)
National Register: January 18, 1985
1627-29 Locust Street

In 1917, St. Louis architect Albert B. Groves received a commission to design a building that would consolidate advertising agencies and related firms into one location. Largest among the original tenants was Gardner, a leader in establishing the influential American Association of Advertising Agencies, the first agency to use recipes in food ads and the first to sign celebrities to endorse products (cowboy Tom Mix for client Ralston Purina). After Gardner left in late 1936, the building was home to the Mary Muffet line of clothing. That name will be reestablished in a scheduled conversion to loft apartments.

26
Fashion Square Building
National Register: October 9, 1985
1307 Washington Avenue

Sam and Rose Pollack, envisioning a garment center—"The Aristocrat of Washington Avenue"— for the wholesale trade, brought in architect/contractor David R. Harrison of New York to design a 1926 interpretation of Gothic Revival industrial architecture complete with the modern advantage of an underground parking garage.

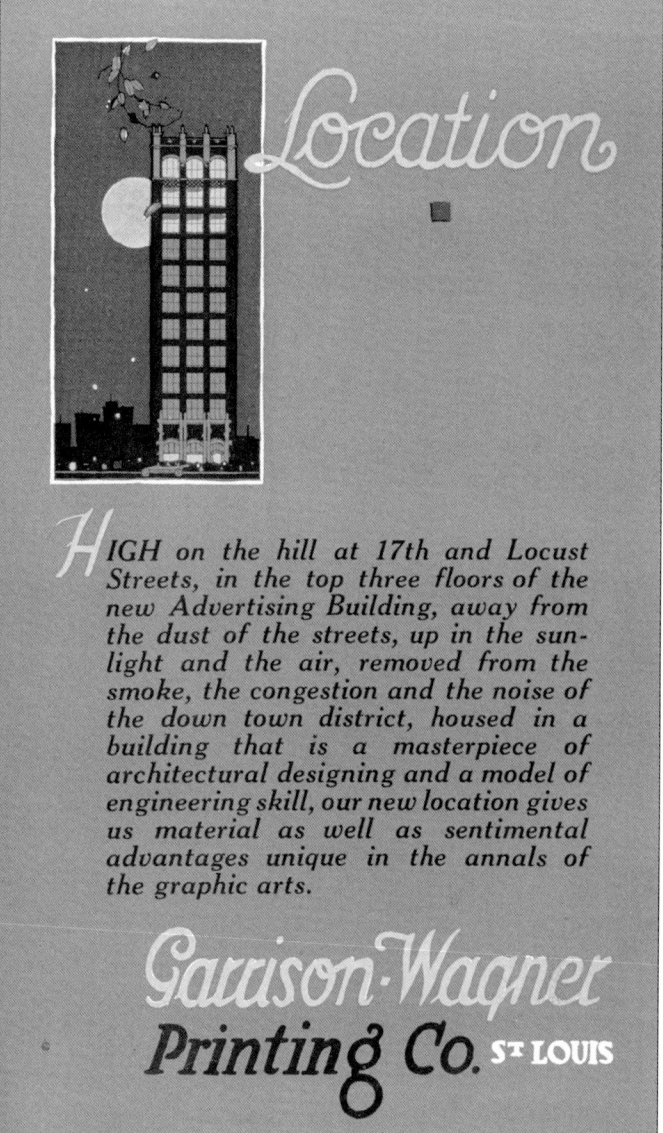

Advertisement from Greater St. Louis: the Official Bulletin of the Chamber of Commerce, *September 1919*

Landmarks Collection

27
Lesan-Gould Building
National Register: November 6, 1986
1320-24 Washington Avenue

The newly merged Lesan Advertising and Gould Directory Companies hired the versatile St. Louis firm of Mauran, Russell & Garden (St. Louis) to design a building for their headquarters. Built in 1907, the building combined forthright expression of its early system of reinforced concrete construction (patented by engineer Julius Kahn, Detroit) with Arts & Crafts enameled brick ornament. The structural system survived the vicissitudes of two decades of abuse at the end of the 20th century after the property was acquired by the city for back taxes. Sold by the city for a greatly discounted price, the building sat vacant for years during which time successive owners raised

Chapter 3   Central Business District: West

Willys-Overland: East Elevation
Gray Design Group

the acquisition price. A development underway by McGowan Brothers (designed by Fendler & Associates, St. Louis) forecasts the Grace Lofts with twenty condo units for sale from $135,000 to $270,000.

28
Peters Shoe Company (Rudman Building)
National Register: January 26, 1984
1232-36 Washington Avenue

In 1901, St. Louis architect Isaac S. Taylor designed the corporate headquarters of Peters Shoe, a ten-year-old company whose dramatic rise paralleled St. Louis' emergence as a national manufacturing center of boots and shoes. Peters merged with Roberts, Johnson & Rand in 1911 to form International Shoe Company but each kept separate corporate identities, brand names and sales branches. In 1930, Peters moved to the building at 15th and Washington erected in 1909 from plans by Theodore Link for Roberts, Johnson & Rand. An attempt to adapt the building at 1232-36 Washington to housing in the early 1990s brought financial disaster to the would-be developers. A decade later the project seems viable.

29
1300 Washington Avenue (Knickerbocker, earlier Lucas Park, Lofts)
National Register: September 2, 1982
1300-10 Washington Avenue

A millionaire by age 46, Robert S. Brookings retired to serve as President of the Board of Directors of Washington University from 1895-1928. It was his keen business acumen that led to numerous university investments including this property designed in 1899 by Eames & Young—Brookings' favorite architectural firm. Eames & Young also designed new buildings at **Cupples Station** for the university *(page 22)* and Brookings' home at 5125 Lindell in the Central West End. The eastern three bays at 1300 Washington were occupied for nearly thirty years by Marx & Haas Jeans Co., the leading local manufacturer with sales in 1901 of more than one million garments. Those same three bays were converted to loft apartments by Carpenter-Pitzman, developers, in 1983 from plans by Brownstein & Associates, St. Louis.

30
Willys-Overland Building (SJI Companies)
National Register: December 30, 1999
2300 Locust Street

John Willys started his career in transportation as a bicycle dealer who also sold Overland cars. In 1907, he took over the presidency of the ailing company, renamed it and propelled it by 1913 to a distant second in national sales after Ford. Constructed in 1917, St. Louis' Willys-Overland Building was both a dealership and a regional distributorship serving Missouri, Illinois, Kentucky and Arkansas. The giant in a linear concentration of auto sales buildings stretching west to Midtown, its reinforced concrete construction was based on a system developed by architects Mills, Rhines, Bellman & Nordhoff of Toledo. The company remained at this location until 1932 and sold the building in 1935. Partially vacant from the 1960s through the 1990s, the entire building was renovated for SJI Companies (a marketing firm) in 1999 at a cost of $8 million. Gray Design Group provided the plans.

CHAPTER 4 Midtown

Continental Building
Gary R. Tetley, 1989

Chapter 4

Midtown

1 Midtown District
2 Samuel Cupples House
3 Fox Theatre
4 Isaac H. Lionberger House
5 Masonic Temple
6 St. Francis Xavier "College Church"
7 St. Louis Theatre (Powell Symphony Hall)
8 Sheldon Memorial
9 St. Louis Club, then Woolworth Building
10 St. Alphonsus Liguori
11 Ford Motor Car Company Building
12 Scott Joplin House
13 Plaza Hotel Complex
14 Robert H. Stockton House
15 Washington Tabernacle Baptist Church
16 Phyllis Wheatley Branch YWCA

St. Louis Landmarks and Historic Districts

1

Midtown District
National Register: July 7, 1978

Located at the crossroads of Lindell and Grand Boulevard three miles west of the riverfront, Midtown's skyline asserts the strong silhouette of a second downtown. The district's collection of buildings from the half-century of eclecticism (1880–1930) includes larger-than-life creations designed by the most prestigious St. Louis and out-of-town firms of the period. Stolid and playful, secular and mystical, historical and avant-garde, the buildings in Midtown invite a pleasant stroll and beckon the visitor inside.

By 1890, Midtown was graced by substantial homes, elegant churches and the new campus of St. Louis University. **The St. Louis Club** *(page 88)*, one of the first private clubs to build in Midtown, erected a competition-winning building on Lindell in 1899.

Others followed in the first two decades of the 20th century, as did theaters and high-rise residential hotels, office buildings, dancing schools, fashionable shops and doctors' offices. The last two Midtown monuments to the Twenties were built the year of the Crash: the Fabulous **Fox Theatre** *(page 83)* and St. Louis' epitome of Art Deco, the Continental Building—an atypical product from William B. Ittner's office.

The Depression had relatively little effect on the public perception of Midtown. Magic musicals played to full houses while a chorus line from the Missouri Theatre, "The Missouri Rocket Girls" (later transformed into the Rockettes of Radio City Music Hall), kicked in astonishing unison. Luxury trains carried theatergoers and performers from Chicago through Alton to St. Louis and on to Kansas City. Performing in Midtown was Big Time; the remaining step up the ladder was either Hollywood or New York.

Washington Avenue looking west toward the future site of the Fox Theatre on Grand Avenue circa 1917

Landmarks Collection

St. Louis experienced its first population loss between 1930 and 1940 but wartime construction brought overcrowding and a false sense of confidence. Post-war funds for "slum clearance" left the 1950s face of the city scarred by massive demolition. One such project was the Mill Creek urban renewal effort that cut a broad path from downtown to the doorsteps of St. Louis University and displaced hundreds of residents. Although most of the Mill Creek institutions and houses had "trickled down" from whites to blacks, documentary photos *(see next page)* taken for the Historic American Buildings Survey suggest that many of the fine buildings were in good condition at the time of demolition. Remaining housing near Midtown was converted to multi-family or boarding houses as the district began to experience steady erosion that lasted a generation. The pioneering rehabilitation of the old **St. Louis Theatre** *(page 87)* to Powell Symphony Hall in 1968 did little to reverse the trend.

Opposite page
University Club circa 1917
Landmarks Collection

First Congregational Church circa 1915, now the Grandel Theatre
Mercantile Library

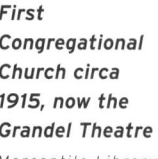

Chapter 4

3127 Laclede Avenue, razed for the Mill Creek urban renewal project
Historic American Buildings Survey photos, 1960

Below:
Third Baptist Church circa 1950
Landmarks Collection

Former Temple Israel (designed by Grable & Weber in 1888) was home to the Union Memorial African M. E. Church from 1907 to the 1959 demolition for the Mill Creek urban renewal project.
Historic American Buildings Survey photo, 1960

Chapter 4   Midtown

Detail: Continental Building
Ken Konchel, 1999

Cupples House
Robert C. Pettus, 1988

In 1974, the first redevelopment corporation for the neighborhood (New Town/St. Louis, Inc.) was organized followed by the City Centre/Redevelopment Corporation, which in turn was succeeded by Grand Center, Inc. With the reopening of the **Fox Theatre** and the **Sheldon Memorial** *(page 88)* in the 1980s, the lights began to come back to Midtown. The transition has been slow, but steady. Portfolio Gallery & Education Center founded in 1989 has showcased the work of more than 500 African-American artists from the United States. The St. Louis Black Repertory Company performs six mainstage shows each year at the Grandel Theatre, an 1884 Congregational church reopened in 1992 as space for non-profit groups and cabaret shows brought in by the redevelopment corporation. In 1993, EarthWays Home—conversion of

the Block brothers' residence and photography studio by Ralph Wafer (St. Louis)—became a showcase for environmentally safe products and "green" construction techniques.

The Pulitzer Foundation for the Arts by Tadao Ando (Japan) opened to rave reviews from the international press in October 2001. Next door, a new building (currently under construction) designed by Brad Cloepfil (Portland, Oregon) for the Forum for Contemporary Art will share an outdoor plaza, green space and sculpture by Richard Serra. But the most anticipated symbol of progress may well be the rescue of the Continental Building. After twenty-two years of vacancy and countless unsuccessful attempts by various developers to put together a renovation project, Steve Trampe, president of Owen Development, succeeded. A $28 million rehabilitation scheme designed for Owen by Trivers Associates got underway in 2001, a beacon in the ongoing creation of a vital theater and performing arts center.

2
Samuel Cupples House
City Landmark: September 1973
National Register: October 8, 1976
3673 West Pine Boulevard

Currently owned by St. Louis University and managed by the Samuel Cupples House Foundation, this Romanesque Revival mansion designed by Thomas B. Annan (St. Louis) was built for the extravagant sum of $500,000 in 1890. Craftsmen from western England executed stone carvings in purple Colorado sandstone; stained glass windows are by Louis Comfort Tiffany. With forty-two rooms and twenty operative fireplaces, it took eighteen servants just to keep the house running. Born in Harrisburg, Pennsylvania in 1831, Cupples left for Cincinnati at age fifteen where he worked for a pioneer woodenware dealer before opening his first St. Louis store in 1851. It would become the largest enterprise of its kind in the country. Three decades later with Robert Brookings, Cupples began development of the monumental **Cupples Station** complex *(page 22)*.

The house was purchased from his heirs in 1919 by the Order of Railroad Telegraphers. St. Louis University's acquisition in 1946 could have meant demolition had not Maurice B. McNamee, S.J., a determined professor of Art History at the university, taken up the cause. Today, the resplendent Cupples House is open to the public including lower level (originally a bowling alley) gallery space named for Father McNamee, Executive Director of the Cupples House Foundation until his retirement in 1995 and foremost among those involved in its preservation and restoration.

Detail:
Cupples House
John William Nagel, 1986

3
Fox Theatre
City Landmark: November 1975
National Register: October 8, 1976
523 North Grand Avenue

A conglomeration of Moorish, Far Eastern and Indian motifs, the $6 million Fox Theatre opened on January 31, 1929 as the second largest theater in the country with an organ that would "...reproduce sound never believed possible in such an instrument" and elevators operating to all balcony levels. C. Howard Crane of Detroit designed the 5,060-seat house for William Fox (theater promoter, developer and founder of 20th Century Fox). Interiors came from Eve Leo Fox in a flamboyant decoration-without-limitation manner dubbed "Eve Leo Style" by husband William. (In an uncanny instance of history repeating itself, another husband and wife team would buy, restore and reopen the magical venue in 1982. In this case Leon Strauss loved to relate that he gave Mary an unlimited budget and she exceeded it.)

The Fabulous Fox fell into receivership during the Depression, managing to stay alive by adding vaudeville shows and celebrity appearances to first-run films from Hollywood. Stan Kann first touched the Mighty Wurlitzer in 1953; stars including Frank Sinatra, Dean Martin and Ella Fitzgerald still managed to draw crowds from the suburbs into the late 1960s. A tougher crowd turned out for the "exploitation" movies offered before the theater closed in 1978.

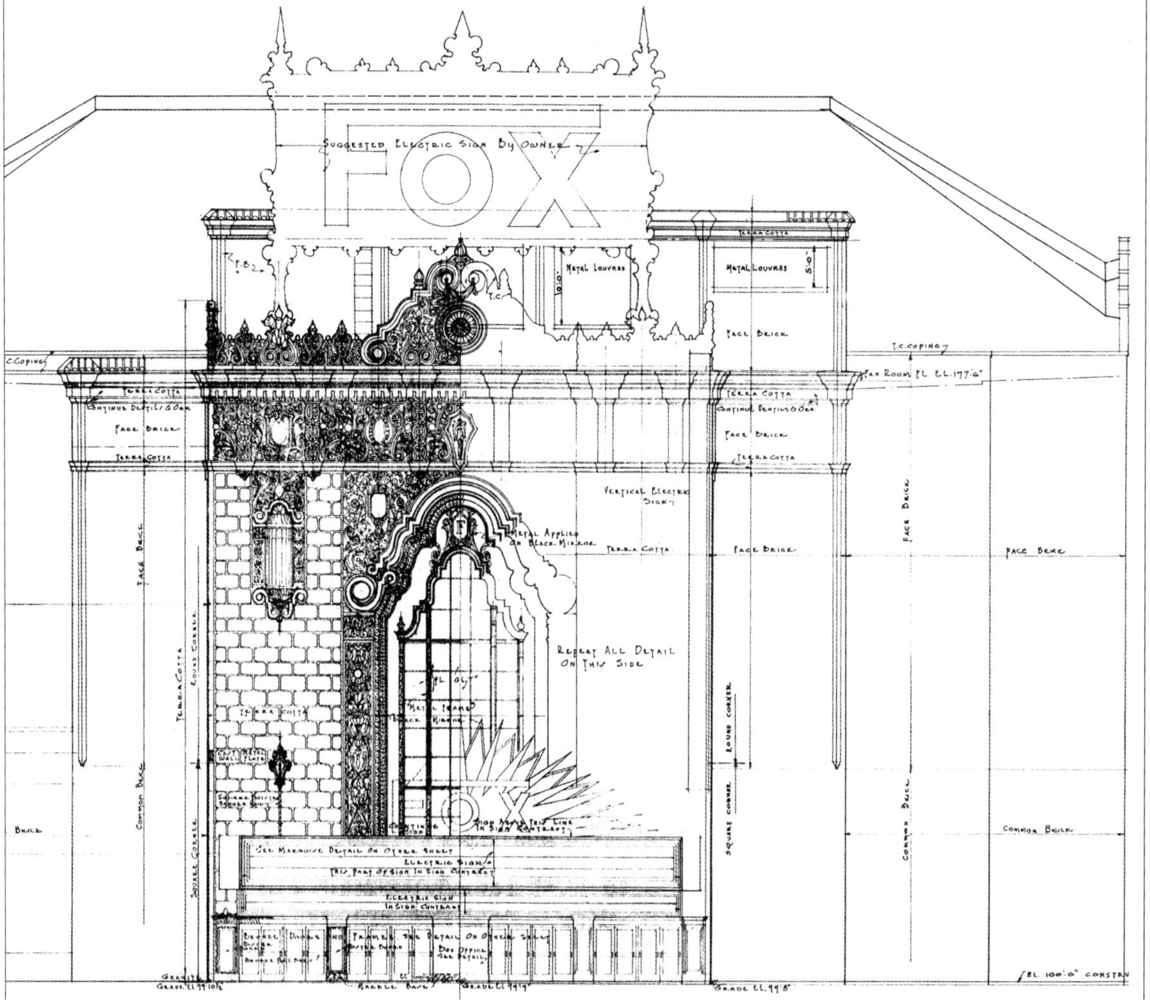

Chapter 4

Fox Theatre drawing from 1928
C. Howard Crane

Lionberger House, exterior and interior views
Landmarks Collection

Lovingly restored for the Fox Partners by Mary Strauss with Claybour Architects (St. Louis) in 1982, the theater was expanded in 1994 to lengthen stage depth from 30 to 50 feet to accommodate ever more elaborate Broadway touring company productions. Few can match, however, the drama every four years when the Fox's 2,000-pound chandelier (twelve feet wide, 160 light bulbs with 2,264 pieces of jeweled glass) is lowered and cleaned.

4
Isaac H. Lionberger House
City Landmark: April 1975
3630 Grandel Square

When his wealthy father had this house constructed as a wedding gift in 1886, Isaac Lionberger was a young attorney not long returned from a brief adventure attempting to raise cattle in Montana. It was one of three houses that John Lionberger commissioned from the office of America's most important architect at the time, H. H. Richardson of Boston (whose chief assistant, George Shepley, was Isaac's brother-in-law). Although all three commissions were received in 1886, only the John Lionberger residence on Vandeventer Place was listed in the catalog of designs completed prior to Richardson's death that same year. Working drawings for the Isaac Lionberger House were apparently

approved by Richardson (his comments appear on several drawings), so the house can justifiably be included among the great architect's projects.

The house originally was only two bays wide, its front entrance recessed in a deep-set porch at the west corner of the façade. In 1894, Lionberger had Richardson's successor firm (Shepley, Rutan & Coolidge) add a third bay to accommodate a large library and more bedrooms for his growing family. Placed on the west side of the building, the addition obliterated the original entrance and elaborate window pattern of the west wall, created a symmetrical front elevation and replaced the broad central dormer with three French-inspired brick wall dormers not out of keeping with Richardson's work.

When the Lionbergers moved to Westmoreland Place in 1907, Isaac was one of the city's leading citizens. The Lionberger House remains in relatively good condition (considering that most of its neighbors have been demolished) due to the care of two long-term owners. The Benton College of Law purchased the house in 1917 and operated here until it went out of business in 1937. In 1945, the trustees of Cooks and Pastry Cooks Local 26 purchased the house. The union's successors were headquartered here until 1999, when a partnership interested in adaptive reuse bought the house for $180,000. The other two Richardson houses in St. Louis were not so lucky: John Lionberger's fortress-like mansion in Vandeventer Place was demolished with the rest of the block. Isaac's sister's house, the Potter House on Cabanne, was undoubtedly the city's most important example of the Shingle Style before the city tore it down in 1958 to make a park.

5
Masonic Temple
City Landmark: November 1976
3671 Lindell Boulevard

Architects Thomas Crane Young and Albert B. Groves (St. Louis) set out to create a Bedford stone monument that would "incorporate the temples of ancient Babylon, of mighty Egypt and of Classical Greece." Opened in 1926 as a new home for various Masonic groups with lavish ceremonial rooms, the main lobby contains the only known statue of President George Washington in Masonic attire. But the massive $4 million building was not completely finished. A large theater space on the first floor is still a concrete shell, offering tantalizing opportunities for use by either St. Louis University or Grand Center.

The Masonic Temple seen to the right of the now-demolished Castleman/ Mackay House.
Historic American Buildings Survey photo, 1960

Chapter 4 Midtown

6
St. Francis Xavier "College Church"
City Landmark: November 1974
Southwest corner of Grand and Lindell Boulevards

Irish-born architect Thomas Waryng Walsh designed St. Francis Xavier Church and DuBourg Hall in 1883 as the first buildings for the new campus of St. Louis University. The cornerstone was laid June 8, 1884, but work continued over many years. Walsh died before the Gothic Revival church was completed; Henry Switzer (Chicago) modified the design and continued work on the project. The tower was finally complete in 1915 with 18th century bells cast in Spain that had once summoned worshippers to the old college church downtown. Stained glass windows from Emil Frei (St. Louis) followed in 1929 and 1936-38. Controversial alterations in 1990 by Kurt Landberg (St. Louis) inserted a central altar platform, removed the pipe organ and introduced a new baptismal font at the entrance to the lofty interior of English fan vaulting.

College Church circa 1930
Missouri Historical Society

"New St. Louis Theatre" from 1927 postcard. Message on back states: "Dear Sis, This is some vacation. Beats everything I've ever tried all hollow."
Landmarks Collection

7
St. Louis Theatre (Powell Symphony Hall)
City Landmark: November 1975
National Register: May 25, 2001
712 North Grand Avenue

Little more than a decade after the first movie theaters were built in St. Louis, filmgoing had become an immensely popular pastime. Late in 1925, the city's building commissioner counted 102 "motion picture shows" with a total of more than 96,362 seats. With the inauguration of the St. Louis Theatre on November 23, total capacity was pushed past 100,000.

Not only was the St. Louis Theatre the city's largest movie house, it was also the largest in the Orpheum circuit. Orpheum was one of two major "big-time vaudeville" promoters; its territory covered the entire western United States from the Great Lakes to the Pacific Ocean. With a mission to "provide clean, wholesome entertainment so varied in its appeal that every man and woman, boy and girl, will find enjoyment in each program," Orpheum put together bills combining nationally known entertainers with full-length motion pictures. Opening night at the St. Louis Theatre featured a film shot during construction, a light show accompanied by the house's magnificent Kimball organ (claimed to be the world's largest), an address from Mayor Victor Miller, the featured film *Drusilla with a Million*, orchestral numbers, a seven-act vaudeville program including comedians, dancers, singers and a romantic scene. The "World Famous Singer's Midgets" concluded the program with a "spectacle" of twenty little people.

Theaters competed with each other not only on the basis of their awesome programs but also on the lavishness of their architectural adornments. Inspired by Versailles, nationally known theater designers Rapp & Rapp used all of their art to create a richly detailed environment of elegance, from the magnificent three-story lobby to the basement ladies' lounge (which featured a working fireplace). While such environments became particularly popular during the Depression, large theaters with high overhead were hard hit. Dropping ticket prices to remain competitive, the St. Louis laid off its chorus girls, stagehands and musicians in 1934 (and still ended up closing its doors for two years).

The last films at the St. Louis were screened in the mid-60s, when special 70mm equipment was installed for the eighteen-month run of *The Sound of Music*. The theater became the vanguard of revitalization efforts in Midtown when the St. Louis Symphony Society purchased the building in 1966. With careful renovation led by Wedemeyer, Cernik & Corrubia (St. Louis), the theater reopened in 1968 as the permanent home of the St. Louis Symphony Orchestra.

Chapter 4   Midtown

Woolworth Building (St. Louis Club)
Gary R. Tetley

Sheldon Memorial
Kevin Grace, 2001

8
Sheldon Memorial
City Landmark: April 1975
3646 Washington Avenue

Built in 1912 from plans by Louis C. Spiering of St. Louis, the Classical Revival home of the St. Louis Ethical Society was named for Walter L. Sheldon, founder of the society and pioneer in the Ethical Culture movement. The auditorium, nationally known for its exceptionally fine acoustics, hosted famous singers (including Helen Traubel) and sponsored subscription chamber music concerts. After the society moved in 1964 to a striking new building in St. Louis County by Harris Armstrong, its Midtown home continued to present chamber music at a deficit for ten years. Sold in 1974 to St. Michael's Spiritual Churches, Inc., the building changed hands several times before purchase by California businessman Eugene Golden. Golden hired St. Louisan Walter Gunn to direct a $1.4 million renovation; the hall reopened to great acclaim in 1986. Two years later Executive Director Gunn founded the Sheldon Arts Foundation—an entity headed by civic leader Leigh Gerdine after 1991.

The foundation's most impressive achievement, a $5 million expansion by St. Louis architect Raymond E. Maritz completed in 1998, brought elevators to all floors as well as greatly enlarged lobby space for the 708-seat hall and associated ballroom and meeting space. Meandering galleries, opened in 1999, offer 6,000 square feet of art for browsing before performances. Five stained glass windows by St. Louis artist Rodney Winfield entitled "Theme and Variation" were commissioned for the east wall of the auditorium in 2001.

9
St. Louis Club, then Woolworth Building (St. Louis University Museum of Art)
City Landmark: September 1973
3663 Lindell Boulevard

Built for the St. Louis Club in 1899 from plans by the New York firm of Friedlander & Dillon with Lawrence Ewald of St. Louis(winners of a national competition), the $195,000 French Renaissance red brick building hosted the most sought-after New Year's Eve celebration in town. The club disbanded after a 1925 fire destroyed most of the original interior including the third-floor ballroom, billiard rooms and library. Converted first to office space and headquarters for F. W. Woolworth Company, then converted again in the mid 1980s as a classroom building for St. Louis University, the elegant club (now dwarfed between flanking Masonic giants) is currently an art museum for the University.

10
St. Alphonsus Liguori ("Rock Church")
City Landmark: November 1974
1118 North Grand Boulevard

French-speaking Catholics of color numbered foremost among free blacks and mulattos counted in the census of pioneer St. Louis. By 1800, they comprised nearly 6% of village residents. Today, although there are seventeen predominately black parishes in the St. Louis Archdiocese, "Rock Church" is without doubt the regional symbol for more than 27,000 black worshippers. Built for Redemptorist missions and spiritual retreats, the church of local limestone (designed by Reverend Louis Dold, modified by architect Thomas Waryng Walsh in 1893) stood in a virtually unpopulated area beyond the city limits at the cornerstone laying in 1867. Westward population growth changed its status to a parish church in 1881.

Thirty-one stained glass windows by Mayer of Munich installed just before the 1904 World's Fair presented a vibrant showcase for the German firm's booth at the fairgrounds. Streetcar tracks (laid on Grand Avenue in 1894) brought thousands of area Catholics to Rock

Our Lady of Perpetual Help Altar
W. C. Persons, 1931
Missouri Historical Society

Church for devotions, especially during the 1920s when a shrine presented by Pope Pius IX attracted capacity crowds. Although a prominent diocesan historian predicted parish decline in 1928 because of the "influx of Negroes and Jews," St. Alphonsus Liguori would evolve relatively painlessly from Irish to integrated in the 1940s, long after the soaring stone steeples from 1894 by Conradi & Schrader (St. Louis) enhanced the simple English Gothic Revival building. Today, the congregation works with the Grand Rock Community Economic Development Corporation to promote housing and economic growth in the Covenant-Blumeyer and Vandeventer neighborhoods.

11
Ford Motor Car Company Building (Goodwill Industries)
National Register: determined eligible March 6, 2002
4100 Forest Park Boulevard

The Ford Motor Company established its regional branch office in St. Louis in 1907 and followed up with plans for a manufacturing plant (its tenth nationwide) in 1912. By the time the new factory opened in 1914, Ford with 1,561 registered autos on the road was by far the most popular car in St. Louis. Its closest competitors (Cadillac, Packard and **Dorris**—*see pages 117 and 118*) had each sold approximately 390 cars. Ford doubled the size of its St. Louis plant in 1916, stopped production during a brief hiatus as a government warehouse during World War I and then installed an assembly line similar to one in Highland Park, Michigan. Local production peaked in 1923 with almost 80,000 Model T's and 8,000 Fordson tractors. After the shutdown imposed by World War II, Ford moved its St. Louis operations to Hazelwood.

Designed in two phases by locals Clymer & Drischler and Detroit architect Albert Kahn, the Ford Motor Company Building employed reinforced concrete—a technique still being developed in the second decade of the 20th century. Kahn became internationally known for his pioneering concrete buildings structures. If current plans are realized, the old Ford plant will continue the legacy of experimentation as an incubator for technology companies.

12
Scott Joplin House
National Historic Landmark: December 8, 1976
2658-60 Delmar Boulevard

The "King of Ragtime" first arrived in St. Louis about 1885 but left for the profitable entertainment districts of Chicago during the Columbian Exposition of 1893. After returning to St. Louis for a brief stint, Scott Joplin departed for Sedalia, Missouri where he wrote the "Maple Leaf Rag." Published by his friend John Stark, the piece became a national sensation. Joplin moved back to St. Louis in the spring of 1900 with his new wife Belle and rented a second-floor flat at 2658 Morgan (now Delmar). While living there he composed "The Entertainer," "Elite Syncopations," "March Majestic," "Ragtime Dance" and *A Guest of Honor*—a lost opera set at the Governor's mansion in Jefferson City.

Scott Joplin House and Rosebud Café (rear)
Esley Hamilton, 2001

Plaza Hotel Complex, from **Problems of St. Louis 1917**
Missouri Historical Society

Although Joplin lived at a number of locations in St. Louis, all except the Delmar building have been demolished as has the St. Louis mecca for ragtime—The Rosebud Café at 2220 Market Street owned by Thomas Turpin. In 1977, $100,000 in Community Development Block Grant funds were allocated for much-needed repairs to the Joplin House. The money was not spent, however, until after the Missouri Department of Natural Resources acquired the property and the rest of the necessary funds to complete rehabilitation. The only State Historic Site in St. Louis, the Scott Joplin House opened in 1991. Next door, a $500,000 recreation of the "Rosebud Café" built by the State of Missouri opened in 2000.

13
Plaza Hotel Complex
National Register: May 7, 1985
3301-39 Olive Street

Portending a subject that would occupy future generations, the new St. Louis City Plan Commission undertook a disruptive street modification as its first project. Motivation was the automobile—its sale, its use and its conflict with existing streetcar lines. Completed in 1915 at a total cost just over $200,000, the diagonal cutoff cleared the block bounded by Channing, Leonard, Olive and Locust. Lindell and Locust were then joined to create two asymmetrical blocks ripe for new development alongside bustling "auto row."

Detail: **"The Coming of St. Louis,"** *Plaza Hotel Complex*
Stephen R. Dolan, 1985

In the early years of the 20th century, St. Louis' burgeoning automobile trade was concentrated along Locust Street from east of Jefferson to Midtown. The theater district was growing a few blocks west along Grand Boulevard. Seizing the moment, the Pickel Realty Company (owner of the very visible site) hired Preston J. Bradshaw to design a high profile, mixed-use complex including a café, dinner and dance room to complement a hotel and automobile showrooms. The western block in Mission Revival style is finished with bright pink stucco. The Arts & Crafts eastern block, also by Bradshaw, includes the former Plaza Hotel with "The Coming of St. Louis" sculpted by Robert P. Bringhurst, St. Louis. Renovation of the long-vacant complex in the mid 1980s by Campbell Design (St. Louis) distorted the carefully orchestrated traffic pattern so admired in 1915.

Chapter 4 Midtown

Robert H. Stockton House front elevation and floor plan
Pat Hays Baer

14
Robert H. Stockton House
National Register: August 10, 1988
3508 Samuel Shepard Drive (formerly Lucas Avenue)

This distinctive Romanesque Revival stone house designed in 1890 by Barnett, Haynes & Barnett of St. Louis (the earliest known example of the firm's fine residential work) was featured in an illustrated article in the May 31, 1891 *Republic*. A two-story addition from 1900 by the same firm completed the front elevation. Robert H. Stockton's success in post-Civil War St. Louis began at the Simmons Hardware Company where he served ten years as Secretary and another ten as Vice President.

By 1887, Stockton had left Simmons to become Secretary of the Culver Brothers Wrought Iron Range Company. A few years later, he and Culver formed the **Majestic Stove Company** *(page 63)*. In 1904, Stockton, by now a wealthy widower, hired Barnett, Haynes & Barnett to design another house at 4528 Maryland Avenue in the Central West End. Bountiful gifts from both families prompted officials at the Christian University in Canton, Missouri to rename the school Culver-Stockton College in 1917. Painstaking restoration of the Stockton House in Midtown under the direction of the architecturally trained owner Frederick Medler began in the early 1980s.

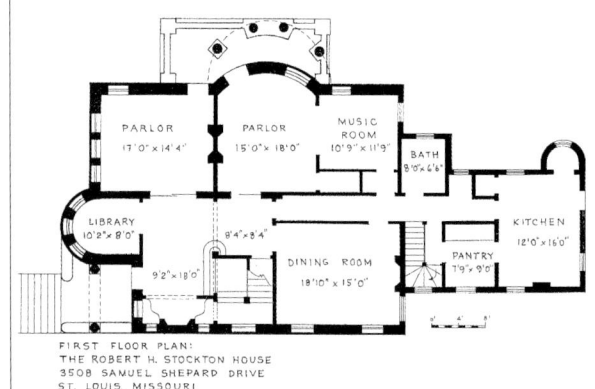

Robert H. Stockton House
Landmarks, 1987

15
Washington Tabernacle Baptist Church
City Landmark: April 1984
3200 Washington Boulevard

Designed in 1877 by John H. Maurice (St. Louis) and constructed of local limestone, this building for a dissident offshoot of Second Presbyterian closely resembles the Lafayette Park Presbyterian Church designed by Maurice for his own congregation a year later. Both employed nearly square sanctuaries, a new architectural trend designed to improve visibility and acoustics. The Presbyterians left Midtown in 1926 for Skinker Boulevard where they built Memorial Presbyterian.

The next owner, Tabernacle Baptist (organized in 1902), recognized the building's spacious sanctuary as appropriate to the denomination's traditional emphasis on preaching. The church was almost lost after a raging fire in November 1945 gutted the interior and roof. With one wall in danger of collapse, the congregation and friends both black and white gathered at a fund raising rally at nearby Third Baptist Church on Grand Avenue as workmen were prepared to raze the building. The congregation under the leadership of the Reverend John E. Nance decided to repair rather than build anew. Historic Tabernacle, for many generations the church home of local black leaders, was selected by Dr. Martin Luther King, Jr. as the site for a major civil rights rally in May of 1963. Held just before the March on Washington, King's St. Louis appearance attracted 3,000 participants.

16
Phyllis Wheatley Branch YWCA
National Register: July 24, 1984
2709 Locust Street

Phyllis Wheatley Branch YMCA
Landmarks, 1997

An African-American branch of the St. Louis YWCA was organized in 1911 by a small group of women from the Union Memorial A.M.E. Church. Renamed in honor of poet slave Phyllis Wheatley the following year, the branch moved to newly renovated headquarters at Garrison and Lucas in 1915. It would remain there until the city condemned the building twenty-two years later. The next stop for two years was the parish house of the Metropolitan Zion A.M.E. Church, then on to the parish house at Holy Communion Episcopal at 2809 Washington. Meanwhile, Anna Lee Scott had been appointed branch director. Between 1936 and 1939, Phyllis Wheatley gained representation on the Metropolitan Board of the Y, established Camp Derricotte (the first in the state for "Negro" girls) and formed an interracial committee to determine how the growing organization could find a suitable permanent home.

In 1941, an opportunity to purchase a nearby facility for only $75,000 solved the problem. Constructed in 1926-27 by plans from LaBeaume & Klein (St. Louis), the still-new Colonial Revival building had been designed for the St. Louis Women's Christian Association to provide young white working women with inexpensive, safe shelter. The home came complete with living room, fifty-nine bedrooms for permanent guests and fourteen for transients, a dining room, playrooms, library, clubrooms and a large backyard.

The Phyllis Wheatley building soon became a center for other groups and individuals to host receptions and hold meetings. In 1953, a new gymnasium built on an adjoining lot completed the complex. The branch continued to prosper at this location through its Diamond Jubilee in 1987. Soon after, however, the site was closed and programs moved to a new facility on West Pine. Vacant for years and in growing need of repairs, the building so important in African-American history will be returned to use as the Phyllis Wheatley Apartments for transitional housing for women making less than $10 an hour. Receiving historic and low-income tax credits was key to the project sponsored by the YWCA of Metro St. Louis.

Plans include linking this building with other cultural landmarks for a heritage trail. Groundbreaking is scheduled for late summer, 2002.

Chapter 4   Midtown

Powell Hall
Sam Fentress, 2000

CHAPTER 5 | West End

29 Westmoreland Place
Robert C. Pettus

Chapter 5

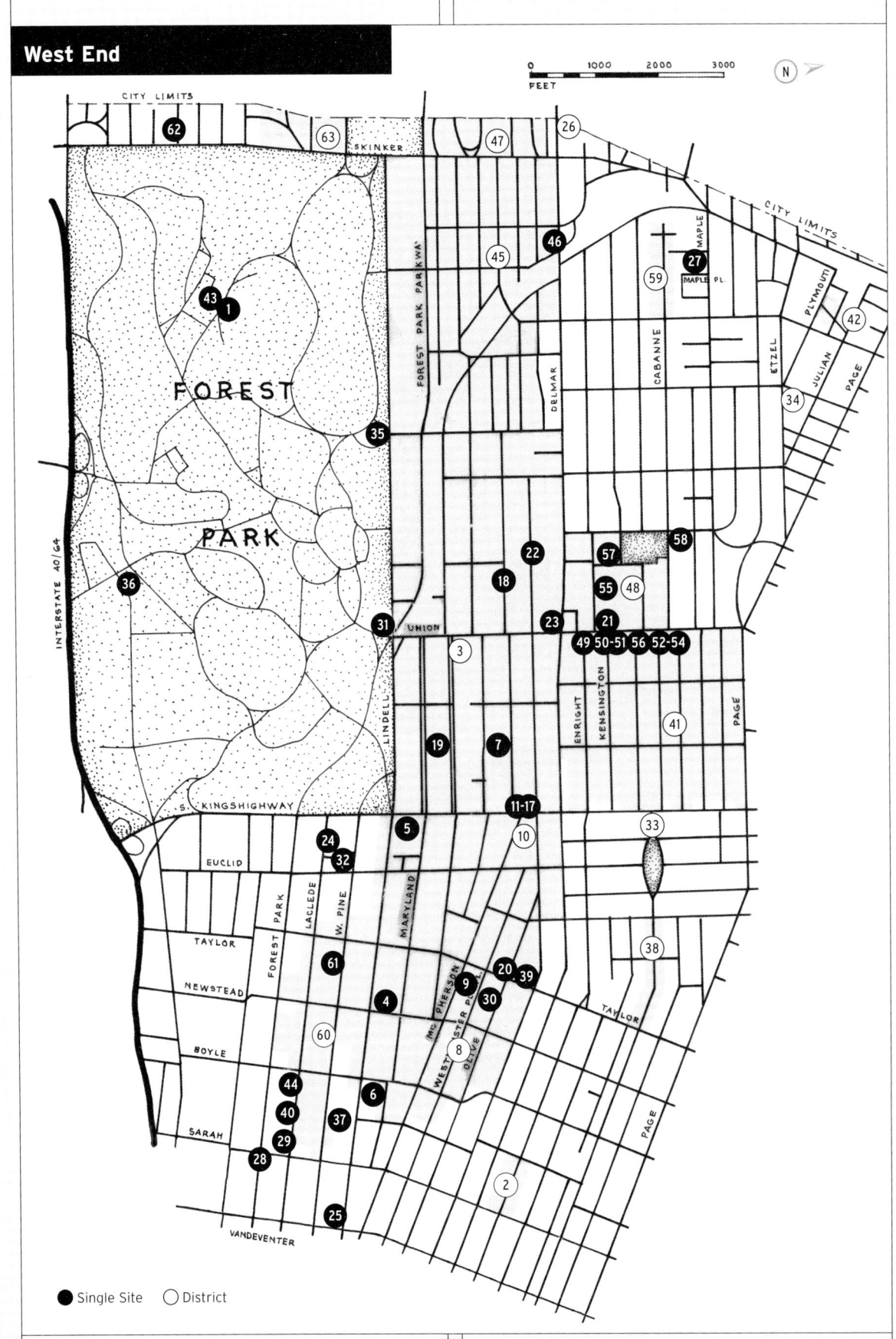

96

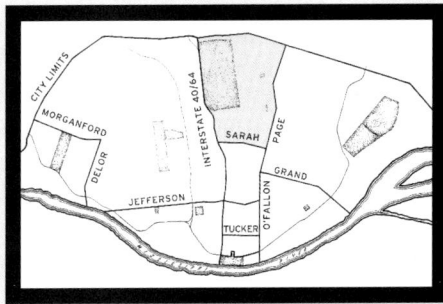

1. Apotheosis of St. Louis
2. Block Unit #1 District
3. Central West End District
4. Cathedral Basilica of St. Louis (New Cathedral)
5. Chase Park Plaza Hotel
6. Kate Chopin House
7. Joseph Erlanger House
8. Fullerton's Westminster Place
9. Eliot House
10. Holy Corners District
11. Temple Israel
12. St. John's United Methodist Church
13. Tuscan Temple
14. First Church of Christ, Scientist
15. Racquet Club
16. Second Baptist Church
17. Washington Hotel
18. Kingsbury Place
19. Portland and Westmoreland Places
20. Second Presbyterian Church
21. Union Avenue Christian Church
22. Washington Terrace
23. Westminster Presbyterian Church
24. Chouteau Apartments/Parkway Dwellings
25. Crabtree Court Apartments
26. Delmar Loop/Parkview Gardens District
27. De Hodiamont House
28. Dorris Motor Car Company
29. Dorris Motor Car (Dorris Lofts)
30. Eugene Field School
31. Forest Park Headquarters "Cabanne House"
32. Forest Park Hotel
33. Fountain Park District
34. Goodfellow/Julian Concrete Block District
35. Jefferson Memorial Building
36. Jewel Box
37. Leonardo Apartments
38. Lewis Place District
39. Lister Building
40. Luyties Building
41. Mount Cabanne/Raymond Place District
42. Oakherst Place Concrete Block District
43. Saint Louis Art Museum
44. Sanitol Chemical Company Building
45. Skinker-DeBaliviere/Catlin Tract/Parkview District
46. A & P Food Stores
47. Parkview District
48. Visitation Park District
49. Young Men's Hebrew Association
50. Church of the Messiah
51. St. Louis Artists' Guild
52. Soldan High School
53. William Clark Grade School
54. Cabanne Branch Library
55. Smith Academy
56. Pilgrim Congregational Church
57. Frederick von Harten House
58. Winston Churchill Apartments
59. West Cabanne Place District
60. West Pine/Laclede District
61. James Gay Butler House
62. Wiltshire and Versailles Apartment Buildings
63. Wydown/Forsyth District

North side of Lenox Place: houses designed between 1902 and 1907, Central West End District
Pat Hays Baer

Chapter 5 — West End

"Apotheosis of St. Louis"
circa 1940
Charles Trefts

1
"Apotheosis of St. Louis"
City Landmark: July 1966
Forest Park in front of Art Museum

An equestrian statue of Louis IX in 13th century armor was one of the most viewed pieces of temporary art exhibited during the 1904 World's Fair. It stood at the Plaza of St. Louis (the entrance concourse) along with a subordinate group in the piece entitled the "City Welcoming Her Guests" by artist Charles H. Niehaus. Working in staff (a short-lived material of plaster), Niehaus contrasted the "Grand Marshall" of the Fair with a personification of the city—a softly draped, queenly figure seated between two "Guiding Spirits."

Charged with a major restoration of Forest Park after the Fair, the Louisiana Purchase Exposition found itself in a singular position for sponsors of World's Fairs: it had made money. Some would go toward a permanent building at the entrance site, the **Jefferson Memorial** (page 122); much more would be needed for reforestation under the direction of landscape architect George Kessler. But first, the directors decided to preserve the strongest image from the Fair in bronze. Artist Niehaus protested that the work needed refinement. His request for $50,000 to furnish the permanent work was refused. Instead, the bronze casting by Winslow Brothers in Chicago was merely enlarged from the original quarter-size figure and the result presented by the directors to the city in 1906. The noble king (with many replacement swords) served as the symbol for the city until the completion of the **Gateway Arch** (page 9).

2
Block Unit #1 District
National Register: July 14, 2000
4100-91 Enright Avenue

While the **Ville neighborhood** (page 170) was the undisputed center of African-American social and cultural life from the 1920s through the 1950s, many middle-class black families preferred to live on the blocks directly south. Larger lots and houses made the area an attractive alternative to the smaller housing stock available in the Ville, but resistance from white homeowners meant that some blocks were harder to settle than others. In January 1923, white residents of the 4100 block of Enright met "to discuss reports that Negroes had purchased property further west on that avenue and to agree that no property owner should sell any tract in that block to Negro purchasers." (When the *Globe-Democrat* reported that a local grocer was present, his mostly black clientele led what the *St. Louis Argus* considered the first successful boycott in St. Louis.) Despite efforts by homeowners and the Real Estate Exchange (which threatened its members with expulsion if they sold to blacks in certain white areas), Enright was considered part of the city's "aristocratic Negro residential district" by 1927.

In 1932, neighbors in the 4100 block of Enright came to the St. Louis Urban League to request assistance in organizing against nuisance problems. Every resident was invited to join the new block unit. Many did. Within a year the Urban League formed a Federation of Block Units with twelve member blocks. Although original programs were primarily aimed at nuisance abatement, the block units soon stretched into cooperative buying, political action, health initiatives and even organizing credit unions. In 1950, the Urban League recognized the program as its most important and successful contribution to the St. Louis community during thirty-two years of existence. Five decades later more than 1,400 block units have been formed in the St. Louis area.

3
Central West End District
City District: June 19, 1974
Bounded roughly by DeBaliviere, Delmar,
Sarah and Lindell Boulevard

The Central West End includes most of the city's private streets and luxury apartment buildings along with some of its finest commercial and religious architecture. While there is neither one prevalent style nor dominant building type, an overall richness of detail and quality of construction create a strong sense of prosperity in the district. Although a few buildings date to the 1880s, the first construction boom began in the 1890s as the upper and middle classes continued their cyclical moves to the edge of the developing city.

The district's first generation of residents belonged to elite clubs, owned automobiles, advocated public playgrounds for the less fortunate and worked politely for women's suffrage. Their children attended Mary Institute, Smith Academy and City House; families spent the summer months on the East Coast or in Michigan. Home to most members of the "Big Cinch," the men who made big money and controlled city policy, the Central West End epitomized the reality of the American Dream in the Midwest.

Lindell Boulevard from Grand Avenue to the gates at the 1904 World's Fair at DeBaliviere had become a showcase of St. Louis wealth in time for the wonderment of 20 million visitors. By the teens, young marrieds and the upwardly mobile could find fashionable courtyard apartments or purchase smaller townhouses; in the 1920s, stylish high-rise apartments and hotels located near the smart shopping nodes on Maryland and Euclid. The Depression era saw sporadic demolition of family mansions. But it was not until zoning changes in the 1950s that the Central West End felt the full impact of problems facing the wider city as crime and white flight sent traditional institutions to St. Louis County.

A city historic district was first proposed during the 1973 campaign for the old 25th Ward Aldermanic seat. The winner, Mary Stolar, was one of the newer residents on Kingsbury Place where houses had been selling for less than $25,000. Working with neighborhood activists and the City Plan Commission, Stolar successfully guided the historic district legislation through unfriendly bureaucratic waters. A generation later, most of the district has enjoyed a rehab renaissance attracting owners, renters, singles, marrieds, straights, gays, retirees, students, blacks and whites.

The magical but temporary world of the 1904 Louisiana Purchase Exposition as viewed from the Grand Basin toward the Sunken Gardens. The Government Building is in the background; the Palace of Mines and Metallurgy is at the right and the Palace of Liberal Arts is at the left. The only building constructed with permanent materials for the Fair was the Art Museum.
Missouri Historical Society

Chapter 5

Apartments under construction on Lindell Boulevard looking west from Taylor Avenue circa 1929
Landmarks Collection

Southwest corner of DeBaliviere and Delmar, circa 1926, designed by Isadore Shank
Landmarks Collection

4
Cathedral Basilica of St. Louis (New Cathedral)
City Landmark: September 1973
Lindell Boulevard at Newstead Avenue

Land for the New Cathedral was purchased in 1895 by Archbishop John L. Kain, who built a provisional chapel on the site and directed architects Barnett, Haynes & Barnett to draw up cathedral plans. Kain died during fund raising for this design; his successor Coadjutor John Joseph Glennon started anew. A competition program calling for a million-dollar church was distributed in 1905 with international response. Entries came from Von Ferbulis (Austria and Washington, D.C.); McGinnis, Walsh & Sullivan (Boston); J. De Mentureal (Paris); Rüdell & Odenthal (Cologne) and Barnett, Haynes & Barnett—the only local firm. To the dismay of architects who had anticipated an open review, a special committee appointed by the new Archbishop quickly selected Barnett, Haynes & Barnett. The winning firm would wrestle with a headstrong client for the next decade.

Ground was finally broken May 1, 1907. With the exterior of somber gray granite laid over a "new and original" concrete form nearing completion, architect and client outdid each other in promises about the interior. Architect George D. Barnett "intended the interior to be almost barbaric in the grandeur of its color." Glennon pledged that the colossal building would not be finished until "it has set on its walls the luster of every jewel, the bright plumage of every bird, the glow and glory of every metal, the iridescent gleam of every glass." The interior received the first of some 83,000 square feet of mosaics in 1912; the last was installed in 1988.

Cathedral Basilica of St. Louis in 1962
Arteaga Photos

Chapter 5 — West End

Chase Hotel and Apartments circa 1929
Landmarks Collection

5
Chase Park Plaza Hotel
City Landmark: June 1977
Kingshighway at Lindell Boulevard

The Chase Hotel with adjacent Chase and Chester Apartments was designed in 1922 by Preston J. Bradshaw; the Art Deco Park Plaza, inspired by New York's Savoy Plaza, was designed in 1929 by Schopp & Bauman for Sam Koplar. After losing the Park Plaza during the Depression, Koplar gained control of both buildings which were combined and renamed in 1961. The lobby at the Park Plaza is still noteworthy as are the panoramic views from the best of the 265 units renovated as apartments from plans by Mackey & Associates in 1987-88 after a subsidiary of General Electric purchased the complex.

The Chase closed in 1989. Two years later, contents were auctioned in an atmosphere of dire forecasts for the property. It would be 1997 before ownership passed to a young developer who began work on renovation. Reopened to loud acclaim drowning out some quiet skepticism in 1999, the born-again Chase boasts popular restaurants, well-attended movies, a trendy health club and banquet rooms alive with prestigious events. The $35 million renovation was made possible by state and federal historic rehab tax credits.

6
Kate Chopin House
National Register: February 14, 1986
4232 McPherson Avenue

In the autumn of 1903, Kate Chopin moved from her house at 3317 Morgan (now razed) to the 1897 house on McPherson where she wrote her last poem and short story. After a visit to the World's Fair, Chopin (the author of over one hundred short stories, poems, essays and novels) suffered a cerebral hemorrhage on August 22, 1904 and died at home. Later recognition of her significance as an important literary figure and an exemplar of the changing role of American women can be traced to the 1899 publication of *The Awakening*.

7
Joseph Erlanger House
National Historic Landmark: December 8, 1976
5127 Waterman Boulevard

This conventional 1904 house, one of several in the block built by the Fair Building Company, was the residence for forty-eight years of Dr. Joseph Erlanger—an 1895 graduate of Johns Hopkins Medical School who came to Washington University in 1910 as Chairman of the Physiology Department. For his innovative work in neurophysiological research, Erlanger was awarded the Nobel Prize for Medicine in 1944.

8
Fullerton's Westminster Place
National Register: April 10, 1980
4300 and 4400 blocks of Westminster

Exclusively the work of St. Louis architects, Fullerton Place houses date from 1892 through 1909. Grable, Weber & Groves, Barnett, Haynes & Barnett and W. Albert Swasey were responsible for forty-one of the original fifty-seven designs from sixteen different firms. (Six houses have been demolished.) Deed restrictions imposed in this private street developed by General Joseph Scott Fullerton included a minimum construction cost of $10,000 with twenty-five feet established as the required setback from the street.

The vast majority of the houses were designed in variations on Georgian, Romanesque and Renaissance Revival themes ranging from studied formalism to Baroque and Mannerist whimsy. A wide palette of brick and stone colors enhanced by fine wood and terra cotta ornament also contributes to the vibrancy and sustained interest on the street. Located too close for comfort to the once-lively Gaslight Square and subjected to ward boundary vagaries and downzoning, Fullerton Place experienced hard times in the late 1960s and early 70s when many homes were converted to rooming houses. Inclusion in the Central West End Historic District in 1974 helped promote and protect this valuable part of St. Louis' architectural heritage.

9
Eliot House
City Landmark: September 1973
4446 Westminster Place

T. S. Eliot, the youngest of seven children, had left for Harvard before his parents moved to this 1905 house designed for them by Montrose P. McArdle, St. Louis. Henry Eliot was President of Hydraulic Press Brick Co. and son of William Greenleaf Eliot, notable Unitarian clergyman and the founder of Washington University. Henry Eliot's products are on prominent display along Fullerton Place. Charlotte, a particularly well-educated woman, was a lifelong poet who encouraged her son to follow a literary career.

Fullerton's Westminster Place: 4463 Westminster
Landmarks, 1979

Chapter 5 West End

Fullerton's Westminster Place: 4457 Westminster
Landmarks, 1979

Fullerton's Westminster Place: Interior, 4300 block Westminster
Landmarks, 1979

Fullerton's Westminster Place: 4388 Westminster

Landmarks, 1979

Chapter 5　　West End

St. John's United Methodist Church
Robert C. Pettus, 1974

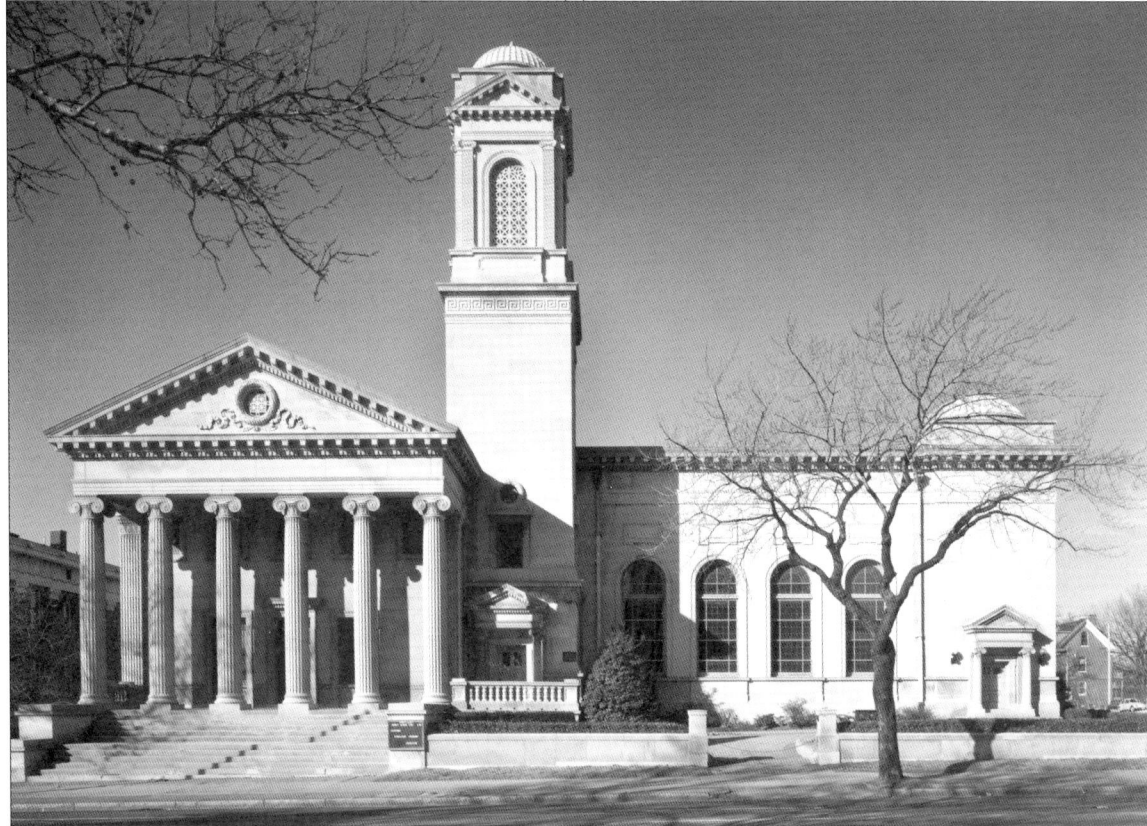

Below, left to right:

Temple Israel
Robert C. Pettus, 1974

Temple Israel circa 1936
Mercantile Library

106

10
Holy Corners District
National Register: December 29, 1975

A monumental urban space focusing on Kingshighway that includes one of the finest collections of early 20th century institutional architecture in America, Holy Corners displays a textbook progression of Classical orders beginning with the Doric (Christian Science), then Ionic (St. John's) and ending with Corinthian (Temple Israel). Those three congregations plus Second Baptist across the street all elected to leave the "Piety Hill" neighborhood just west of Jefferson Avenue within a five-year period. All had fostered interfaith relations in their 19th century neighborhood. That spirit thrived for many years when the move to Kingshighway brought them into even closer proximity. Although six different architectural firms contributed pieces of the *tout ensemble,* all eight buildings in the district are unified by fine materials, judicious siting and construction dates between 1901 and 1907.

11
Temple Israel
City Landmark: January 1972
5001 Washington Boulevard

Temple Israel was organized in 1886 by prominent German Jews as a liberal offshoot of Shaare Emeth, St. Louis' first Reform congregation. For their new home in the Central West End, Barnett, Haynes & Barnett produced an impressive design (in Caen stone) reportedly derived from the Roman Temple of Vespasian. Completed in 1907, it was the westernmost address of all St. Louis synagogues. A companion education and community center designed in 1936 by Benjamin Shapiro reaffirmed the congregation's confidence in the Central West End. But by the 1950s, Temple Israel was one of the few synagogues remaining within the city limits.

The congregation purchased land in Ladue in 1953, but the Ladue Council denied the building application on the grounds that overcrowding would result at the site. The congregation then bought a lot in the city of Creve Coeur. Construction was delayed again until a 1959 Missouri Supreme Court decision overturned objections. Finally, in 1962, Temple Israel moved from the Kingshighway temple to Ladue and Spoede Roads. After a chapter as a public school, the former Temple Israel complex entered another period as the Angelic Temple of Deliverance.

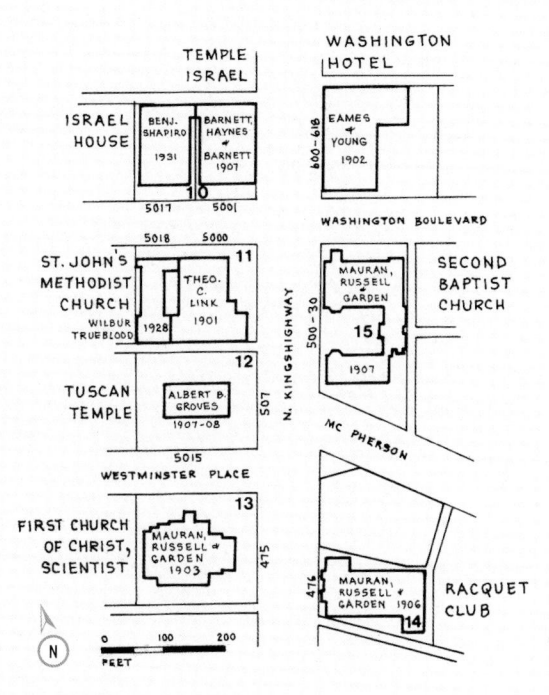

Holy Corners District Map
Pat Hays Baer

12
St. John's United Methodist Church
City Landmark: January 1972
5000 Washington Boulevard

St. John's pioneered construction on Kingshighway, breaking ground in 1901 for a Classical Revival building designed by Theodore C. Link's office. The third home for the congregation organized right after the Civil War, St. John's features full-figure portraits in stained glass by Emil Frei (St. Louis) of John and Charles Wesley, the English founders of Methodism. Later work by St. Louis artists includes windows by Siegfried Reinhardt and Rodney Winfield. Wilbur Trueblood designed the Education Building to the south with adjoining Singleton Chapel to the west in 1928.

Even though membership dropped drastically from 1,600 in the 1930s, the congregation voted to remain in the city. Today, some 140 or so members of St. John's worship in the chapel while 300 members of the Metropolitan Community Church, primarily a gay and lesbian congregation, meet in the main sanctuary. Theater groups, a private school and assorted community organizations renting office and low-cost performance space in the complex provide weekday and evening activity.

Detail: St. John's Church
Robert C. Pettus, 1974

Chapter 5   West End

13
Tuscan Temple
City Landmark: January 1972
507 North Kingshighway

The portico of this Doric order Greek Revival temple was deliberately sited to address the Kingshighway elevation even though the main entrance is around the corner on Westminster Place. Built in 1907–08 from plans by Albert B. Groves, St. Louis, the gray brick building is still the home of Tuscan Lodge No. 360 A.F. & A.M.

Tuscan Temple
Robert C. Pettus, 1974

14
First Church of Christ, Scientist
City Landmark: January 1972
475 North Kingshighway

After a 1901 design by Mauran, Russell & Garden was estimated to cost $300,000, the St. Louis firm returned to the drawing boards to produce a variation in brick to meet the budget of $100,000. Ground was broken September 1903; by the next summer, guests from the World's Fair were able to view the completed auditorium at First Church. Founded in 1894 as one of the first five Christian Science churches in the world, the congregation has remained on Kingshighway.

15
Racquet Club
City Landmark: January 1972
476 North Kingshighway

Mauran, Russell & Garden (St. Louis) gained their second district commission in 1906, this time for a secular client. For the $112,000 Racquet Club, the firm turned to an Arts & Craft vocabulary displayed in reddish-brown brick topped by a striking copper cornice. This is the first home for the club whose charter members established both the Davis (tennis) and Walker (golf) cups. The third Racquet Club organized in the United States also backed Lindbergh's 1927 flight with a contribution of $10,000. Full membership privileges are still limited to men as of 2002.

First Church of Christ, Scientist circa 1905
Missouri Historical Society

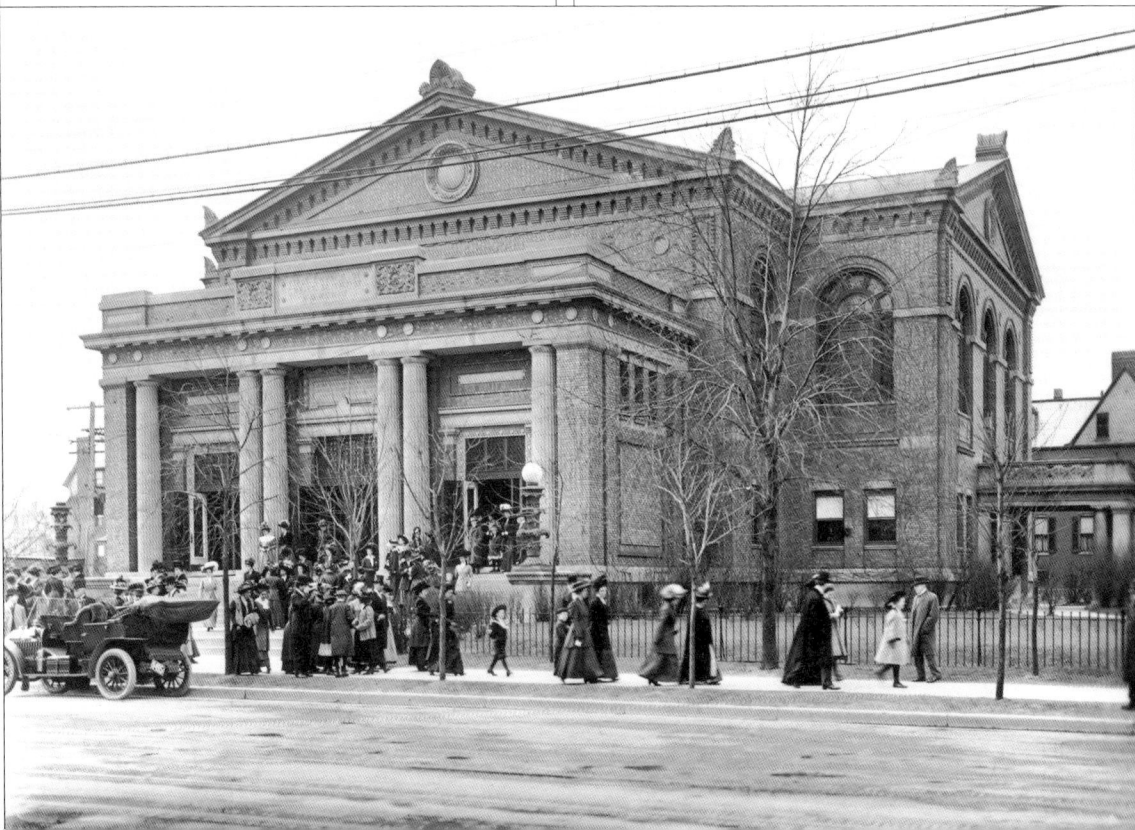

17
Washington Hotel
600 North Kingshighway

One of the most expensive buildings in the district was built for the Louisiana Purchase Exposition, an ethereal event scheduled to vanish in months after it opened. In 1902, permits were obtained for the construction of a $305,000 Bedford stone, seven-story hotel for the Forest City Building Company. Designed by Eames & Young (St. Louis) to accommodate visitors to the 1904 World's Fair, the hotel was adapted to housing by SRT Architects & Planners (St. Louis) in 1979.

Clockwise, top to bottom:

Racquet Club
Robert C. Pettus, 1974

Washington Hotel
Robert C. Pettus, 1974

Second Baptist Church
Robert C. Pettus, 1974

16
Second Baptist Church
City Landmark: January 1972
500 North Kingshighway

This composition of multi-hued golden brick trimmed with dark red granite, terra cotta, red tile and Minnesota sandstone stands as a tribute to inspired masonry. Built in 1907-08 from plans by Mauran, Russell & Garden (St. Louis) for a reported cost of more than $300,000, the church could trace its history back to 1818 and the founding of the first Protestant congregation in St. Louis. More recently home to the Baptist Church of the Good Shepherd, the now vulnerable Lombard/Renaissance masterwork may need a suitable adaptive reuse plan.

Chapter 5 — West End

Kingsbury Place Entrance Gate
Barbara E. Martin, 1973

18
Kingsbury Place
City Landmark: February 1973

Entered through the most regal of private street gates (a 1900 design by Barnett, Haynes & Barnett with bronze statue by Clara Pfeifer), Kingsbury Place is less grandiose than envisioned by its promoters and first few homeowners who selected the city's premier designer of Monumental Beaux Arts to create an entrance symbolizing great wealth. Two of the palatial houses designed by Barnett, Haynes & Barnett (#7 from 1902 and #3 from 1905) have been demolished; #11, designed in 1902, is extant.

Houses in the western block where lots are narrower were generally designed by less prominent architects who also received commissions on nearby **Windermere Place** *(page 135)*. Not as consistent in architectural significance as **Fullerton's Westminster Place** *(page 103)*, Kingsbury Place is blessed with a central planting strip—a feature common to several of the private streets laid out by Julius Pitzman. (Pitzman moved from Compton Hill to #6 Kingsbury in 1912.)

25 Portland Place, Eames & Young, 1893

Robert C. Pettus, 1988

19
Portland and Westmoreland Places
National Register: February 12, 1974

St. Louis' age of opulence is best reflected in Portland and Westmoreland Places where resplendent mansions built for the elite continue to amaze visitors to the city. Opened for development in 1888, these streets offered larger lots in a pastoral location free from the encroachments of the 19th century city that had begun to tarnish Vandeventer Place (razed) in **Midtown** *(page 77)*. A few houses have been altered or painted, obscuring the rich original materials. A few have been razed, but the remaining collection is an outdoor museum of American domestic architecture designed for the wealthy.

32 Portland Place, Weber & Groves, 1898

Robert C. Pettus, 1988

Chapter 5 West End

6 Westmoreland Place, Eames & Young, 1890
Robert C. Pettus, 1988

23 Portland Place, Eames & Young, 1892
Robert C. Pettus, 1988

33 Portland Place, Mauran, Russell & Crowell, 1911
Robert C. Pettus, 1988

40 Portland Place, Frederick Bonsack, 1897
Robert C. Pettus, 1988

Chapter 5 — West End

Tiffany Window from Second Presbyterian Church, installed 1922
Church Archives

20
Second Presbyterian Church
City Landmark: September 1973
National Register: September 11, 1975
4501 Westminster Place

The first piece of this outstanding Romanesque Revival limestone complex was the 1896 chapel by Shepley, Rutan & Coolidge (Boston). The sanctuary designed by Theodore C. Link (St. Louis) got underway three years later. LaBeaume & Klein, St. Louis, furnished plans for the large education building from 1930. Eleven luminous windows in the sanctuary are by Tiffany of New York; windows in the chapel are from Emil Frei, St. Louis. Kurt Landberg, St. Louis, renovated both the chapel and the sanctuary in 1986-87. The congregation (organized in 1838) built its first church at 5th and Walnut in 1840; a second at 17th and Lucas Place was completed in 1870. Electing not to move west from this third home in the 1960s, the congregation has been active in neighborhood preservation and social services.

Second Presbyterian Church
Robert C. Pettus, 1975

21
Union Avenue Christian Church
City Landmark: November 1974
733 Union Avenue

The first church to break ground in the cluster on North Union *(see map on page 135)* was designed by Albert B. Groves in two stages: the chapel at the rear in 1904 and in 1907 (with partner August Weber) the Lombard Romanesque sanctuary fronting Union. Both enliven smooth limestone walls with bands of rough-faced stone. An outgrowth of Central Christian Church (organized in 1871 after dismissal from the First Christian Church for insisting that instrumental music had a legitimate place in religious worship), the congregation currently hosts well-regarded secular performances including an opera series.

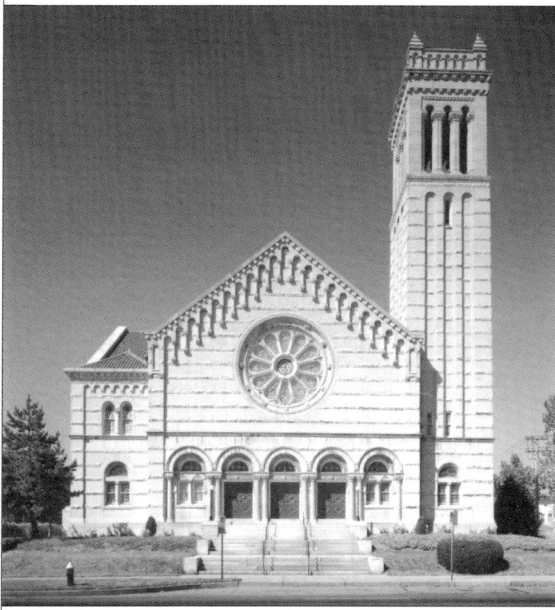

Union Avenue Christian Church
Robert C. Pettus, 1988

22
Washington Terrace
City Landmark: April 1973

Washington Terrace is announced by romantic entrance gates designed in 1893 by Harvey Ellis of Ellis & Mann, St. Louis. (The bountiful terra cotta ornament was formed at the local Winkle Terra Cotta Company; the heraldic lions were sculpted later by J. Rollin.) Reminiscent of the 15th century portal at Lübeck (a Hanseatic city in north Germany), the photogenic gates were meant to entice purchasers to the Terrace, rather than to rival Portland or Westmoreland Places, by the Bell Realty Company.

Although the minimum allowable cost for a house on the Terrace was higher than Portland or Westmoreland, few of those built on the Terrace are as palatial. The most extravagant, the Barnett, Haynes & Barnett house at #5, was razed in the 1940s. The street includes seven other houses by that firm, five by Will Levy (St. Louis) and four by Albert Groves, also of St. Louis. Only four of the forty on the street were built before 1900; twenty-three were built in the decade between 1900 and 1909.

Washington Terrace Entrance Gate
Robert C. Pettus, 1975

Chapter 5   West End

North side of Washington Terrace with 1895 house by Barnett, Haynes & Barnett at the right
Landmarks Collection, 1989

23
Westminster Presbyterian Church
City Landmark: November 1974
5300 Delmar Boulevard

Albert B. Groves, either alone or with partners Grable and Weber, designed twelve extant St. Louis churches. Six were Presbyterian. For the congregation dislocated by construction for the **Fox Theatre** *(page 83)*, Groves selected an impressive English Gothic design executed in Bedford stone with Caen stone interior. Interior oak finishes were designed by Groves who also collaborated with Marx & Jones in the design of the windows. Several memorial windows from the old church on Grand Avenue were incorporated in the new building constructed in two phases between 1913 and 1915.

24
Chouteau Apartments/Parkway Dwellings
National Register: February 10, 1983
4937-43 Laclede Avenue

Designed in 1909 by Mauran, Russell & Garden of St. Louis, the four Parkway Dwellings resemble stately Georgian townhouses. Each of the sixteen units featured the first two-story, double-decked apartments in the city. Sold in 1919 to August Chouteau, Sr. (namesake and direct descendant of one of St. Louis' 18th century French founders) the buildings were converted to condominiums in 1983 from plans by Stan McKay of St. Louis.

Chouteau Apartments
Stan McKay, 1982

Dorris Motor Car Company Building (Dorris Lofts)
W. C. Persons, 1919
Missouri Historical Society

25
Crabtree Court Apartments
National Register: August 23, 1984
Southwest corner Lindell and Vandeventer

"St. Louis, world renowned for its beautiful homes and attractive residence districts, soon will become equally as famous for its commodious and imposing apartment houses." The 1909 feature article in *The St. Louis Republic* on apartment design could not have been written ten years earlier when residents of Lindell Boulevard and other prestigious streets viewed apartment buildings with suspicion. Contemporary accounts suggest that hostility sprang not from increased density but rather from the opinion that the late 19th century "so-called apartment houses" of St. Louis were in reality only "joined flats."

The press announced construction of the Louise (later Crabtree Court) Apartments as one of the "big projects" giving impetus to an unprecedented movement in apartment construction. Designed in 1908 by MIT-trained Charles Deitering, the two red brick, three-story buildings offered thirty suites with interiors artfully finished in Arts & Crafts oak woodwork plus a janitor on the premises. A deep courtyard on Vandeventer Avenue, high-grade brickwork, projecting bay windows and up-to-date interior plans distinguished the "Louise" from the ubiquitous but scorned St. Louis flats.

26
Delmar Loop/Parkview Gardens District
National Register: February 16, 1984

John C. Jannopoulo's Delmar Garden Amusement Park and Louis Cella's racetrack opened on Delmar west of Skinker at the turn of the 19th century after the streetcar line was extended beyond St. Louis city limits. Both attractions remained active until the teens when their owners embarked on redevelopment plans including commercial buildings on Delmar and small-scale apartments to the north. The "Loop," named for the streetcar turn-around, became University City's downtown. After a ragged period in the 1970s, the street now offers some of the best specialty shopping in the area. (Except for the short strip along Delmar from Skinker to Limit Street, the 84-acre district is outside St. Louis' city limits.)

27
De Hodiamont House
City Landmark: October 1972
951 Maple Place

Belgian-born Emmanuel de Hodiamont built the original rectangular stone house circa 1829. Gothic Revival details and an addition date from the 1870s after de Hodiamont had sold the property and retreated to the Trappist Abbey of Gethsemani in Kentucky. His first ten years in the New World (including a year in Florissant between 1808 and 1809) had been spent with the same contemplative order. Possibly a disinherited Baron, de Hodiamont left the order around 1818 for marriage and a secular life in real estate and farming. (Notes from the papers of John F. Darby, Mayor of St. Louis in 1835-37 and 1840, indicate that de Hodiamont had "an immense sum of money.")

28
1907 Dorris Motor Car Company Building (Center for Emerging Technologies)
National Register: February 10, 2000
4063-65 Forest Park Avenue

Although St. Louisans regarded George Preston Dorris' arrival from Nashville in 1898 with his experimental car as "the best joke since the McKinley-Bryan election returns," his St. Louis Motor Carriage Company was the first in the city to manufacture autos. When

Chapter 5

Dorris Motor Car Company Building
W. C. Persons, 1919
Missouri Historical Society

the company moved to Peoria in 1905, Dorris resigned and formed the Dorris Motor Car Company. Two years later its success was such that John Ludwig Wees was commissioned to design a new factory on Forest Park Boulevard. Capacity was approximately 300 cars annually; many were shipped out of town. In late 1907, a local publication reported that the approximately forty Dorris cars in St. Louis performed so well that "you very rarely see a Dorris car stalled...."

The use of this building as both an engineering and manufacturing center was short-lived. Even with a third story added in 1909, production couldn't meet demand. A larger facility was constructed about a block away in 1911 (next entry), and the original factory was turned into a service and repair center. After serving the rest of the 20th century as a shoe factory and office furniture warehouse, the former factory returned to its engineering roots. A full rehabilitation completed in 2001 (by Mackey Mitchell Architects, St. Louis) readied the building for new life as a high-tech incubator, part of the Center for Emerging Technologies.

29
Dorris Motor Car Company Building (Dorris Lofts)
National Register: May 1, 1986
4100 Laclede Avenue

Built in 1911-12 from plans by John Ludwig Wees, the Dorris Motor Car Company's Laclede Avenue factory was the incubator of many of Dorris' important innovations in the evolution of the American automobile, including the first valve-in-head four-cylinder engine and the first float-feed carburetor. Dorris continued the tradition established at its earlier location *(previous entry)* of producing high-quality cars by hand. In its most prolific year, 1920, production peaked at almost 400 cars and 117 trucks; that same year Chevrolet established a St. Louis plant producing over 100,000 cars annually. A late effort to enter the low-cost car market could not save the company. Dorris was dissolved in 1924. The 1911 factory is architecturally significant as the earliest known St. Louis example of mushroom capital/paneled slab technology. It was recycled as loft condominiums in 1986 from plans by Mitch Wall (St. Louis).

30
Eugene Field School
National Register: September 2, 1992
4466 Olive

William B. Ittner (**Carr School**, *page 54*) reconciled a small lot with a large budget in the 1900 Field School, resulting in a nicely ornamented three-story building with a U-shaped plan. The arms of the "U" extend almost to the sidewalk line, forming a courtyard; a one-story kindergarten projects from the rear. Terra cotta is used to great effect in blind arcades, decorated sills, shields, panels and brackets. Twin stair towers in the courtyard's corners add to the overall Italian effect. In the Board of Education's 1899-1900 Annual Report, Ittner wrote: "The Eugene Field School may be taken as embodying the improvements which we have been able to make through a careful study of our earlier buildings, and represents, perhaps, as near an ideal school building as it is possible to effect." After several years of disuse, the Field School was renovated in 2001 to accommodate students displaced while their own facilities underwent modernization.

31
Forest Park Headquarters Building ("Cabanne House")
City Landmark: July 1971
National Register: June 11, 1986
115 Union Avenue

Conceived as part of the original Master Plan for Forest Park, this informal picturesque structure is the only surviving 19th century building in the park. Known locally but inaccurately as the "Cabanne House," the house designed in 1875 by James H. McNamara (St. Louis) underwent extensive renovation in 1986 by David Mason, St. Louis, to adapt it to offices and event space for The Saint Louis Ambassadors.

32
Forest Park Hotel
National Register: March 22, 1984
4910 West Pine Boulevard

By the early 1920s, the Central West End had developed into an important tourist destination largely through the appeal of Forest Park which more than fulfilled 19th century predictions as an attraction. The blocks facing the park along Kingshighway had been reserved and developed exclusively as a prestigious subdivision of apartments and hotels by neighborhood resident/investors. Preston J. Bradshaw, whose **Chase Hotel** *(page 102)* was just getting underway at the corner of Lindell and Kingshighway, was also selected in 1923 to design the first portion of the red brick Forest Park Hotel. A seven-story addition from 1926 by George D. Barnett featured exquisite small dining rooms with elaborate historic period ornament.

Still in use as a shabby but genteel lodging into the 1980s, the Forest Park Hotel closed after fitful attempts at renovation. Ownership passed to Maharishi Vedic University from Boone, North Carolina, whose announced plans to transform the property into a center of Transcendental Meditation did not materialize. Acquired through eminent domain for $680,000, the building is scheduled to reopen with 100 apartments in late 2002 after completion of a $20 million tax credit project designed by Duncan Architects, Kansas City.

Forest Park Headquarters "Cabanne House" before renovation
Landmarks, 1985

Chapter 5 — West End

Statue of Dr. Martin Luther King, Jr., Fountain Park District
Landmarks, 1979

33
Fountain Park District
National Register: October 18, 1982

Grandly envisioned and first platted in 1857 as a much larger, self-contained suburban development, Fountain Park (originally Aubert Place) saw only limited development before the 1890s when the park was landscaped by the city. Although many of the late 19th and early 20th century houses were designed by architects (especially Barnett, Haynes & Barnett), most were built for developers rather than individual clients. Beautifully sited, the 1896 Third Congregational Church by Grable, Weber & Groves has been home to the congregation of Centennial Christian since 1945. Both the exterior and interior of this Italian Romanesque Revival structure have been carefully maintained in contrast to many of the surrounding houses and the beautiful ruins of a commercial building outlining the opposite end of the park. The heroic statue of Dr. Martin Luther King by St. Louis sculptor Rudolph Torrini dates from 1978.

Fountain Park District: Centennial Christian Church
Robert C. Pettus, 1985

34
Goodfellow/Julian Concrete Block District
National Register: August 13, 1987

The St. Louis Portland Cement Company (Missouri's first plant) opened in 1902 at a site about one mile north of the city limits where high-grade Des Moines shale and Mississippian limestone were readily available from the Missouri River bluffs. Although concrete pillars, sill, caps, steps and floors were the first products manufactured, the introduction of a concrete building block offered new applications for the material.

Built just after exhibitions of the new concrete block technology appeared at the 1904 World's Fair, this development by the Crescent Realty Company offered the first architect-designed houses using blocks in St. Louis. Block construction (viewed as a readily available alternative to depleted timber resources) was promoted for its easy maintenance, durability and resistance to fire and earthquake. St. Louis architects A. Blair Ridington and Edward F. Nolte provided three basic designs for sixteen district houses built in 1905-06.

Fountain Park District, corner of Fountain and Bayard
Landmarks, 1979

Fountain Park District, Centennial Christian Church Interior
Robert C. Pettus, 1985

Chapter 5 — West End

Detail: Jefferson Memorial Building
Gary R. Tetley, 1996

35
Jefferson Memorial Building
City Landmark: May 1979
Lindell at DeBaliviere Avenue

Designed by Isaac Taylor, Director of Works for the 1904 World's Fair, the first memorial building honoring Thomas Jefferson was constructed in 1911 on the site of the main entrance to the Fair with proceeds from the unusually successful event. A carved-in-place marble statue of Jefferson by Karl Bitter, Director of Sculpture for the Fair, sits inside the rotunda. Behind Jefferson toward the park lies the $30 million addition to the History Museum (formerly Missouri Historical Society) opened in 2000. Designed to complement rather than mimic the original Classical Revival building, the addition is named for Emerson Electric Company in recognition of its lead gift of $3 million in 1997. HOK's St. Louis office won a 1999 award for the addition from the American Institute of Architects as one of the ten most environmentally friendly buildings that year.

The Jefferson Memorial Building in 1914 faced empty residential lots and the recently built concrete wall designed to buffer railroad noise.
Missouri Historical Society

122

Enclosing the River des Peres (1914) in Forest Park, Jefferson Memorial Building at the right
Missouri Historical Society

36
Jewel Box
National Register: March 14, 2000
Junction of Wells & McKinley Drives in Forest Park

City Engineer William C. E. Becker set out to build a different kind of greenhouse when funds were allocated for a new floral conservatory in Forest Park. The challenge was to create a design which would resist hail and prevent sun damage to delicate plants. After extensive consultation and testing, his solution was to design a step-roofed structure with tall glass verticals and solid horizontal surfaces, all supported on an arched steel structure. The result was an innovative, durable greenhouse. Opened to the public in 1936, its immediate popularity was overwhelming and prompted the installation of electric lights so that hours could be extended. In the 1938–39 season, some 416,000 visitors came through—25,000 more than the Art Museum during the same period. Although the public's ravenous appetite for floral display has somewhat diminished, the Jewel Box is still a perennial favorite with park visitors. A $3.2 million renovation designed by Christner Partnership (St. Louis) was underway by early 2002.

Jewel Box in 1938
Preston Raymond Papin, Landmarks Collection

Chapter 5   West End

Entrance Arch, Lewis Place District

Landmarks, 1975

37
Leonardo Apartments
National Register: August 11, 1983
4166 Lindell Boulevard

The Worth Investment Company, deciding to add a "residence hotel" and garage to its portfolio in 1925, hired Boaz & Kiel as contractors for the $200,000 Lindell project. Company president Henry W. Kiel had just completed an unprecedented three terms as Mayor. The developer engaged the services of T. J. Craven to draw up a nine-story building in the general terra cotta and red brick formula made popular by architect Preston J. Bradshaw.

38
Lewis Place District
National Register: September 15, 1980

Behind the monumental triumphal arch designed in 1894 by Barnett, Haynes & Barnett (St. Louis) lies Lewis Place. Planned as a street of ambitious houses displaying various revival styles popular in the 1890s, Lewis Place is instead dominated by the Bungalow, or "Bungle-oh" to contemporary detractors. The Bungalow craze first flourished in Southern California, then, proving adaptable to a wide range of climates and tastes, swept the housing market in the second decade of the 20th century. Many offered Arts & Crafts details (with revolutionary but informal plans) and a cozy hearth to buyers with modest budgets.

39
Lister Building
National Register: February 10, 1983
4500 Olive Street

The red brick Renaissance Revival building designed by John L. Wees (St. Louis) was built for Dr. Herman Tuholske, one of eight physicians to establish the first post-graduate medical institution in the United States. Prussian-born Tuholske, the first Chief of Staff and Head of Surgery of the new (1902) Jewish Hospital on Delmar, was awarded an honorary LLD by Westminster College in Fulton, Missouri in recognition of his contributions to the field of medicine. Construction of the Lister Building in 1904-05 (among the earliest St. Louis buildings planned especially for doctors' offices) coincided with the emergence of new professional and ethical standards following the unregulated chaos of the 19th century. (An annex to the west, also designed by John Wees, was built in 1914.)

The site was located on a popular streetcar line opened in time for the World's Fair in the midst of the rapidly developing Central West End neighborhood. Up until the sudden demise of Gaslight Square to the east in the late 1960s, this section of Olive Street bustled. Drug stores, the Hispanic Trading Company, Greenwalds Fine Linen, Fine Arts Frame, a post office, the Beethoven Conservatory of Music, the Lorelei Natatorium,

Presto printing and Ben Selkirk's auction house were all part of the eclectic commercial node. But by the 1990s, the Lister Building was vacant and the street silent. The annex, in even worse condition than the original building, was razed in 1999. In late 2001, years of stalwart attempts to find an owner willing to pick up the challenge came to fruition when Central West End Builders acquired the Lister Building and two of the other three corners at Olive and Taylor. Plans for adaptive reuse are underway.

40
Luyties Homeopathic Pharmacy Company Building
National Register: pending
4200 Laclede Avenue

Herman C. G. Luyties came to America in 1850, already considered a doctor at the age of sixteen or seventeen after training in conventional medicine and homeopathy in his native Bremen. In 1853, he set up a downtown St. Louis pharmacy specializing in homeopathic remedies—a popular alternative to a medical establishment still based on bleedings and toxic mercury treatments. After the turn of the century, Luyties' company (now run by his sons) moved to a developing light industrial area in the central corridor. Company lore relates that when the first new factory burned to the ground, the company president insisted that the replacement be completely fireproof. Architect Frederick C. Bonsack responded with one composed entirely of concrete poured on-site: walls, floor and even the exterior ornament. Although the technology had been available for more than a decade, Bonsack's 1915 design may be the first St. Louis example of a fully poured-in-place building.

Luyties, already one of the world's largest when its new factory was constructed, weathered homeopathy's early 20th century decline in popularity when many other companies could not. Annual sales of $13 million with thirty-one employees still headquartered at 4200 Laclede were reported as late as 2000. When the company sold the building in 2001, the interior retained original work areas, partitions and shelving as well as a walk-in safe (said to have been installed for the controlled substances used in manufacturing). Designs are underway to convert the building into residential lofts—a use already pioneered by the nearby **Dorris** (page 118) and **Sanitol** (page 129) factory buildings.

41
Mount Cabanne/Raymond Place District
National Register: pending
Bounded roughly by Union, Delmar, Kingshighway and Page Boulevard

It is only some seven or eight years ago since the lover of the spectacular, who risked the dirt, danger and delay of the old narrow gauge [railroad] cars, used to ride through this tract to Kensington Gardens. Anything less attractive or more objectionable could scarcely be imagined. The ground looked as though a series of embryo earthquakes had struck it, and it was simply an eyesore and a hindrance to investment. The influence of the Portland place [sic] and adjoining improvements has redeemed this plain of wilderness between the Aubert subdivision and the eastern bound of Cabanne.

The two subdivisions attracting the colorful attention of the *St. Louis Republic* in that 1895 article opened in 1887 and 1893. Offering an alternative to the

Median park and bungalows in the 4700 block of Lewis Park
Landmarks, 1979

Chapter 5 | West End

Oakherst Place Concrete Block District site map
Pat Hays Baer

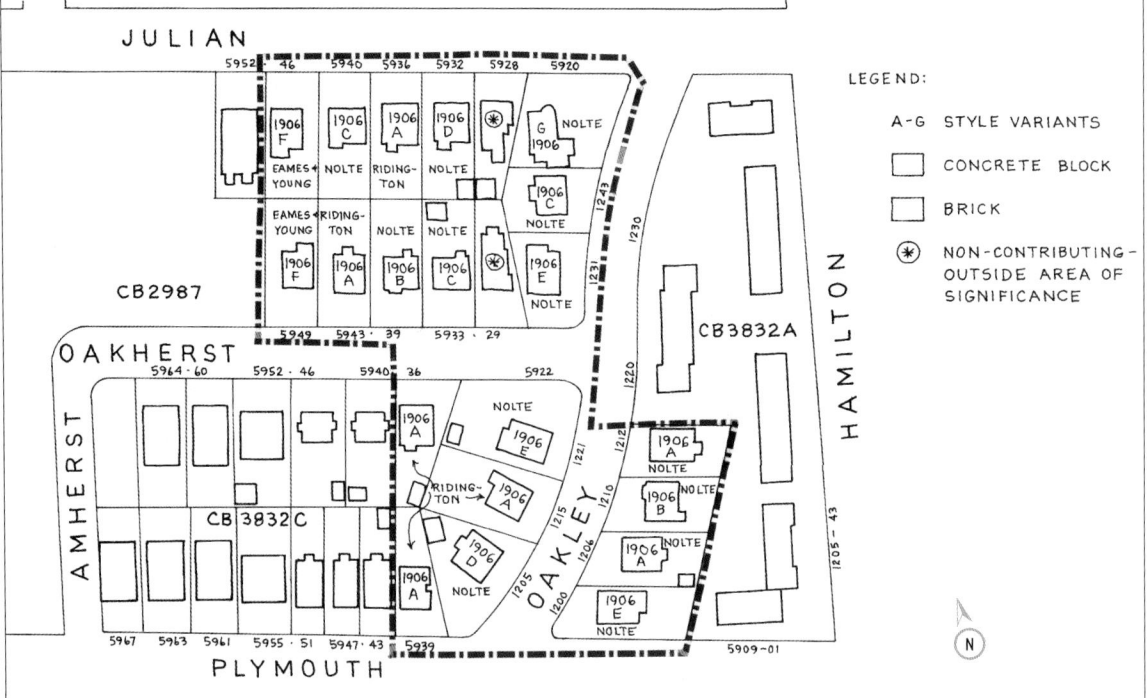

Concrete Block House at 5920 Julian
Landmarks, 1986

emerging **Central West End** (page 99) for the city's growing middle class, the Mount Cabanne-Raymond Place district was built out with upscale revival-style dwellings between 1890 and about 1910. Among the many notable buildings is one of the city's best and most varied collections of work by builder/architect/developer Alexander A. Fischer. Fischer's trademark broken frieze can be seen throughout the neighborhood in more than 70 single and two-family houses.

The district is also rich in cultural history. Sally Benson's autobiographical novel *Meet Me in St. Louis* was set on the 5100 block of Kensington. (Her family's house has been razed.) In the same block is the subject of another memoir, *The Boy Next Door* by Henry Eisenkramer, detailing life two decades after the World's Fair. Eisenkramer's family was part of a significant Jewish population in and around the neighborhood in the 1920s and 30s. Many moved here to be

Saint Louis Art Museum in the distance from the World's Fair pavilion overlooking Forest Park
Landmarks Collection, 1920

within walking distance of the B'nai Amoona Temple at Academy and Vernon. Widely considered to be the most important Orthodox congregation in the community, the group evolved into the city's first Conservative congregation during its time at this location. Other Jewish institutions in the district were United Hebrew (its temple at Kingshighway and Enright has been demolished) and the **YMHA** in the **Visitation Park Historic District** *(page 135)*.

B'nai Amoona left Mount Cabanne/Raymond Place in 1943 for University City where it hired Erich Mendelsohn to design one of the region's finest examples of Modern architecture. As most of the other first- and second-generation institutions and populations moved west, the neighborhood began to suffer from disinvestment. So did the Central West End. But this neighborhood did not share in the renaissance that occurred to the south of Delmar. It is hoped that historic designation, appreciation of the superb housing stock, an annual house tour and new interest from developers will bring much-deserved recognition and revitalization to Mount Cabanne-Raymond Place.

42
Oakherst Place Concrete Block District
National Register: May 5, 1987

The second development designed for concrete blocks in the West End, this subdivision was originally called Woodland Place. Pendleton Realty retained architects A. Blair Ridington and Edward F. Nolte, who had designed the nearby houses in the **Goodfellow/Julian District** *(page 121)*, plus Eames & Young. Of the seven basic designs produced by the three firms, Nolte was responsible for the largest number and the greatest diversity. All of the houses demonstrated the potential for interpreting Arts & Crafts idioms in a new material. Sadly, the district now contains many buildings in deplorable condition. Two have been demolished.

43
Saint Louis Art Museum
City Landmark: May 1969
Forest Park

Cass Gilbert's first designs for the Palace of Fine Arts, the only permanent building constructed for the 1904 World's Fair, date from 1901. In spite of strong differences of opinion between Gilbert and Museum Director Halsey Cooley Ives, Gilbert's powerful friends on the board kept him involved in work at the Museum long after the exposition closed. In 1915, he was asked to prepare a grandiose plan for expansion. Gilbert's scheme, which would have increased cubic footage tenfold in phased construction projects, remained a remote possibility until St. Louis architect Louis LaBeaume assumed presidency of the board in 1931. LaBeaume implemented a different vision.

Chapter 5 West End

Saint Louis Art Museum
W. Philip Cotton, Jr., 1989

Sanitol Chemical after renovation
Architectural Illustrations, 2000

Donating his firm's work, LaBeaume created fanciful period rooms of great appeal and slim authenticity. After his retirement and the end of World War II, new director Charles Nagel brought in Murphy & Mackey of St. Louis to re-think expansion proposals. Two additions from the 1950s by that firm were unabashedly contemporary. Charles E. Buckley, who became director in 1964, turned to the New York firm of Hardy, Holzman & Pfeiffer for the preparation of another master plan in 1971. The "interpretative restoration" of Sculpture Hall and the East Wing followed in 1977. The New York firm retained a role in the 1979 Administration Building that enveloped the 1950s additions but the project architects were HNTB of Kansas City. They in turn had only a minor role in the new West Wing opened in 1987 by project architects Smith & Entzeroth of St. Louis in collaboration with Moore-Ruble-Yudell of Santa Monica. Meanwhile, Buckley had been succeeded by James N. Wood who was followed by James D. Burke. Brent Benjamin, brought in as director in the late 1990s, inherited an as yet unbuilt but still controversial expansion proposal in Forest Park.

The opening paragraph from Osmund Overby's definitive monograph released on the occasion of the West Wing opening offers a subtle summation of the often painful evolution of Cass Gilbert's building and the institution it houses: "The Saint Louis Art Museum has never looked better than it does now. It was boldly conceived amid controversy, hastily built, changed, enlarged, struggled with, restored. Clear-headed, strong-willed people, whose visions of the Museum have been as different as their personalities, have shaped its architecture."

44
Sanitol Chemical Company Building (Crown Loft Apartments)
National Register: October 21, 1985
4264 Laclede Avenue

The Sanitol Chemical Company was the first light-manufacturing concern to erect a new building at the eastern edge of the Central West End. That prescient 1906 decision may have been made by company president Frederick August Luyties whose residence at 4475 Lindell was within walking distance. George W. Hellmuth (St. Louis) designed the $250,000 offices and laboratory for the firm that had made St. Louis the greatest manufacturing center for tooth powder in the world. Sanitol soon expanded its line to include shaving supplies, face powder, toilet water, etc. The building was later used as a shoe factory, then for storage by Borden, Inc. and Crown Foods. After threats of demolition and a period of vacancy, Owen Development acquired the building and opened the Crown Loft Apartments designed by Trivers Architects in 2000.

Chapter 5 West End

Arts & Crafts houses designed between 1914 and 1916 on the 5900 block of Waterman Avenue
Landmarks, 1983

St. Roch's Church and School
Robert C. Pettus, 1988

Hamilton School
W. L. Persons, 1918

45
Skinker-DeBaliviere/Catlin Tract/ Parkview District
City District: September 1978
Bounded roughly by City Limits, Delmar, DeBaliviere and Lindell Boulevard

Massive expenditures for the 1904 World's Fair left this undeveloped area with the most modern capital improvements in the city and a new commuter-based university campus at its threshold. **Parkview Place** *(page 133)*, platted by Julius Pitzman, was the first (1905) of the district's subdivisions to be opened for development followed by Washington Heights (1907) and the Catlin Tract (1909). Although sporadic construction continued into the 1930s, most of the 850 historic buildings in the district were built in the decade between 1907 and 1916. This dramatic construction surge along with deed restrictions establishing uniform setbacks and minimum costs produced streetscapes of remarkable continuity.

The vast majority of single-family houses were designed in styles popular with the growing St. Louis middle class: Classical and Tudor Revival, Arts & Crafts and Bungaloid. Apartments and flats, many sporting the ubiquitous West End sun porch, echoed the styles chosen for single-family houses. (A sampling of French Chateaux, English Manor House and Spanish Colonial appeared later on the larger lots of the Catlin Tract on Lindell.) Although prestigious architectural firms were active in the district, especially in Parkview and the Catlin Tract, contractors designed the majority of the buildings with the prolific Alexander A. Fischer responsible for some 75 structures. His trademark, the "broken" or interrupted frieze at the roofline, is stamped on entire streetscapes.

Wabash Station before renovation
Landmarks Collection, 1983

Important institutional buildings include Grace Methodist Church at Skinker and Waterman (originally designed in 1897 by Link & Rosenheim and moved to this site in 1914), Jacobethan-style Hamilton School (5819 Westminster) from 1917 by Rockwell M. Milligan, Delmar Baptist Church at Washington and Skinker designed in 1918 by William B. Ittner and St. Roch's Church at Waterman and Rosedale—a Tudor Gothic Revival landmark from 1921 by Lee & Rush. The former Wabash Station, designed in 1929 by company architect R. E. Mohr, marks the location of the Delmar MetroLink station opened in 1993.

The "English Renaissance" Dorr and Zeller Building (401 DeBaliviere) designed by Preston J. Bradshaw in 1922 is now home to the Central West End Bank. Central West End Bank grew from concerted neighborhood efforts to confront the urban problems of the 1960s. Finding real estate companies less and

Chapter 5

5855 Lindell Boulevard (in the Catlin Tract) designed in 1926 by Maritz & Young
Landmarks, 1983

The typical "walk-up" apartment building in Skinker-DeBaliviere circa 1915 favored Arts & Crafts details, a tile roof and a traditional British name.
Landmarks Collection

less willing to show houses, determined volunteers established a residential service in 1970.

Abandoned and deteriorating multi-family buildings proved the most difficult (and controversial) part of the neighborhood. Pantheon Corporation (lead developers of DeBaliviere Place in the Central West End) created a mini-neighborhood of new housing called Kingsbury Square; Westminster Builders assumed the task of renovation in Nina Place. Throughout the bad years and into the optimistic present, St. Roch's and other neighborhood-based churches have taken activist roles in the district's future along with the Skinker-DeBaliviere Community Council.

Dramatic recent improvements along the northern boundary include the transformation of a derelict grocery store (**A & P Food Stores**, see next entry), the opening of the MetroLink light rail system and subsequent street improvements on Delmar plus construction of the new Pageant nightclub/concert venue developed by Joe Edwards. Edwards has since

purchased the former University Presbyterian Church (built in 1924) at 6166 Delmar. His plans to adapt it to a performing arts space helped entice the Regional Arts Commission to move to the district.

46
**A & P Food Stores Building
(Saint Louis Design Alliance)**
National Register: October 5, 2000
6014-18 Delmar Boulevard

The Atlantic & Pacific Tea Company (A & P) with over 15,000 locations by 1930 was one of the nation's most successful chain stores in the first half of the 20th century. Competition from supermarkets led the company to reduce the number of its stores while building at new, larger locations with ample parking. This streamlined Art Deco paragon, designed in 1940 by Saum Architects, was one of the chain's first supermarket locations in St. Louis. Sixty years later, layers of paint and siding totally obscured the original design. Saint Louis Design Alliance, an architectural firm with verve, bought the building, restored the exterior and put their own offices in the flexible, open interior space.

47
Parkview District
National Register: March 14, 1986
Bounded roughly by Melville, Delmar, Skinker and Millbrook Boulevard

Parkview Place, the last and largest of the private street subdivisions laid out by Julius Pitzman, was opened for development in 1905. Deed restrictions established a uniform setback of fifty feet, a minimum construction cost of $7,000 and specified materials of brick, stucco or stone. Of the more than 250 houses built in the seventy-acre district, 85% were constructed between 1906 and 1914. The vast majority are brick, designed in variations on Arts & Crafts, Tudor Revival and Colonial Revival themes.

Favored by original street trees and Pitzman's horseshoe plan with triangular park spaces, the district is bisected by the boundary between St. Louis and University City. Local architectural firms and contractors responsible for numerous houses in Parkview include contractors George Bergfeld, O. F. Humphrey and A. A. Fischer and architects Roth & Study, Preston J. Bradshaw, Klipstein & Rathmann, William P. McMahon, Stephens & Pearson, Louis B. Pendleton and Edward F. Nolte.

Many of the original residents were faculty from the newly built Washington University campus at its southern edge. With an unusually large number of houses for a private street subdivision occupied by solidly upper-middle-class residents, Parkview developed a tradition of participatory government within its boundaries. Attendance at meetings of the trustees was high, though often vocal, and loyal residents grew to expect consensus rather than imposition from above. A study in 1970 found that 20% of the Parkview families were either the original owners or grew up in the neighborhood.

A & P Food Stores Building (Saint Louis Design Alliance)
Landmarks, 2001

Parkview District Gate
Landmarks, 1983

Clockwise, top to bottom:

Parkview District: 6236 Waterman Avenue, designed in 1908 by architect William A. Hirsh for his family.
Landmarks Collection, 1983

Interior of 6236 Waterman Avenue
Courtesy Mrs. O. B. Hirsch

Map of Parkview District
Pat Hays Baer

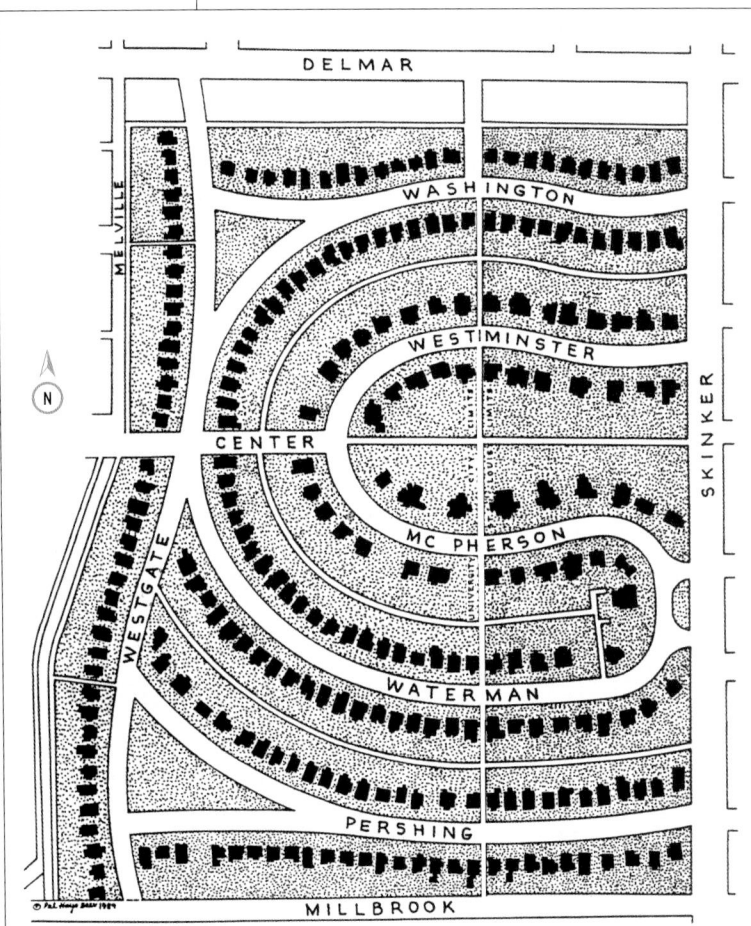

But the soft demarcation between city and county boundaries experienced only as a pedestrian path within the enclave was sharply differentiated in the 1970 school statistics. None of the children from the city side of the district attended public schools; 40% of those living on the county side went to public schools in University City. Concern for the future of Parkview in the path of "growing slums" was expressed in the open and in private as large houses came on the market for less than $30,000. Those who stayed put or bought during that period (in spite of discouraging realtors) now own property worth more than ten times that figure.

Left:
23 Windermere Place, Visitation Park District
Landmarks, 1985

Below left:
Detail: 23 Windermere Place
Landmarks, 1985

Map of Union Avenue Promenade, Visitation Park District
Pat Hays Baer

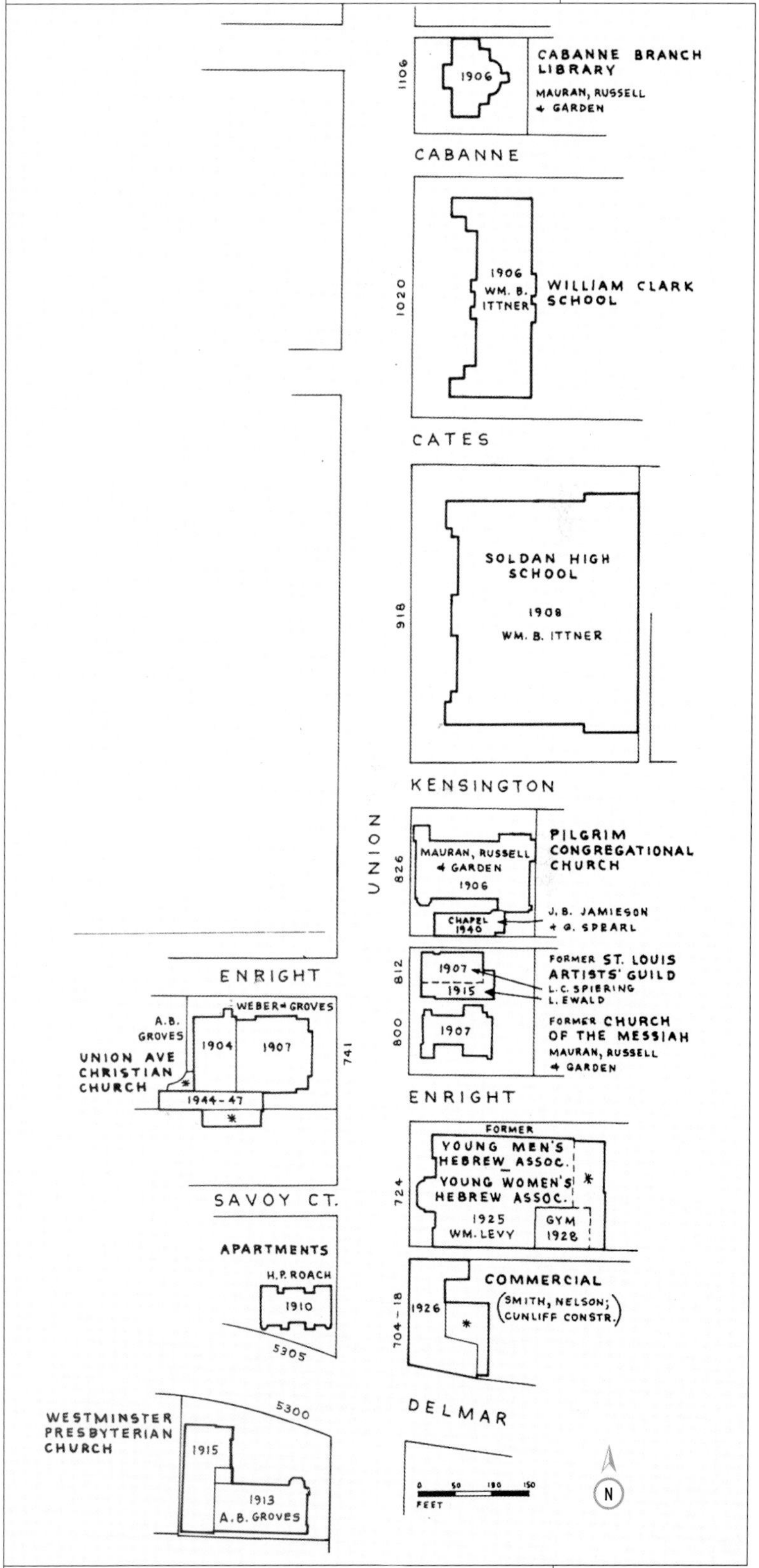

48
Visitation Park District
City District: March 21, 1975

Central to the residential portion of Visitation Park is Windermere Place, opened as a one-block private street by Thomas and Emilie Wright in 1895 with deed restrictions setting a minimum cost of $5,000 and a setback of forty feet. Although the streetscape developed a somewhat suburban aspect with its welcoming front porches, the two houses of most architectural interest are townhouses: #6, built in 1905 from plans by Henry W. Roach (St. Louis), a sophisticated Arts & Crafts three-story house in buff Roman brick and #23, designed in 1907 by Edward Garden of Mauran, Russell & Garden for his family, an even more outstanding Arts & Crafts achievement recognized with extensive coverage in a 1910 issue of *The Brickbuilder*. Windermere Place would receive media attention again, this time national, as an exemplar of racial integration in the 1950s.

While nearby **Holy Corners** *(page 107)* can be viewed as a single panorama, Union Avenue north of Delmar in the Visitation Park District is a grand promenade that must be traversed in stages. The promenade showcases the work of the same firms as Holy Corners plus William B. Ittner, Will Levy and Louis Spiering to demonstrate further the elevated state of architecture in early 20th century St. Louis.

Chapter 5   West End

Detail: Young Men's Hebrew Association
Paul Ladensack, 1993

49
Young Men's Hebrew Association (West End Community Center)
724 Union Boulevard

Designed in 1925 by Will Levy (St. Louis) for the established Jewish community in the neighborhood, the Classical Revival building with profuse terra cotta ornament from the Winkle Terra Cotta Company of St. Louis was the last to join the progressive architectural feast on Union. The new building offered all the amenities of clubs open only to gentiles plus many unique to the YMHA but attractive to the public at large. High on that list was "The Liberal Forum" series. A January 1939 appearance by feisty seventy-year-old Frank Lloyd Wright brought an audience of more than 1,000. Sold to Washington University in 1959, the property was given to the city for a temporary police station. When the police moved out, the city turned it into a community center but could not supply funds to keep the large facility from deteriorating. An exceptional story of collaboration began in 1993 when volunteer John Mann took on the enormous challenge to bring in financial resources from the original constituency to help today's community renovate the building.

50
Church of the Messiah (Parrish Temple Christian Methodist Episcopal Church)
800 Union Boulevard

Architect John Lawrence Mauran
Landmarks Collection

William Greenleaf Eliot organized the first Unitarian church west of the Mississippi in 1834. Members became a prosperous, altruistic force in St. Louis, responsible for founding numerous cultural and education institutions. All seventeen original incorporators of Washington University in 1853 held membership in Eliot's church. For years the only open abolitionist in St. Louis, Eliot, in touch with President Abraham Lincoln, formed the St. Louis Provident Society when it seemed clear that the Civil

Church of the Messiah (Parrish Temple)
Landmarks, 1985

136

St. Louis Artists' Guild
Landmarks, 1985

War was inevitable. When it was over he and James Yeatman led the movement to provide free education without public funds for local black children. High school classes were held in Eliot's church basement at 9th and Olive Streets.

Early churches for the Unitarian congregation were among the most distinguished in the city: the second church at 9th and Olive was reportedly the largest Protestant church in 1850, and the third church at Locust and Garrison was an 1879 Peabody & Stearns (Boston) design *(page 259)*. Sumptuous stained glass windows from that building were brought for installation in the fourth and final Church of the Messiah designed by member John Mauran of Mauran, Russell & Garden. Recently elected to the American Institute of Architect's elite Board of Directors, Mauran was also Chair of the Municipal Art Committee, a resident of Vandeventer Place and one of six on the executive committee for the Civic League's 1907 *City Plan for Saint Louis*.

William Greenleaf Eliot's son Henry Ware Eliot participated in the dedication service for the 1907 Church of the Messiah. The founder of the Hydraulic Pressed Brick Co, Henry Eliot supplied the building material for the unassuming new Gothic Revival church. Thirty years later the Union Avenue church, faced with flagging membership during the Depression, voted to consolidate with the Church of the Unity on Waterman at Kingshighway and adopt the name First Unitarian Church of St. Louis.

51
St. Louis Artists' Guild
(Dignity House Christian Art Center)
812 Union Boulevard

William Greenleaf Eliot, "the most influential man in St. Louis" according to *Spectator* in 1882, selected Peabody & Stearns (Boston) to design the Museum of Fine Arts associated with Washington University. This bulwark of Massachusetts brownstone at Lucas Place and 19th Street hosted early meetings of the free-spirited St. Louis Artists' Guild. Organized in 1886 for the purpose of developing a high standard of art appreciation and expression, the guild chose appropriately when it selected Louis C. Spiering (St. Louis) to design a small headquarters on Union in 1907. An expansion to that Arts & Crafts building in 1915 by Lawrence W. Ewald (St. Louis) added a Rathskeller and theater enjoyed by community players and architecture students from Washington University until the Artists' Guild left for Webster Groves in 1973.

Making a World of Difference, a magazine published by the Missouri Department of Conservation, has recognized the innovative programs now run from the old Guild building thanks to a ministry financed by the United Church Neighborhood Houses. One of a series located throughout the city, the Dignity House on Union developed the Dolphin Defenders cadre of children who plant trees in honor of young people touched by violence, create participatory games about the environment and raise enough money to adopt acres of South American rain forest.

Chapter 5 — West End

Soldan High School
Robert C. Pettus, 1988

52
Soldan High School
918 Union Boulevard

Named in honor of Louis Soldan, Superintendent of Schools from 1895-1908, the three-story $630,244 Tudor Revival high school by William B. Ittner opened September 1909 as the brightest gem in the city's public school collection. (A sampling of well-known graduates over the years includes Virginia Mayo, Agnes Moorehead, Clark Clifford, Tennessee Williams, Robin Boyce and David Thirdkill.) Closed as a regular high school after the 1989-90 year, Soldan reopened in 1993 as the International Studies magnet high school with a spiffy new gym, cafeteria, art gallery, model United Nations assembly room, library with glass atrium and restored wooden windows.

Seldom can one single feature story with two black and white illustrations change public policy, but that occurred in 1988 when the *Post-Dispatch* published E. F. Porter's provocative "Aluminum Window Frames: An Act of Vandalism?" The article appeared just as the Board of Education was gearing up for a massive renovation program necessitated by court order. Without Porter's reproachful story, the board would have replaced the original wooden multi-paned windows on its architecturally magnificent schools with short-lived, prefabricated, anodized aluminum windows with large one-over-one panes.

53
William Clark Grade School
1020 Union Boulevard

Spirited Clark grade school, located immediately north of **Soldan**, was designed by William B. Ittner a year earlier than the more sedate high school. Both feature elaborate central entrances and front yards embraced by projecting wings; both display fine brickwork, stone quoins and balustrades. Each is topped with brilliant copper flourishes at the roofline. Together, they form a syncopated sequence of color and form unmatched in the city.

54
Cabanne Branch Library
1106 Union Boulevard

The grand opening July 29, 1907 of the second Carnegie branch library attracted 5,000 to the $75,000 building designed by Mauran, Russell & Garden. Many patrons walked from the surrounding neighborhood named, like the library, for the family that opened a series of residential subdivisions starting in 1877. Located in one of the more serene settings of all the branch libraries (in contrast to those in immigrant neighborhoods), Cabanne librarians set up a collection strong in the classics, literature, fine arts, travel and biography to read at home or by the fireplace in cozy reading rooms. The formal Beaux Arts entrance that suggested stability and prosperity in the early 20th century was viewed later as a bit imposing according to the branch manager in 1994, who credited an interior renovation of 1990 with attracting more readers and community groups.

55
Smith Academy & Manual Training School
5407-51 Enright Avenue

Built in 1905 for $275,000 from plans by Mauran, Russell & Garden (St. Louis) for Washington University, this restrained Classical Revival, red brick, terra cotta and stone preparatory school for boys suited its elite clientele. Smith Academy and Manual Training School, along with its expansive campus, was sold to the Board of Education in 1917. Renamed for Superintendent Ben Blewett, the complex functioned as a junior or senior high school through 1948. It then housed Harris Teacher's College (white counterpart of **Stowe Teacher's College**, *page 176*) until return to the regular school system as Enright Middle School in 1963. The Board of Education closed the facility in the 1990s; its future is unknown.

56
Pilgrim Congregational Church
City Landmark: November 1974
826 Union Boulevard

Henry Isaacs (St. Louis) designed an imposing 1867 Gothic Revival church in "Piety Hill" with the tallest steeple in town for Pilgrim Congregational, named for the English separatists from the Church of England who landed at Plymouth Massachusetts in December 1620. Although nearby congregations moved west before the end of the century, Pilgrim did not make the decision to move from the landmark at Washington at Ewing until after the World's Fair. Their next building was equally impressive.

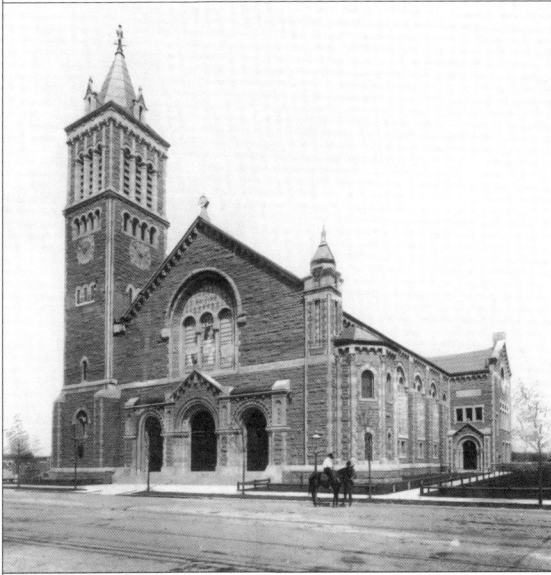

Pilgrim Congregational Church circa 1910
Missouri Historical Society

Designed by Mauran, Russell & Garden, the pink granite modified Romanesque Revival church on Union was completed in 1907. New doors installed in 1933 came from designs by architect Charles Eames, a member, who also drew plans to rebuild the tower damaged by lightning in 1935. A Tudor Gothic chapel of matching granite designed in 1940 by Jamieson & Spearl adjoins the south wall of the church. Pilgrim voted to integrate its membership in 1953, a year before the U.S. Supreme Court struck down segregated schools in *Brown vs. Board of Education*. In 1999, Pilgrim welcomed its first black and first female to the pulpit.

Smith Academy & Manual Training School in a postcard dated 1907
Landmarks Collection

Chapter 5 — West End

Visitation Academy (razed)
Landmarks Collection

57
Frederick von Harten House
City Landmark: February 1980
5433 Enright Avenue

Built in 1896 at an estimated cost of $5,500 from plans drawn by Herbert C. Chivers (St. Louis) for Edward W. von Harten, the apricot-colored brick, two-story Georgian Revival with Palladian window and circular front porch was owned and inhabited by the original family for almost 100 years. (Chivers' best-known building is the 1903 Magazine Building, now City Hall, in University City, Missouri.)

58
Winston Churchill Apartments
National Register: April 4, 1985
5475 Cabanne Avenue

The increased popularity of apartment living in the first decades of the 20th century resulted in a pattern of tall, elevator-dependent buildings dotting major transit lines in established and emerging middle-class neighborhoods. Delmar Boulevard, primarily west of Union, developed into one of the city's major corridors. Three blocks to the north, backing up to the Hodiamont streetcar line, the 1927 Winston Churchill Apartments were located directly across the street from Visitation Academy—Barnett, Haynes & Barnett's 1891 architecturally extravagant High Victorian school and convent, which was razed in 1962 to create the district's namesake park.

The eight-story apartment building combines Modern-influenced massing with neoclassical details. Building permits list the architects as Avis, Hall & Proetz (the only known alliance between the three). Francis C. Avis is best known for a distinguished collection of 1930s modernistic residences in Clayton. Ralph Cole Hall and Victor Proetz practiced together in St. Louis from the mid-twenties until 1934. Hall would later become the chief architect for the State Department, designing embassies in Iran and Peru. Proetz's extraordinary career brought him a one-man show at the St. Louis Art Museum in 1944. At the time of his death in 1966, he was curator of the Smithsonian Museum's Barney House Studio.

59
West Cabanne Place District
National Register: November 21, 1980

Conceived as a semi-rural retreat at the edge of the city and platted as a private street in 1888, West Cabanne Place offered a deliberately unpretentious setting for local experimentation with the Shingle Style. Part of a post-Centennial search for a truly "American" architecture, the Shingle Style first appeared on the eastern seaboard and arrived in St. Louis with H. H. Richardson's much acclaimed Potter House of 1886 located a block east of the district. (Sadly, it has been demolished as have three of the Shingle Style houses in the district.)

Ten of the twelve houses completed or under construction in West Cabanne Place by 1893 were frame. Several combined Queen Anne details and forms with shingles, clapboards and sweeping front porches. Although St. Louis' flirtation with the Shingle Style was brief, the district's distinctive bucolic character attracted a disproportionate number of architect

Above:
5944 West Cabanne Place (razed) designed by Theodore C. Link for his family
St. Louis Public Library,

Left:
Entrance to West Cabanne Place
Landmarks Collection circa 1920

Chapter 5 | West End

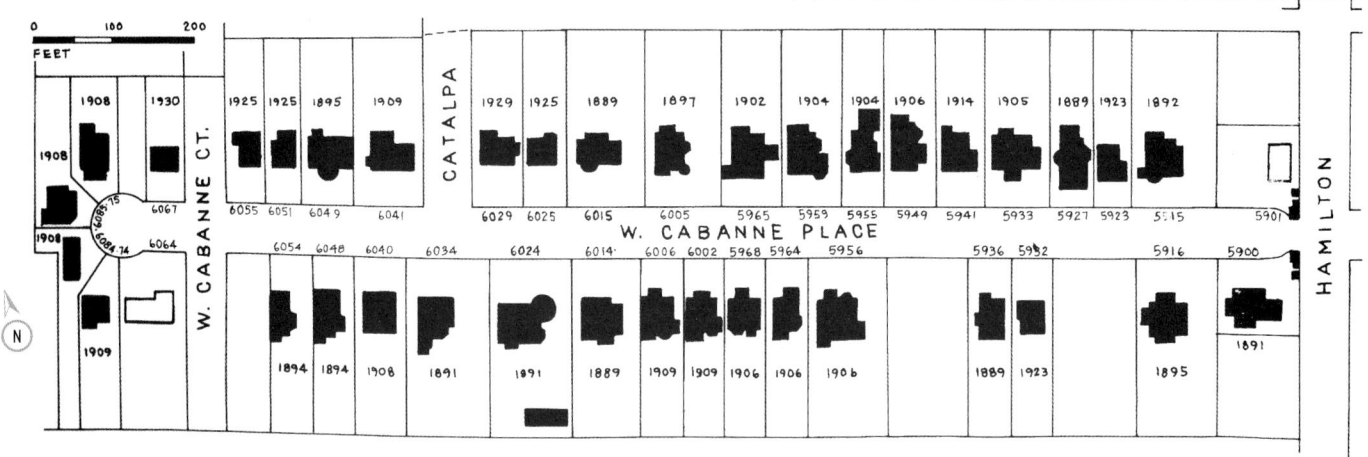

West Cabanne Place District Site Map
Pat Hays Baer

owners: 6015 West Cabanne, designed in 1889 by Charles K. Ramsey; 5900 West Cabanne, designed in 1891 by Theodore Link; 5955 and 5959 West Cabanne, designed in 1905 by Robert Walsh of Widmann, Walsh & Bosselier—one house for himself and another for his mother; 6084 West Cabanne, designed by Lawrence Ewald in 1908.

The larger Cabanne neighborhood remained relatively stable until after World War II. When the first black family bought a house on West Cabanne Place in 1956, some residents moved, but this private street and Windermere Place (**Visitation Park**, *page 135*) were models of successful integration. Residents, weary of the costs of maintenance, returned the street to city ownership at the end of the 20th century.

60
West Pine/Laclede District
National Register: May 9, 2002
Bounded roughly by Taylor, Lindell, Sarah and Forest Park Avenue

In boosterism typical of the late 19th century, an 1888 writer noted the new improvements in Forest Park, described the advantages of those improvements to nearby property owners and predicted that West Pine Boulevard would soon become "the handsomest resident way in the city." The next decade, the most active building period within district boundaries, seemed to fulfill that prophecy with the construction of large and impressive single-family houses on Lindell and West Pine. Scale, richness of detail, quality of construction

6015 West Cabanne Place designed in 1889 by Charles K. Ramsey for his family
Landmarks, 1980

and strong sense of prosperity matched their contemporaries in the abutting **Central West End District** described above. High-end developers were also attracted. Charles Hill (tobacco magnate whose eccentric mansion once stood on the site of the **Chase Hotel**, *page 102)* had developed almost the entire north side of the 4400 block of Laclede with single-family houses by 1897. Grable & Weber (later with Groves) of St. Louis were responsible for all Hill's design work. Meanwhile, James B. Legg (St. Louis) had received the commission for seven houses across the street for developer Orian Gregg. By the turn of the century, other investors had built attached townhouses and the first grocery store.

The decade of the World's Fair introduced garden apartment buildings, new styles in single-family houses and the city's most elaborate police station on Newstead Avenue. Arts & Crafts influences became pervasive in the 1920s, except for the newly popular high-rise apartment buildings. The worst natural disaster in West End history occurred on September 29, 1927 when a deadly tornado swept northeasterly through the neighborhood. "When the darkness lifted, desolation reminiscent of a shelled French village remained." Obvious tornado damage and repair appear throughout the eastern part of the district. Two divergent buildings date to the slow-moving 1930s: the Spanish Mission-style gas station at Newstead and Laclede and the medical clinic for Dr. Samuel B. Grant at 114 North Taylor, a small jewel designed by the pioneering modernist of St. Louis architects, Harris Armstrong.

The neighborhood remained relatively intact through the Depression, but the 1940s brought the first rooming house conversions. Sporadic demolition and zoning changes combined to erode this district and the abutting Central West End. In the 1970s, Washington University Medical Center (the area's primary employer and one of the largest in the region) decided to assume an active role in the future of its immediate neighborhood by forming and directing a well-funded redevelopment corporation. This effort coincided with the creation of the Central West End district to the north. A generation later the overall neighborhood has seen dramatic improvements. Within the proposed West Pine/Laclede district, the 4400 block of Laclede received gates, a median planting and massive reinvestment by new owners. Today, varied commercial enterprises include a catalogue of all-budget restaurants while infill construction is monitored by the watchful eyes of an increasingly active neighborhood association.

61
James Gay Butler House
National Register: September 2, 1982
4484 West Pine Boulevard

The elaborate Queen Anne house designed in 1892 by Albert Knell (St. Louis) for millionaire tobacco manufacturer James Gay Butler cost more than any other house on West Pine. His building permit recorded an estimate of $25,000 on top of $9,300 already paid for the lot. Butler could afford it. A major in the Union forces, Butler settled in St. Louis after the war and entered the lucrative fine-cut and plug tobacco business. With consolidation of much of the tobacco industry as the American Tobacco Company in 1904, Butler emerged a major stockholder and member of the board. In 1912, four years before his death, he founded the Bank of St. Louis.

The cachet of West Pine faded by the 1930s. After a bleak period as a rooming house, Butler's house was adapted for the offices of the International Institute of St. Louis. The organization remained here for thirty years. In 1982, the Overlook Group purchased the property and hired the Brownstein Group of St. Louis to design an exemplary renovation project.

West Cabanne houses designed in 1905 by Robert W. Walsh for his family: 5959 (left) and 5955 (right)
Landmarks, 1980

Detail: James Gay Butler House
Pat Hays Baer

Chapter 5 West End

Skinker Boulevard looking north from Versailles Apartments in 1934
Landmarks Collection

62
Wiltshire and Versailles Apartment Buildings
National Register: October 18, 1982
725 and 709 South Skinker Boulevard

The Wiltshire (designed in 1924 by William H. Mills) and the Versailles (designed in 1927 by Preston J. Bradshaw) were built in the heyday of speculative luxury apartment buildings in St. Louis. Considered high-rise in the Twenties, the nine-story red brick Wiltshire is embellished with Jacobethan ornament; the Versailles, of buff brick, is trimmed with Renaissance Revival details in terra cotta.

63
Wydown/Forsyth District
National Register: May 23, 1988
Bounded roughly by University Lane, Forsyth, Skinker and Farquier Boulevard

Although most of the 184 houses in this well-to-do district are in St. Louis County, three impressive places of worship are located on prominent sites overlooking Forest Park within the city limits. The most arresting is the former United Hebrew Temple at 225 South Skinker, built 1924-27 from plans by Maritz & Young with Gabriel Ferrand, Dean of Washington University's School of Architecture. The temple was converted to the Library and Archives of the Missouri Historical Society in 1992 following plans by Ted Wofford (St. Louis) whose firm also designed an unassuming addition. To the north at 201 Skinker is Memorial Presbyterian Church with Gothic Revival tower and chapel from 1925 by Albert B. Groves and the perpendicular Gothic main auditorium from 1931

by Aegerter & Bailey. Aegerter & Bailey's Italian Gothic Eighth Church of Christ, Scientist, from 1928 is at 6211 Alexander.

Much of Wydown-Forsyth was included in the 1904 World's Fair grounds and held after the conclusion of that event until development considered harmonious with the interests of Washington University began in 1911. (The hilltop campus is also listed on the National Register; the boundaries for that district lie outside the city limits.) A remarkable number of the Wydown-Forsyth district's "period houses" (Georgian, Tudor, Spanish Colonial, French Country, etc.) were designed by the rising St. Louis firm of Maritz & Young. Other architects who gained repeated important commissions include Nolte & Nauman, Study & Farrar and finally, in the late 1930s, Nagel & Dunn.

United Hebrew Congregational Temple
St. Louis Public Library, 1924

144

CHAPTER 6 Northeast

St. Liborius Church and Rectory
Gary R. Tetley, 1992

Chapter 6

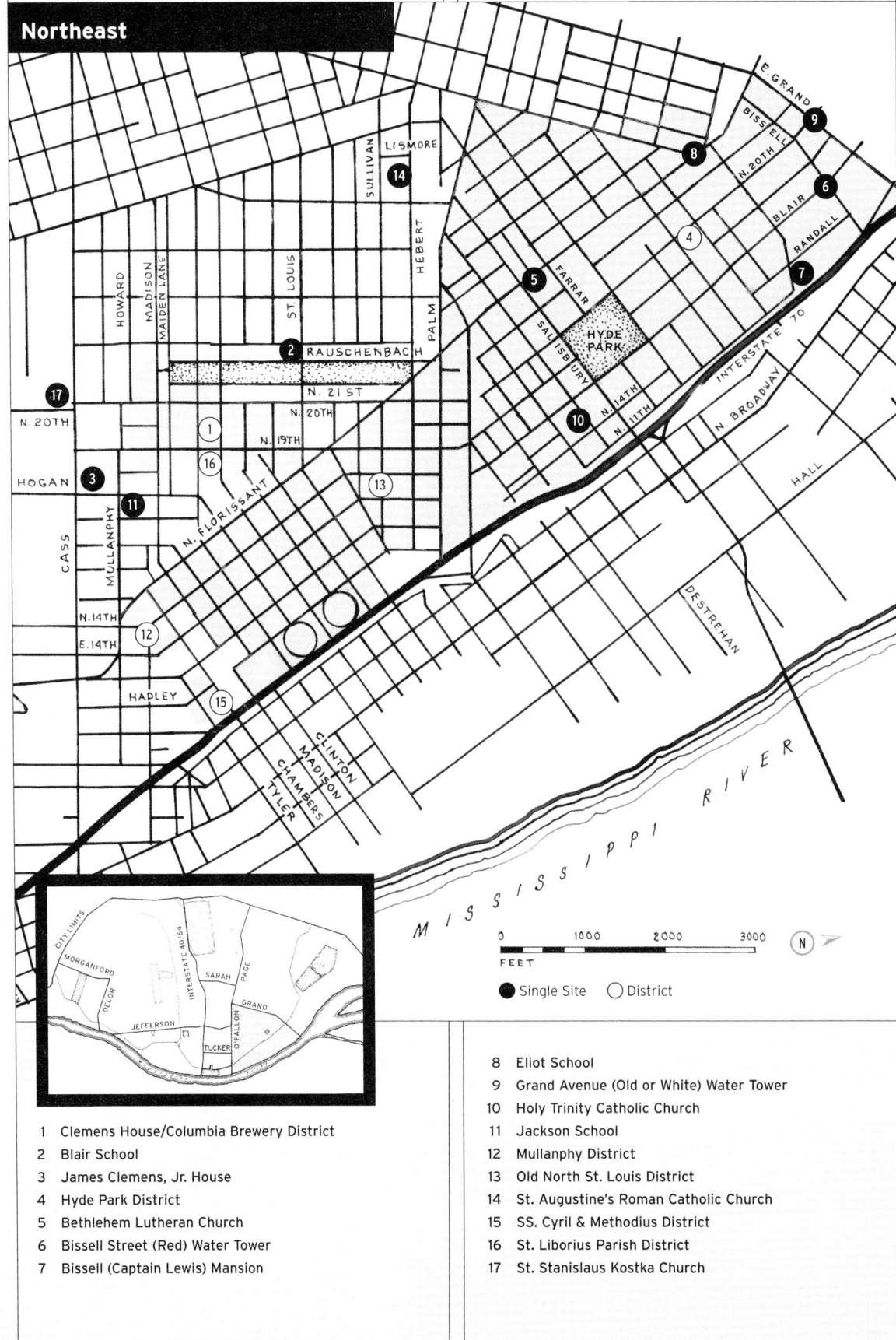

Northeast

1. Clemens House/Columbia Brewery District
2. Blair School
3. James Clemens, Jr. House
4. Hyde Park District
5. Bethlehem Lutheran Church
6. Bissell Street (Red) Water Tower
7. Bissell (Captain Lewis) Mansion
8. Eliot School
9. Grand Avenue (Old or White) Water Tower
10. Holy Trinity Catholic Church
11. Jackson School
12. Mullanphy District
13. Old North St. Louis District
14. St. Augustine's Roman Catholic Church
15. SS. Cyril & Methodius District
16. St. Liborius Parish District
17. St. Stanislaus Kostka Church

Hops and barley decorate Columbia Brewery entrance
Landmarks, 1983

1
Clemens House/Columbia Brewery District
National Register: July 19, 1984 and July 22, 1986
Roughly bounded by Cass, North 20th, St. Louis Avenue and Hogan Street

One of only a handful of breweries still standing in St. Louis, the Columbia Brewery at Madison and North 20th was designed in 1891 by E. Jungenfeld & Company—a local firm with twenty breweries to its credit. The announcement that a new corporation would build the third largest brewery in the city was greeted with enthusiasm in the recession-ridden 1890s. With major ads ("Columbia: the Peer of All") in the bulletins and guidebooks promoting the 1904 World's Fair, the company pushed Alpen Brau and other memorable brews. In 1907, Columbia and eight other breweries' consolidation as the Independent Brewing Company left sixteen competitors either in the English-owned alliance or strong enough to remain autonomous.

IBC root beer introduced by Independent during Prohibition (probably the only local soft drink with a market after repeal) helped sustain investors during the drought. Columbia reincorporated as an independent company in 1933; in 1948, it merged with Falstaff. By the mid 1970s, the property had been acquired by the city's Land Reutilization Authority for non-payment of taxes. An Urban Development Action Grant combined with federal historic rehab credits made possible an adaptive reuse opened in 1987. The project by McCormack Baron from plans by Trivers & Associates (St. Louis) also rescued the fine row of brewery workers' housing across the street.

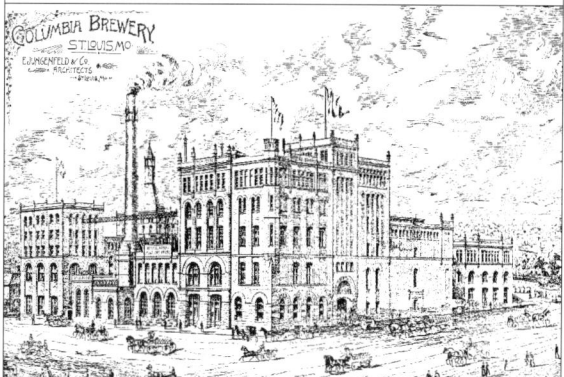

Columbia Brewery circa 1891
Landmarks Collection

The original boundaries of the historic district, which included both the brewery and the former **Clemens House** (next page), were expanded in 1986 to include several industrial buildings, additional housing stock and the complex of buildings associated with Zion Lutheran Church. The Gothic Revival church (designed by St. Louis architect Albert Knell in 1895) contains an unusually elaborate altar and pulpit hand-carved of Italian marble by Schrader & Conradi of St. Louis.

Chapter 6 Northeast

Advertisement from 1902 World's Fair Bulletin
Landmarks Collection

1900 block of St. Louis Avenue
Landmarks, 1985

Located immediately north of what was once Kerry Patch and then Pruitt-Igoe (imploded in 1975), the district is increasingly beleaguered by abandonment, demolition and suburban-style new subdivisions to the east. McCormack Baron's Murphy Park Hope VI project to the west and south offers a more urbanistic philosophy of city rebuilding from Trivers Associates.

2
Blair School
National Register: February 10, 1983
2707 Rauschenbach Avenue

Passage of the Tax Reform Act of 1976 followed by the Economic Recovery Act of 1981 instigated new and different interest in historic properties. Several for-profit development corporations took note and took risks. Among the first was McCormack Baron. Blair School and its detached, intriguingly rare octagonal kindergarten comprise one of the first St. Louis school properties adapted to housing. The High Victorian red brick school with vivid polychromatic glazed brick trim was designed in 1881 by School Board Architect H. William Kirchner with later additions by Kirchner and his brother August. Louis Kledus, St. Louis, was commissioned to draw up the kindergarten in 1891. Trivers Associates produced plans for the 1984 conversion.

3
James Clemens, Jr. House
City Landmark: November 1971
1849 Cass Avenue

Designed as an imposing Palladian villa by Patrick Walsh in 1858, the house for James Clemens, Jr. is an outstanding and rare example of the extensive use of cast iron in domestic architecture. The Clemens House was also the first important commission for Irish-born, St. Louis-trained Porter White. During his long career as a plaster and stucco artist, White worked at the Old Courthouse, Union Station, the Wainwright Building and the 1904 World's Fair. Although it seems impossible to substantiate stories that Mark Twain (Samuel L.

Clockwise from upper left:

Drawing of Blair School
August H. Kirchner, 1894

Detail: James Clemens, Jr. House
Landmarks, 1979

Drawing of James Clemens, Jr. House and chapel addition
Pat Hays Baer

Entrance to James Clemens, Jr. House
Landmarks, 1979

Sisters of St. Joseph of Carondelet *(page 209)* who commissioned the 1896 chapel designed by Aloysius Gillick, St. Louis. Celebrated for their innovative mission to teaching and to the poor and handicapped, the Sisters retained ownership until a 1949 sale to the Vincentian Fathers. After 1979, the Cass Catholic Workers (a lay organization modeled after the work of Dorothy Day in New York City during the 1930s) leased the property. Next came a descending pattern of social service ownership without maintenance. By the beginning of the 21st century, the house and attached chapel were in terrible condition with no real prospects for improvement. Boards applied to windows and doors in summer 2001 did not prevent vandalism to an interior distinguished by original marble fireplaces, vigorous plaster ceiling centerpieces and simple but grand woodwork. A change of ownership in early 2002 offers renewed hope.

Clemens) or General Custer were guests at the Cass Avenue mansion, the documented history of Clemens, his wife Eliza Mullanphy and their star-crossed family includes fur trade, bank failure, cholera, slavery, duels, land speculation, philanthropy, Southern sympathies, elopements, disinheritances, blindness and deathbed conversion.

After Clemens' death in 1878 at the age of eighty-seven, the property was sold by his heirs to the

Chapter 6

Bremen/Hyde Park Ownership in 1850
Pat Hays Baer

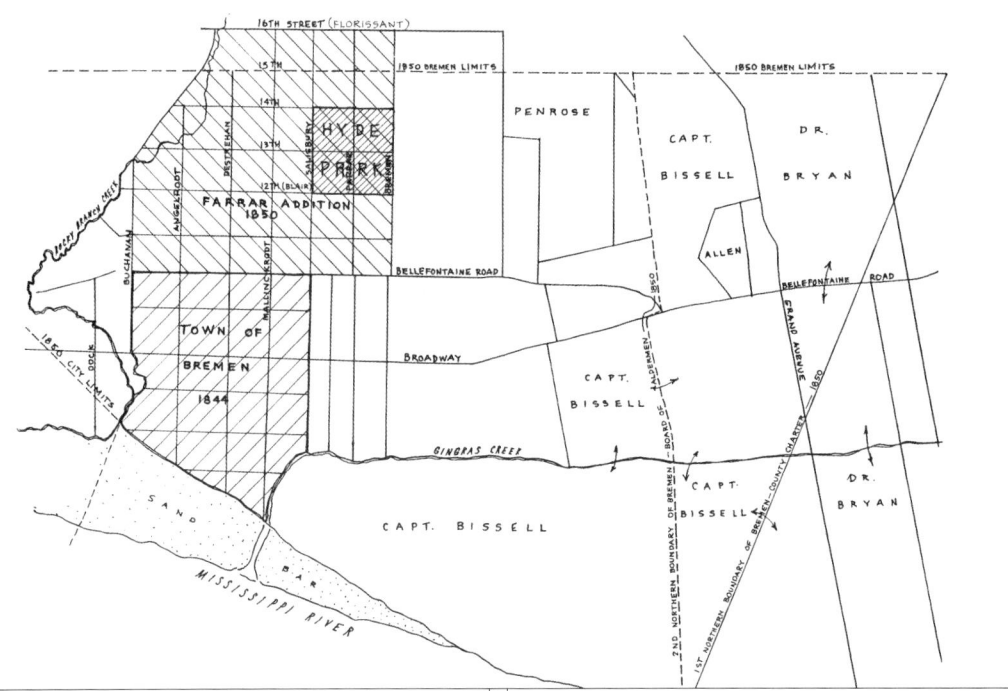

4
Hyde Park District
City District: January 12, 1978

Most of the Hyde Park District is located within the former boundaries of Bremen, a town laid out in 1844 by a group of German landowners including Emil Mallinckrodt. By the time Bremen was absorbed by the city of St. Louis in 1856, the agrarian suburb had been transformed into a thriving town of 3,000 persons employing 1,150 workers in twenty-nine different manufacturing establishments. The park for which the district is named was formerly part of a large estate owned by Dr. Bernard G. Farrar (the first American doctor west of the Mississippi), who died ministering to victims of the 1849 cholera epidemic. Although the city purchased the Farrar country house and land from his widow in 1854 for $36,250, no improvements were made to the park until the 1870s.

North side contractors, carpenters and architects built most of the surviving housing stock between 1850 and 1900. Nine historic churches, three parochial schools, two public schools, a former library, a now-threatened Turnverein and police and fire stations remain to provide important focal points throughout the neighborhood. Two of St. Louis' three dramatic water towers *(pages 152 through 154)* are also located in the district.

Salisbury at North 14th Street in 1953
Landmarks Collection

Clockwise from upper left:

2223 Salisbury Street
Robert C. Pettus, 1975

Farrar and North 25th Street in 1976
Landmarks Collection

Hyde Park Shuffleboard in 1953
Landmarks Collection

Nord St. Louis Turnverein
Ken Konchel, 1999

2223 Salisbury Street First Floor Plan

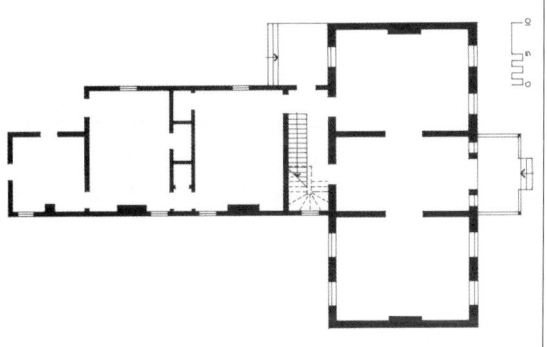

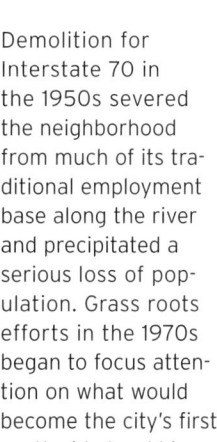

Demolition for Interstate 70 in the 1950s severed the neighborhood from much of its traditional employment base along the river and precipitated a serious loss of population. Grass roots efforts in the 1970s began to focus attention on what would become the city's first north side local historic district. A surge of attention from Mercantile Bank, a model house fitted up with the best energy efficiency rehab techniques, a limited competition to encourage compatible but not replicated new housing and visits from out-of-town developers interested in the historic housing stock brought a hope for the neighborhood that could not be sustained.

Chapter 6   Northeast

Bethlehem Lutheran Church
Robert C. Pettus, 1975

Bissell Water Tower
Arteaga Photos, 1968

5
Bethlehem Lutheran Church
City Landmark: July 1976
2153 Salisbury Street

Dedicated in 1893, destroyed by fire in 1894 (but rebuilt by 1895 following original plans by St. Louis architect Louis Wessbecher), damaged (then repaired) after the 1927 tornado, Bethlehem Lutheran today stands open to the elements—well on its way to demolition by neglect, a tragic end for the Gothic Revival red brick church. Its German-speaking congregation was organized in 1849 before the town of Bremen was incorporated by the city of St. Louis. Dedicated to community involvement and immigrant education, Bethlehem was the mother church for six other north side Missouri Synod Lutheran congregations.

**Bissell Mansion
circa 1960**

Frank T. Hilliker

6
Bissell Street (Red) Water Tower
City Landmark: September 1966
National Register: June 5, 1970
Bissell Street at Blair Avenue

Fewer than ten Victorian-era water towers survive in the United States. St. Louis has three of them. Saved from the wrecker's ball in the 1960s, this landmark was restored in the early 1970s thanks to a matching grant from the U.S. Department of the Interior. Erected in 1885–86 from plans by Deputy Building Commissioner/architect William S. Eames, the 200-foot tower features elaborate brickwork, limestone bands and terra cotta panels. Originally built to control sudden surges of water pressure, the Bissell Street and Grand Avenue *(page 154)* water towers are now beacons in the night thanks to funds for lighting them from the Gateway Foundation.

7
Bissell (Captain Lewis) Mansion
City Landmark: September 1966
4426 Randall Place

Captain Lewis Bissell, son of the first Commandant of Fort Bellefontaine, purchased 1,500 acres overlooking the Mississippi River in 1824; by 1830, he had built a red brick Greek Revival house. (A wing at the northwest corner was added in 1883 by Frederick Kraft.) Considered the oldest remaining brick house in St. Louis, the Bissell Mansion was threatened by demolition for the Mark Twain Expressway in the late 1950s. Landmarks Association intervened and the house was spared. A neighborhood-based corporation converted the Bissell Mansion to a restaurant in 1978, maintained as a mystery dinner theater experience into the 21st century.

8
Eliot School
National Register: September 2, 1992
4242 Grove Street

One of the first designs by William B. Ittner (background in **Carr School**, *page 54*) after his appointment as Commissioner of School Buildings, Eliot School (1898) shows a radically different approach to planning than the box-shaped school plans which came before. Like **Jackson School** of the same year *(page 155)*, Eliot is designed on an H-shaped plan. A large kindergarten room projects from the rear of the building in a single story.

The special positioning of kindergartens would remain an important planning consideration in Ittner's elementary designs, motivated by the requirement for larger rooms, the already-established tradition of separating the kindergarten (in part because they were often added to existing schools), the possibility of making the kindergarten a decorative focal point with special glass or murals and perhaps a certain sentimentality towards the youngest students. Classical Revival detailing is well thought out and impressive, although rather staid in comparison to the "Jacobethan" designs for which Ittner is best known.

Chapter 6　　Northeast

Clockwise from left:

Grand Avenue Water Tower circa 1950
Landmarks Collection

Holy Trinity Church circa 1900
Landmarks Collection

Interior, Holy Trinity Church
Landmarks, 1979

9
Grand Avenue (Old or White) Water Tower
City Landmark: September 1966
National Register: June 5, 1970
North Grand at 20th Street

Two years after the conclusion of the Civil War, the St. Louis Water Department under the direction of engineer Thomas J. Whitman (brother of poet Walt Whitman) began construction of a major waterworks plant designed by prominent architect George I. Barnett. The system initially included low and high service stations at Bissell's Point, a reservoir on South Grand and an amazing water tower clothed in a 154-foot Corinthian column. Completed in 1871 when North Grand was still a dirt road, the tower was retired from service in 1912.

10
Holy Trinity Catholic Church
City Landmark: April 1979
3519 North 14th Street

Swiss-born Joseph Conradi, who worked in St. Louis as both an architect and a sculptor, designed this impressive church of Bedford stone in 1899. Before coming to St. Louis, architect Conradi taught at the National Academy of Design in New York City. In

Holy Trinity Church circa 1900

Landmarks Collection

addition to many fine works in Missouri, Conradi's sculpture may be found at the Library of Congress in Washington, D.C. and the Doheny Memorial Library at the University of Southern California.

The congregation at Most Holy Trinity, St. Louis' third German-speaking parish, looked to Strasbourg Cathedral in Alsace-Lorraine as a model for a "splendid edifice, one that even after a century would still be proof of the faith and sacrifice of the people." Advanced turn-of-the century construction techniques integrated limestone walls with a heavy steel-frame floor and reinforced concrete slabs in the sanctuary. Iron pillars fortified the 215-foot twin towers. (Joseph Stauder, St. Louis, designed the rectory to the south of Holy Trinity in 1909.) A large octagonal crossing tower destroyed by the 1927 tornado was not rebuilt but extensive damage to the apse was repaired.

11
Jackson School
National Register: September 2, 1992
1632 Hogan Street

Like its contemporary **Eliot School** *(page 153)* designed by William B. Ittner, Jackson was constructed in 1898 on an H-shaped plan with Classical Revival detailing. Here, the upper two stories are set on a rusticated brick first story; the red brick composition is set high on a brown brick basement. This early use of polychrome brickwork was far more conservative than many of Ittner's later designs. Limestone is used for belt courses, sills, keystones and an impressive Doric portico topped by a segmental arch.

Chapter 6 Northeast

Mullanphy Home for Emigrants circa 1920
Landmarks Collection

12
Mullanphy District
National Register: February 14, 1983

In addition to important remnants of mid 19th century domestic architecture, this small district includes the former Mullanphy Emigrant Home (1609 North 14th Street) designed by George I. Barnett and Albert Piquenard in 1867 and ingloriously adapted in 1927 for the Absorene wallpaper cleaning company. Another hidden treasure down the street at 1629 North 14th is the first German Swedenborgian Church in the city; constructed in 1859, then enlarged in 1878 and 1885 by the Nord St. Louis Bundeschor—a German singing society which endured at this location for over sixty years. The block-long row of houses on North 14th Street with four gangways or "mouseholes" is particularly noteworthy as are the 1860s houses with Greek Revival entrances on Howard Street. Demolition by neglect and over-the-road truck parking pose continuing threats.

Gangway or "mousehole" at 1612 North 14th Street
Landmarks, 1982

1208-30 North Market Street
Landmarks, 1983

13
Old North St. Louis (Murphy/Blair) District
National Register: January 26, 1984

The eastern edge of the district was once part of the town of North St. Louis, laid out in 1816 with three circles possibly inspired by the contours of Indian mounds. Although most of the earliest residents were from Kentucky, by the 1850s the settlement was overwhelmingly German with a smattering of Irish and a colony of utopian French Icarians. (A few of the district's extant buildings may date from that decade.) By the turn of the century, a major shopping area had developed along 14th Street where residents could purchase furniture and appliances as well as groceries, clothing and hardware. Today almost moribund, the best-known survivor from 14th Street's heyday is the timeless Crown Candy Company at St. Louis Avenue.

With a few notable exceptions, the district's architecture is best described as vernacular. Over 90% of the buildings are residential, including a number of distinctive red brick row houses trimmed with stone lintels from neighborhood quarries. Some industrial

Touring the 1200 block of Hebert Street
Gloria Bratkowski, 1989

buildings have survived, as have several parochial schools. William B. Ittner designed Webster Public School in 1906; the Gothic Revival stone church for Grace Hill Episcopal was built in 1923 from plans by Jamieson & Spearl, St. Louis. The district also includes the last bathhouse built in the city. Designed in 1937 by Building Commissioner Albert Osburg, the Art Deco building at 1120 St. Louis Avenue was built on the foundation of an 1870s fire station.

The World War II era marked the beginning of the neighborhood's decline. War industry jobs attracted poor rural migrants (both white and black) to the area and many older residents fled to the suburbs. Demolition in the 1950s for Interstate 70 cut a swath through the neighborhood. By 1961, the Board of Aldermen declared the area blighted; Murphy/Blair became a Model City neighborhood in 1968. In retrospect, additional demolition during that era for parking lots and the imposition of a pedestrian mall on 14th Street were unwise.

Appreciation of the architectural significance of Old North St. Louis has increased dramatically in the past few years. Brightly colored banners now wave from many corners; in May of 1988, the neighborhood sponsored its first house tour as part of Preservation Week. The Crown Candy Kitchen at 1401 St. Louis

1433-41 Wright Street
John Bratkowski, 1988

Avenue, opened in 1913 by Greek immigrants, continues to attract new customers throughout the region with its sinful malts and specialty chocolate. Innovative grant writing by the neighborhood association secured housing tax credits from the State of Missouri and funding from the Whitaker Foundation to design neighborhood "pocket parks" along Florissant at North Market and at Hebert. On January 8, 2001, creative marketing resulted in a full-page *Post-Dispatch* feature story touting a just-released cookbook and

Chapter 6   Northeast

Crown Candy at North 14th and St. Louis Avenue
Robert C. Pettus, 1988

Bath House at 1120 St. Louis Avenue
Robert C. Pettus, 1988

the ethnic history of the district. Ambitious plans are now underway to secure large plots of nearly vacant parcels for thoughtful infill housing designed by a neighborhood architect.

14
St. Augustine's Roman Catholic Church (Historical Christ Baptist Church)
City Landmark: March 1986
National Register: October 2, 1986
3114 Lismore Street

One of many St. Louis churches built as a national parish exclusively for the use of German immigrants, St. Augustine's hall church plan derives from 13th century German antecedents. Stained glass windows (now mostly boarded) are by St. Louis' foremost designer of church glass, the Emil Frei Art Glass Company. Purchased in 1982 by Christ Baptist, the Gothic Revival buff-colored brick church was built in 1896 from plans by Louis Wessbecher, St. Louis. Henry Hess, St. Louis, designed the Tudor Gothic rectory in 1928.

15
SS. Cyril & Methodius District
National Register: June 28, 1982

Named for the church SS. Cyril & Methodius (built originally as North Presbyterian), this small district when designated included twenty-two buildings spanning the years from 1857 to 1908. Within two decades of listing on the National Register, the most important houses in the district, the **Glassford/Bernays House** *(page 257)* at the corner of Chambers and North 11th Streets and the Charles McCord House at the southeast corner of Chambers and Hadley Streets, had been razed.

Although the church, designed in 1857 by Eugene L. Greenleaf of St. Louis, is among the oldest in St. Louis, it is the 20th century that gives this building unique significance. The Polish National Catholic Church, the largest American schism of Roman Catholicism, originated in Scranton, Pennsylvania in 1896 after repeated altercations over property rights and the selection of church officials. Early in the schism's history, women were allowed to vote in parish government; in 1921, the fourth General Synod abolished compulsory celibacy for priests. The establishment of SS. Cyril & Methodius on November 7, 1907 marked the first Polish National Catholic Church west of the Mississippi and one of the earliest in the country. Today, the church serves a small but devoted parish; some members are third generation.

1100 block of Chambers Street (SS. Cyril & Methodius district) in 1960. Over half the buildings have been razed.
Landmarks Collection

North Presbyterian Church (now SS. Cyril & Methodius) seen at top center in Pictorial St. Louis: 1875

16
St. Liborius Parish District
City Landmark: April 1975
National Register: October 11, 1979
1835 North 18th Street

Named for the patron saint of a section of Westphalia, Germany, the parish of St. Liborius was organized in 1855. While other St. Louis Germans were assimilating into the mainstream of American life, the parishioners of St. Liborius remained a tightly knit enclave of German identity and church solidarity well into the mid 20th century. This enduring ethnicity is symbolized by a masterful Gothic Revival church and rectory of red brick with stone trim built in 1889 and 1890 respectively from plans by German-born William Schickel, New York City. Contractors Bothe & Ratermann, parishioners, gave the high altar. Parishioner Joseph Conradi, architect and sculptor, designed the convent from 1905 for the Sisters of

First Communion
John Bratkowski, 1992

Notre Dame. New windows by Emil Frei portraying German saints were installed in 1907.

Conradi's eighty-foot spire of filigree sandstone based on German models was also installed in 1907, but fifty years of pollution apparently damaged it beyond repair. Removal of the treasured spire in 1965 coincided with emerging problems for many shrinking historic parishes as the Archdiocese directed more and more of its funds to the suburbs. The St. Liborius complex survived as an exceptionally well-integrated urban ensemble in a neighborhood that had seen demolition of tragic proportions until the Archdiocese decided to close the church in October 1991. At auction the following May, a pair of eleven-foot Carrara marble torchieres in the form of archangels brought $5,500, two elaborate oak choir stalls for two went for $3,000 and $2,700, two oak confessionals carved with leafage and fruit and moulded fretwork motifs were bought for $1,700 each. A pair of holy water fonts was a bargain at $1,050.

17
St. Stanislaus Kostka Church
City Landmark: March 1976
National Register: July 10, 1979
1413 North 20th Street

The first Polish parish in St. Louis, St. Stanislaus was established in 1880 under the supervision of the Franciscan Order. Father Urban Stanowski, a Polish-born Franciscan of aristocratic origins, arrived in 1885 to provide innovative and forceful leadership for the next four decades. In May of 1891, the parish was incorporated in the State of Missouri giving its Board of Directors, rather than the Archdiocese, control. The board commissioned the new church from Wessbecher & Hummel (St. Louis) whose 1891 Romanesque Revival design was far more exotic before the great Byzantine dome was removed in 1912. (Most of the interior, including windows by parishioner Michael Olszewski, date from 1929-1930 after a disastrous fire.)

Located in a working class neighborhood at the edge of Kerry Patch, the church was unable to hold the allegiance of 20th century members who could afford to move. By the time adjacent tracts of land were cleared in 1953 for the construction of the Pruitt-Igoe public housing project, the parish was in trouble. After demolition in 1975 of the ill-fated housing project, the board voted to

Clockwise from upper left:

St. Liborius in 1978
Landmarks Collection

St. Liborius Oak Choir Stall
Landmarks, 1978

St. Stanislaus Choir circa 1900
Landmarks Collection

Chapter 6 Northeast

Trackless Trolley demonstration in front of St. Stanislaus Kostka, July 1903
Missouri Historical Society

extend the charter of incorporation from 99 years to perpetuity and began a fund drive to restore the building sparked by the first of many Polka Masses. Since then, the roof has been replaced, the radiant interior restored and a 13,300 square foot Polish Heritage Center constructed. St. Stanislaus endures today as a living symbol of Polish immigration and achievement in America.

CHAPTER 7 Northwest

Wainwright Tomb
Gary R. Tetley, 1989

Chapter 7

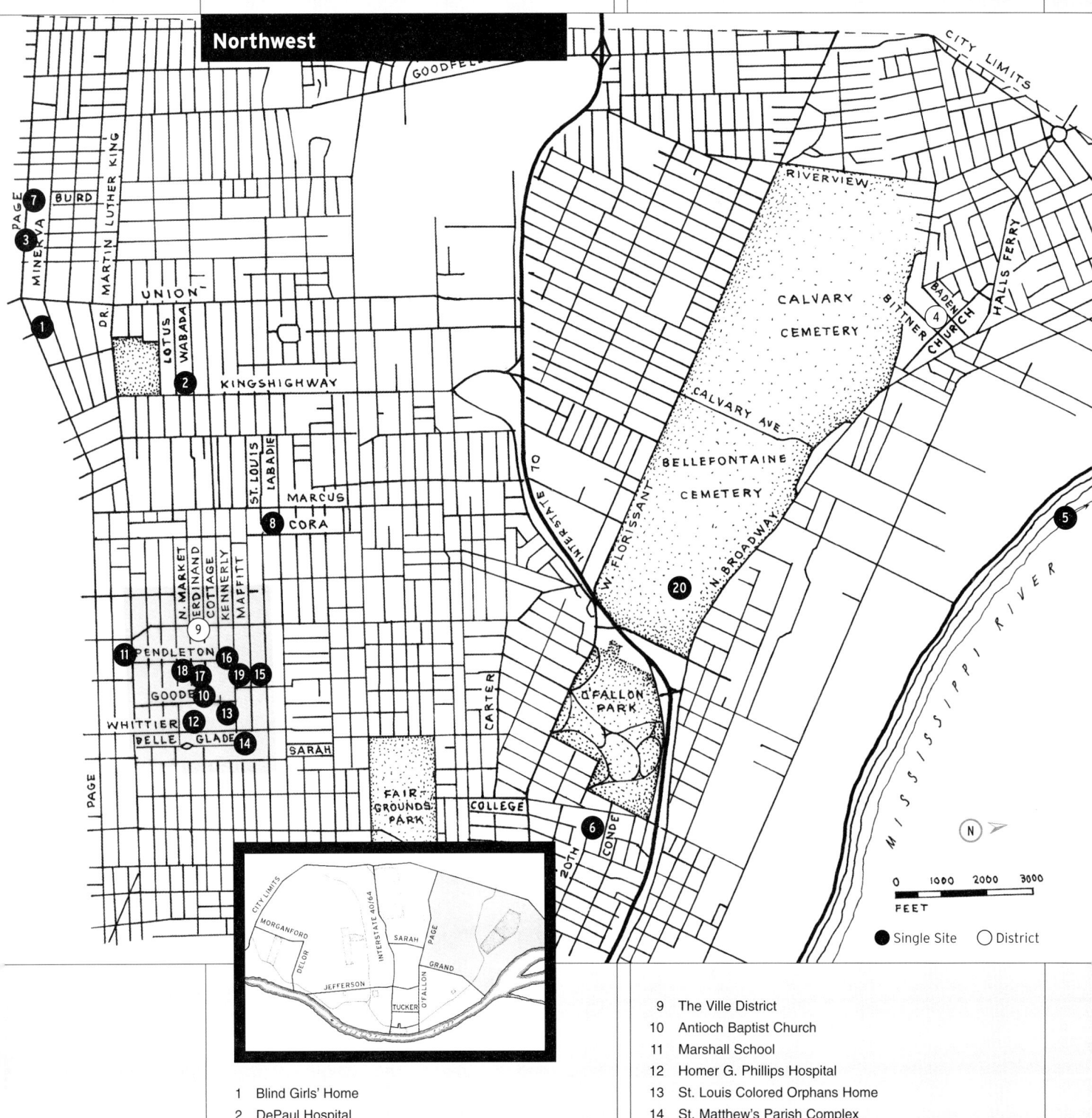

Northwest

1. Blind Girls' Home
2. DePaul Hospital
3. Emerson School
4. Holy Cross Parish District
5. Intake Towers #1 and #2
6. Kulage House
7. The Principia/Page-Park YMCA Gymnasium
8. Shelley House
9. The Ville District
10. Antioch Baptist Church
11. Marshall School
12. Homer G. Phillips Hospital
13. St. Louis Colored Orphans Home
14. St. Matthew's Parish Complex
15. Simmons Colored School
16. Stowe Teachers' College
17. Sumner High School
18. Tandy Community Center
19. Charles Turner Open Air School
20. Wainwright Tomb

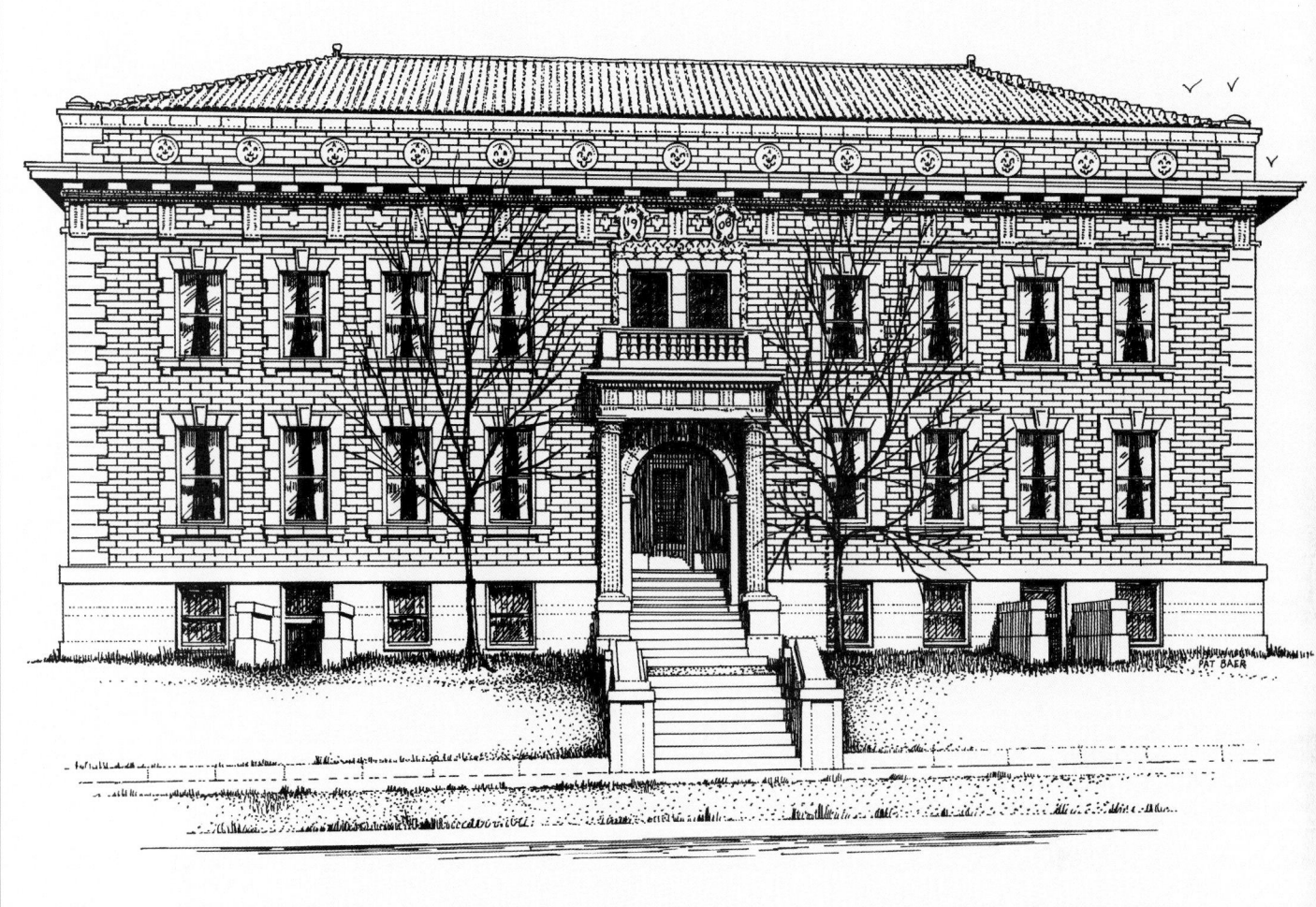

1
Blind Girls' Home
National Register: August 23, 1984
5235 Page Boulevard

Founded in 1867 by five resourceful young women graduates from the Missouri School for the Blind, the home was adopted in 1884 by the socially prominent St. Louis Women's Christian Association. The association, organized in 1868 by thirty women from prominent families, dealt first with the plight of Civil War widows left without means or family. In subsequent years the charity set up a retirement home (the **Memorial Home**, *page 236)*, a training school, a city residence for working girls (later **Phyllis Wheatley YWCA**, *page 93)*, a county retreat for city working girls, Traveler's Aid and a number of other facilities all dedicated to aiding, protecting and enriching the lives of poor working women.

Their new facility exclusively for the blind came from a gift of Mrs. L. L. Culver who also provided an endowment. Inside the handsome Georgian Revival red brick building designed in 1908 by J. Hal Lynch, St. Louis, the girls found fifty single bedrooms and spacious public rooms furnished by local department stores or association members. The home separated from the association in 1956 to become an independent corporation and moved to Kirkwood in 1966. Plans by architect Michael Willis, St. Louis and San Francisco, renovated the Page Avenue building as housing and job training for low-income residents in 1985.

Blind Girls' Home circa 1910

Pat Hays Baer

Chapter 7   Northwest

Blind Girls' Home, cornice detail before renovation
Landmarks, 1983

Below right:

Holy Cross Church drawing circa 1906
Landmarks Collection

2
**DePaul Hospital
(Tower Village Nursing Care Center)**
National Register: March 29, 1983
2415 North Kingshighway

Deliberations about whether to renovate or relocate to meet American Medical Association standards were tilted in favor of a new facility when the 1927 tornado hit Mullanphy Hospital at Montgomery and Grand. Only essential repairs were made to the old complex in anticipation of the 1928 groundbreaking for an Italian Romanesque Revival campus featuring multi-colored mosaic tile panels, quarry tile floors, carved wood altar and ornate beamed ceilings. Most buildings (hospital, convent, chapel, dormitory and nursing school) were designed by O'Meara & Hills, St. Louis. The firm (with earlier practice in Fort Dodge, Iowa, St. Paul, Minnesota and Detroit, Michigan) was recognized throughout the Midwest for its specialty in Roman Catholic ecclesiastical architecture. *Catholic Churches and Institutions by O'Meara & Hills* was self-published the same year ground was broken for DePaul.

DePaul swept in on the crest of a local hospital building boom: St. Mary's in 1924, Deaconess in 1928, McMillan in 1928, St. Louis Maternity in 1928, Shriners in 1928, Firmin-Desloge in 1932 and **Homer G. Phillips** *(page 172)* also designed in 1932. Operated by the Daughters of Charity of St. Vincent de Paul until 1977, this institution is a direct descendant of the first hospital (1828) west of the Mississippi and the first Catholic hospital in the United States. After merger of DePaul, St. Vincent's and St. Anne's in 1969, the governing board authorized the purchase of ground for a new facility in Bridgeton. McMahon Architects, St. Louis, converted the property on Kingshighway to housing for the elderly and an elderly care center in 1984.

3
Ralph Waldo Emerson School
National Register: September 2, 1992
5415 Page Boulevard

Construction for the $122,000 Emerson School began in 1901. In this design architect William B. Ittner fully realized the "open plan" for which he later became famous. (Background in **Carr School**, *page 54.*) Corridors are lined with classrooms on one side only; light is allowed into the classrooms from windows along outside walls and through windows to the corridor. Emerson School is also one of Ittner's early expositions of the hybrid "Jacobethan" style, which he would use in about two-thirds of his St. Louis designs after the turn of the century. This eclectic combination of Elizabethan and Jacobean style is manifested in Ittner's designs in exuberant polychrome brickwork, stone ornament, and (in this case) Tudor-inspired rafter detail.

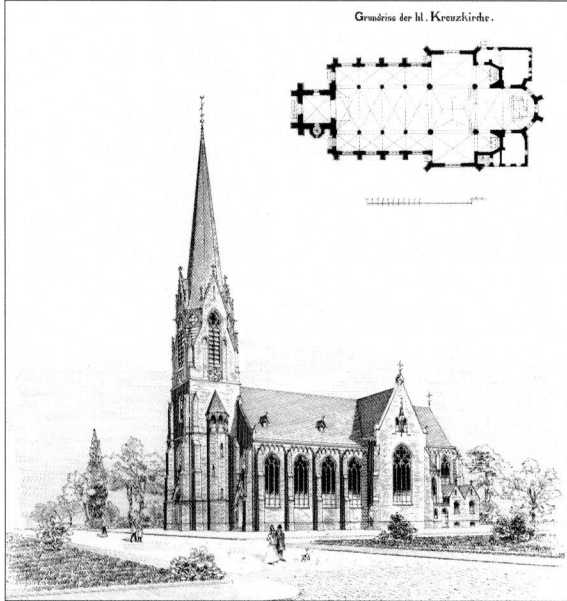

4
Holy Cross Parish District
National Register: March 26, 1980
8121-29 Church Road

"Succeeding generations shall know who built this church. We did not solicit or beg from anyone

Holy Cross Parish circa 1940
Missouri Historical Society

Holy Cross Church high altar
Landmarks, 1979

Engineering competition category at the 1904 World's Fair. His $1,000 prize went toward the building fund. St. Louis sculptor/architect Joseph Conradi modified the original plans, supervised construction and provided the stone carvings embellishing the front entrances. Reverend Wigger designed a white marble altar executed by T.G. Schrader Sons (St. Louis); figural art glass is by the Emil Frei Studio. The Gothic Revival church was completed in 1909 at a cost of $47,000. The model from 1904 is still on display in the Parish Hall.

5
Intake Towers #1 and #2
City Landmark: May 1969

With one million gallons of Mississippi River flowing by every second, the city has always been assured of a bountiful if muddy source of water. The first channel intake tower, attributed to architect William S. Eames (St. Louis), was completed in 1894. Rising ninety-two feet above bedrock perched on massive blocks of Missouri red granite, Intake Tower #1 is the most poetic Romanesque Revival structure in the city. Now

Intake Towers #1 and #2
Landmarks, 1992

outside our own parish. We are too proud. We are no beggars. We are Germans." (Pastor Peter Wigger.)

Located in Baden, a north St. Louis settlement first named Germantown, Holy Cross Catholic Church was founded in 1864 as a mixed Irish-German congregation. The appointment in 1865 of Herman Wigger initiated an astounding seventy-five years of strong leadership by a single family of German priests from Westphalia. In 1872, the Irish withdrew to form their own church and Holy Cross became a German national parish.

The next priest, Peter Wigger, looked to the homeland and his own background in art for the design of a new church. Plans drawn by Rüdell & Odenthal (Cologne, Germany) provided the basis for Father Wigger's wood model of the church entered in the Architectural

Chapter 7　Northwest

Three photos, this page:

Kulage House
Landmarks, 2001

inaccessible due to turbulent waters at the base, the tower (equipped with minimal living quarters) was once reached on foot across a now-submerged dike.

When construction began on Intake Tower #2, the main channel lay between the two towers until an excursion boat rammed the construction site and sank in midstream. A miniature Roman palace of Bedford limestone with green slate roof designed by Roth & Study of St. Louis in 1913, this tower also contains living quarters. Both towers are protected from floating objects by large stone prows pointing upstream.

6
Kulage House
City Landmark: November 1974
National Register: May 10, 2002
1904 College Avenue

The center portion of this house dates from about 1876, transformed and enveloped in a lavish Tudor Revival project designed in 1906 to accommodate the Eurocentric specifications of a determined client. Although fascination with things from abroad was common in St. Louis at the beginning of the 20th century, the Kulage family outdid themselves. The most challenging imported item for local architect Otto J. Boehmer's renovation was the twenty-six foot tall German pipe organ boasting 1,700 pipes and fourteen ranks. The most unaccountable, given the family's long-time association with St. Louis brick making, was the European gray brick used to cover the original red brick walls. Even the radiators came from Italy. Otto and his sister Ida Kulage (both single) deeded this remarkable house complete with hand-painted religious-themed windows from Europe to their servants in 1935. The current owners have owned and carefully maintained the eccentric house since 1973.

The Principia Gymnasium circa 1920
Landmarks Collection

7
The Principia/Page-Park YMCA Gymnasium (Minerva Place Apartments)
National Register: September 2, 1982
Minerva at Montclair Avenue

Founder Mary Baker Eddy's seminal 1875 publication is credited with engendering widespread interest in the Christian Science movement. By the end of the 19th century, churches had been formed in most major Missouri cities. St. Louisan Mary Kimball Morgan had begun a program of alternative education that would evolve to include the only Christian Science four-year college in the world. Wife of an executive of the Ely & Walker Dry Goods Company, and a former Methodist, Mrs. Morgan (with assistance from her husband and later from her two sons) shaped The Principia well into the 1940s.

Supporters purchased a full city block between 1901 and 1903 and steadily built a model campus where the coed curriculum from nursery school through junior college reflected the most innovative and progressive educational programs of the day. In 1923, a site in St. Louis County was selected for a four-year college to be designed by legendary Bernard Maybeck of San Francisco. Seven years later that location was rejected in favor of a breathtaking alternative in Illinois on bluffs overlooking the Mississippi River. Maybeck's campus opened in 1935. Principia's lower and upper school did not begin a gradual transfer to St. Louis County from the city until the mid 1950s. With the students gone, arson and gradual deterioration drastically reduced the number of buildings on the original campus. The only major survivor, a gymnasium built in two stages (1910, Albert B. Groves; 1919, William B. Ittner) was purchased in 1961 by the YMCA. Programs were offered from this branch until 1976; in 1982, the building was recycled to affordable housing from plans by Trivers Associates (St. Louis).

8
Shelley House
National Historic Landmark: December 14, 1990
4600 Labadie Avenue

When J. D. and Ethel Shelley first arrived in St. Louis in 1939 from Starksville, Mississippi, they found a house to rent and then sent for their five children. Next, the family located a two-story red brick house for sale at 4600 Labadie. Built in 1906 from plans by H. C. Miller, the residence came complete with a signed covenant in effect. Private agreements (racially restrictive covenants) to prevent

Aerial of The Principia circa 1920
Landmarks Collection

Chapter 7

Shelley House
Esley Hamilton, 1998

9
The Ville District
City District: February 4, 1987

Significant primarily for historical associations rather than architecture, the Ville neighborhood was first known as Elleardsville from the estate and nursery of Charles Elleard adjacent to St. Charles Rock Road—an old and important route between the first State capital and the city of St. Louis. A small concentration of black residents in the area was enough for the Board of Education to create the Elleardsville Colored School #8 in 1873, three years before the semi-rural suburb was annexed by the city. **Antioch Baptist Church** *(page 172)* became the first African-American neighborhood congregation in 1884; St. James AME followed in 1885.

Unlike the segregated enclaves after 1920, black residents in 1890 lived in four wards and could be found in dispersed locations throughout much of the city. By 1907, enough families had settled in the Ville to influence the relocation of **Sumner High School** *(page 176)*. With completion of the state-of-the-art school in 1910, this became the neighborhood of

the sale or lease of property to "persons of the Negro and Mongolian Race" had been observed in segregated St. Louis for almost three decades. The Shelleys, however, worked with a real estate salesman familiar with the subterfuge of using a white "straw party" to purchase the property, then transfer the deed to black buyers.

Members of the Real Estate Exchange, outspoken supporters of restrictive covenants, selected neighbors Fern and Louis Kraemer of 4632 Labadie to bring suit against the Shelley family a day after they moved in. Circuit Court Judge Koerner ruled in favor of the Shelleys; the Missouri Supreme Court reversed that decision. With assistance from the Civil Liberties Committee (organized by black religious leaders in 1865) and attorney George L. Vaughn, the case was appealed to the U.S. Supreme Court where oral arguments were heard during mid January 1948. When the ruling was handed down on May 3, 1948, nineteen states and the District of Columbia had deed restrictions in effect. *Shelley vs. Kraemer* declared that state enforcement of such covenants was unconstitutional, thus opening the way for dramatic change throughout the nation.

The Ville Map
Pat Hays Baer

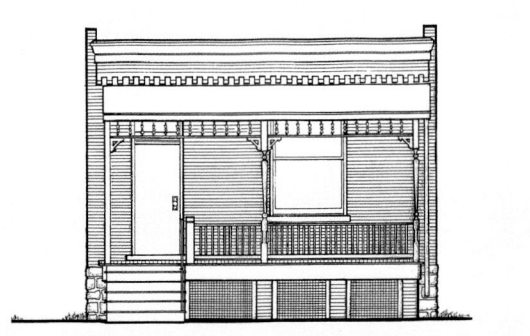

4277 Garfield, a typical Ville cottage in 1975
Joe Bilello

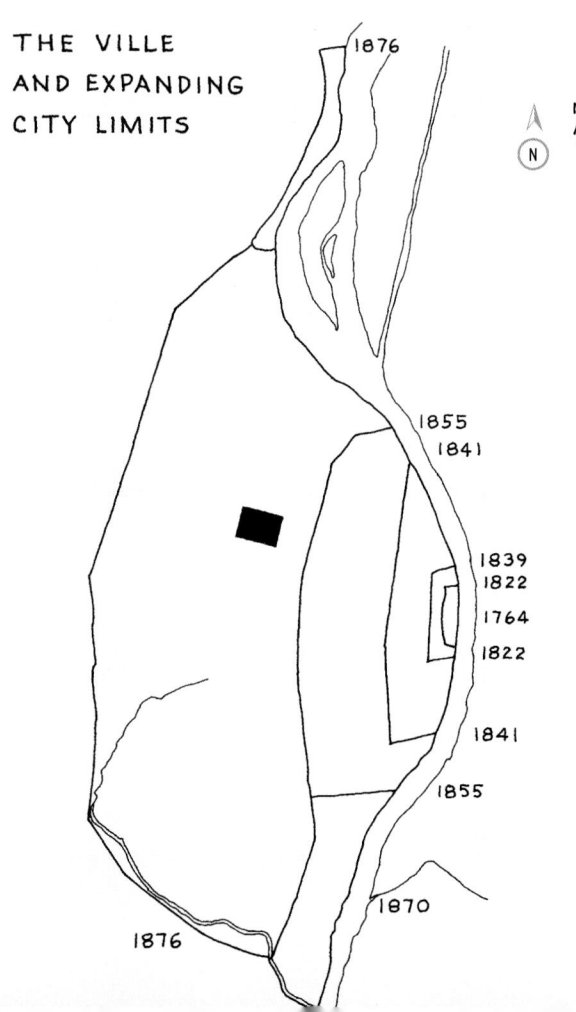

Ville matriarchs (including Julia Davis second from the right) circa 1970
Landmarks Collection

choice for African-Americans who wanted to see their children educated beyond the eighth grade. In the following decade, the black population of St. Louis grew by 60% to 70,000, fueled in large part by the influx of uneducated rural blacks from the South. In response, white St. Louisans began to devise and enforce race-restrictive deeds and covenants. The systematic discrimination of the white real estate establishment also contributed to the growing racial segregation of St. Louis.

While segregation placed enormous stress on the few neighborhoods where African-Americans were welcome, it also laid the groundwork for enormous social and institutional growth within the Ville. In 1919, Annie Malone built Poro College to educate women in the sales and use of her line of hair and beauty products. In addition to cosmetology classes, Mrs. Malone sponsored parties, lectures, plays and concerts by touring black entertainers. Additional public schools were added, the Aldridge Players brought theatrical opportunities, the Elleardsville Branch of the YMCA opened opposite Poro College and the **Colored Orphans Home** *(page 174)* relocated to the neighborhood.

One of the former residents who provided an oral history tape for *The Ville: the Ethnic Heritage of an Urban Neighborhood* in 1974 reminisced fondly about life during the 1920s:

I think the thing that made The Ville unique was that there were so many one-story homes in it, little cottages where people lived in single families. We liked the area, and it was an area where everybody took a lot of pride in their places. People liked flowers. Many

Poro College from 1924 postcard
Landmarks Collection

people had beautiful flower gardens and some people had food gardens. As I look back on it now, it seems to me that more people were just ordinary, poor people. Of course, I might get a lot of debate on that, because maybe some people thought they were affluent. I think the most affluent were possibly the schoolteachers. There might have been a few doctors and a few lawyers, postal employees, railway porters and mail clerks... just plain everyday working people.

The 1930s brought three major Depression-era public works projects: **Stowe Teachers' College**, **Tandy Community Center**, and **Homer G. Phillips Hospital** with its associated training schools for nurses and doctors *(described below)*. When the Lincoln University School of Law moved into Poro College in 1937, the Ville became a rare example of a community where black Americans could choose between three different college-level schools scarcely two blocks apart.

Chapter 7

Antioch Baptist Church
Landmarks Collection, 1996

With the Supreme Court decisions ending restrictive covenants on individual houses in 1948 (**Shelley House**, *page 170*) and segregation in public schools (1954), middle-class blacks began to leave the Ville. The neighborhood has been hit hard by the disinvestment, population loss and neglect afflicting much of the city north of Delmar since the 1950s, but almost all of its institutions remain strong. In 1999, institutional buildings in the Ville not already on the National Register were listed under a Multiple Property nomination similar to those for **Carondelet: East of Broadway** (*page 203*) and the **Public School Buildings of William B. Ittner** (see **Carr School**, *page 54*).

10
Antioch Baptist Church
National Register: September 17, 1999
4213 North Market Street

About a dozen members of the Ville's small black community gathered in a private home in 1878 founded Antioch Baptist Church. Within a few years, the congregation was able to build its first frame chapel on Kennerly Avenue. In 1909, Antioch purchased the Goode Avenue Methodist Episcopal Church (located at the site of Antioch's current education building) from its white congregation. Quickly outgrowing the space, the members planned a new sanctuary which would be attached to the east. Opened in 1921 for more than 700 members, that church expanded to its present size in 1954 with an office and education annex (replacing the previous church building). With its historic connection to the Ville, the church chose to remain in its original neighborhood even as many congregants joined the migration to the suburbs. Antioch Baptist Church still claims at least 2,000 members, most from outside the Ville.

11
Marshall School
National Register: September 17, 1999
4342 Aldine Avenue

Designed in 1900, Marshall School was the ninth of William B. Ittner's schools for the St. Louis Board of Education. The plan illustrates Ittner's groundbreaking experimentation with the "open plan," a concept he introduced in America. Shortly after the completion of Marshall, Ittner settled on an E-shaped plan which he would use, with variations, for the rest of his career. His work was widely copied throughout the country. Originally open only to white students, Marshall reflected the Ville's ongoing demographic shift when it became a black intermediate school in 1918. Capacity was increased through the use of temporary outbuildings during the 1930s; a single-story branch school was added on the grounds to the southeast in 1952.

12
Homer G. Phillips Hospital
City Landmark: February 1980
National Register: September 24, 1982
2601 Whittier Street

Considered by many to be the most tangible accomplishment of St. Louis' black community, Homer G. Phillips Hospital was named for a prominent civil-rights attorney gunned down while waiting for a streetcar at Delmar and Aubert in 1931. Phillips (born in Sedalia, Missouri in 1880) graduated from Howard University Law School in Washington before moving in 1904 to St. Louis where he found a bride, started a law practice and became embroiled in emerging "Jim Crow" controversies. By 1911, the increase in St. Louis' black population precipitated restrictive covenants in an attempt to ban migration into white enclaves.

Opposing blatant segregation laws sharpened Phillip's political skills. A spokesman for the growing minority community, Phillips and other advocates extracted the promise of a new hospital in exchange for black support of the 1923 bond issue. It passed, but the one million dollars promised for a new "Negro Hospital" was questioned by the judiciary and debated in the Board of Aldermen. Phillips finally carried the battle to a successful conclusion in the Board of Aldermen. By the time a shovel turned dirt late in 1932, Phillips was dead. An honorable new Mayor committed himself to completing the project. Mayor Bernard F. Dickmann called the dedication in 1937 "one of the happiest moments in my administration...."

Albert A. Osburg, City Architect, brought St. Louis the best in current hospital design both functionally and artistically. The central administration building with four radiating wings, a service building and a nurses' home are all clad in buff brick trimmed with Art Deco terra cotta. Completed in 1936 at a cost of $3,160,000, Homer G. Phillips Hospital was one of the few fully equipped facilities in the country where black doctors, nurses and technicians could receive training. Its influence spread throughout the nation. But improvement in the patterns of segregation that created a first-rate facility paradoxically spelled the slow loss of status and service starting the late 1950s. Important connections with teaching staff at Washington University were diminished or severed; staff salaries were not competitive with those at **City Hospital #1** *(page 187)*.

A fifteen-year worry that Homer G. Phillips Hospital would close became reality in 1979. Renovation of the former nurses' residence was completed in 1991 for $3 million from plans by Fleming Corporation, St. Louis, but the hospital remained vacant. Ten years later a St. Louis/Minneapolis partnership put together a $43 million financial package to adapt the building to 220 elderly housing units. Completion of the Fleming-designed Homer G. Phillips Dignity House is anticipated in June 2003.

Homer G. Phillips Hospital
Original drawing

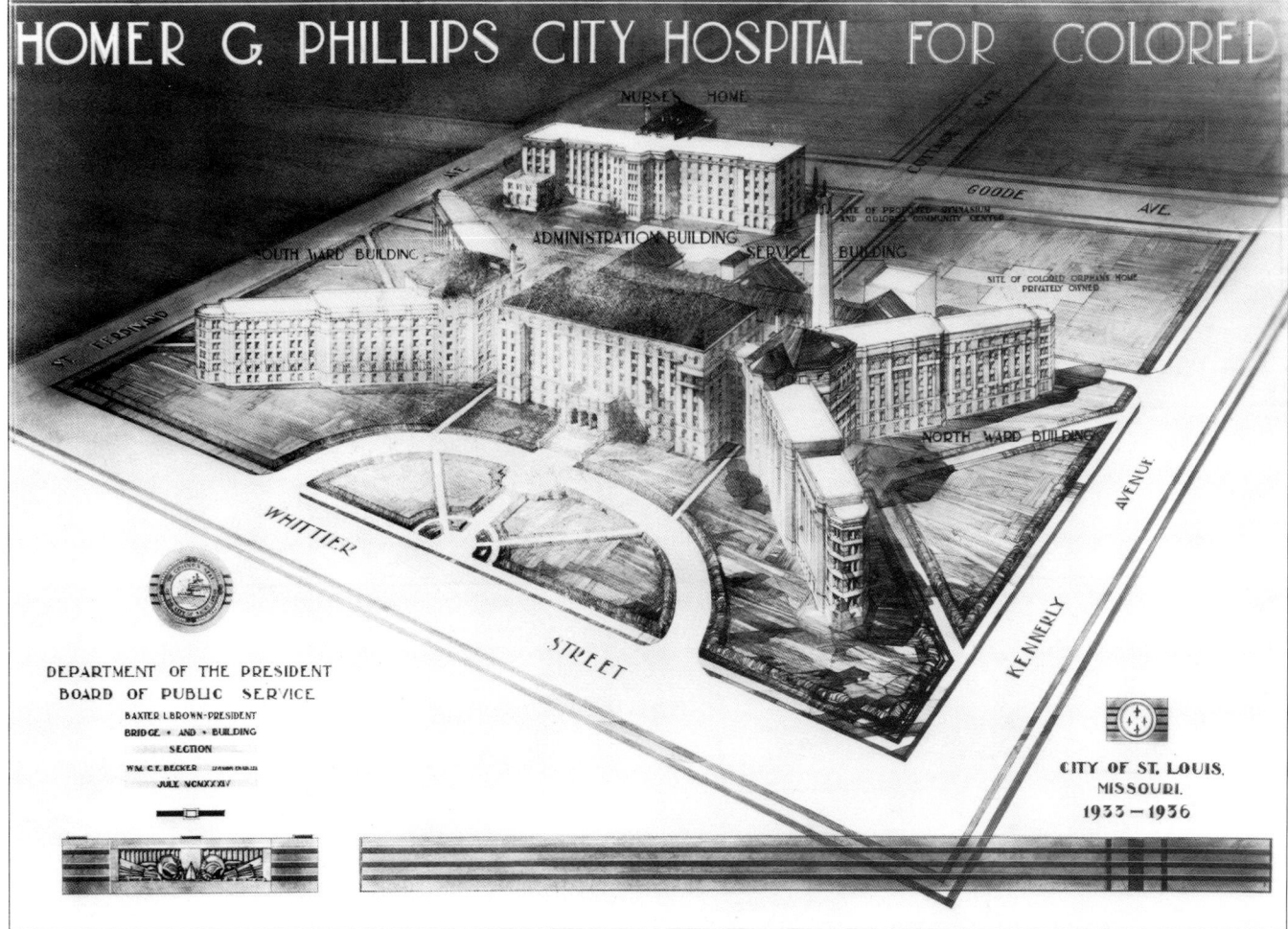

13
St. Louis Colored Orphans Home (Annie Malone Children and Family Service Center)
National Register: September 17, 1999
2612 Annie Malone Drive

The original St. Louis Colored Orphans Home was founded in 1888 with the donation of the former Negro Civil War Veterans Home on North 12th Street (since demolished). In 1901, the orphanage moved to a house on Natural Bridge north of the Ville with enough property to pasture two cows. The home had apparently fallen on hard times when Annie Turnbo-Malone (one of the country's first self-made black female millionaires) assumed the presidency in 1919. Malone, a Southern Illinois native, had just moved to the Ville from Mill Creek Valley in order to expand her hair and cosmetics business (known as the "Poro System").

Completed by 1920 (razed in 1965), Poro College occupied a full city block where more than 200 employees were trained to use and sell her products. That same year Malone donated $10,000 towards the construction of a new orphanage designed by William B. Ittner. The groundbreaking in May 1921 and dedication a year later of the Colonial Revival structure initiated the annual May Day celebrations in the Ville. Although Malone moved to Chicago in 1930, she remained president of the board until 1943 and returned annually for the parade. In 1946, the home was renamed in her honor. To this day, the annual Annie Malone parade in the Ville attracts thousands.

14
St. Matthew's Parish Complex
National Register: August 6, 1986
Sarah and Kennerly Streets

St. Matthew's (one of five Roman Catholic parishes founded in 1893) was part of an east-west corridor of Irish parishes which grew successively from St. Patrick's, the cradle of St. Louis Irish congregations located at 6th and Biddle. Although Irish immigration to St. Louis had slowed dramatically by the end of the 19th century, sympathy with Ireland's struggles to gain political independence spurred a renewed interest in ethnic identity. The new parish under the direction of legendary Father Shields grew rapidly.

St. Louis Colored Orphans Home (Annie Malone)
Landmarks, 1996

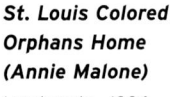

When the new Gothic Revival church by Joseph Conradi (St. Louis) was dedicated September 22, 1907, it ranked in size with the largest in the city.

The parish reached its peak during the World War I era with a congregation of around 1500 families and school enrollment approaching 700. Demographic shifts in the neighborhood brought on by white out-migration during the 1940s considerably reduced the congregation. In the late 1950s the Jesuits took charge of the parish, converting blacks to Catholicism and asserting a new commitment to social service. The old school, designed in an Arts & Crafts vocabulary between 1901 and 1913 by William P. McMahon, was recycled to low-income housing in 1986 by Westminster Builders, St. Louis. But without the appearance of Reverend Matt Ruhl in 1993, the faltering parish could have been merged out of existence. Ruhl appealed to Catholics throughout the region, stressing the city's Catholic heritage and his belief that those who moved out had an obligation to lend generous financial support. In return, parish leaders demonstrated that those funds could be quickly translated into action. With $140,000 in gifts, a renovation in 1997 changed worship orientation to a central altar surrounded by pews and the choir. Across the street, "Fat Matt's" barbecue stand and restaurant opened in a vacant building at 4068 Maffit. In July 2000 ground was broken for a new community center destined to become the nucleus of a $3 million dream for reviving the immediate neighborhood. "Catholic churches should do more to bring the city back," admonished Reverend Matthew Ruhl.

St. Matthew's Church and School
Landmarks, 1986

15
Simmons Colored School (Simmons Middle School)
National Register: September 17, 1999
4306-18 St. Louis Avenue

Elleardsville School for Colored Children No. 8 opened in 1873 in a two-room frame building on the site of the present Simmons Middle School, the first black institution in the Ville. Although the school began with all white teachers, by 1877 black teachers had replaced

Chapter 7

Simmons School
Landmarks, 1987

them and had begun serving in administrative positions as well. The first portion of the current facility was built from plans by William B. Ittner, Commissioner of School Buildings, in 1898. The original two-story building was designed for the possibility of a third floor addition, which followed in 1901. Increased enrollment led to further additions in 1911 and 1929. Simmons was the home of Stowe Teachers College from 1930 to 1940, educating hundreds of students in its teaching and junior college programs.

16
Stowe Teachers' College
National Register: September 17, 1999
2615 Pendleton Avenue

Although the Stowe Teachers College building dates from 1940, the institution itself dates back to 1890 when a one-year normal school program was established at **Sumner High School** *(see next entry)*, then located downtown. Because black teachers could not work at white schools, early enrollment was limited. The normal school moved to the Ville with Sumner and earned official status as a college in 1925. Overcrowding, always a problem in black schools, squeezed the renamed Harriet Beecher Stowe Teachers' College into a new wing of Simmons School at the end of the 1920s.

By the end of the 1930s, Stowe, now with students enrolled in a junior college as well as the teachers program, desperately needed to get out of the elementary school. The Board of Education finally approved a new building, designed in 1938 by George Sanger. The facility was dedicated in 1940 "to provide more abundant higher educational opportunities for many worthy and deserving young colored people whose chances have been sadly limited and restricted." Like the other schools in the Ville, Stowe lost its uniquely black identity but gained additional opportunities for its students after the 1954 *Brown vs. Board of Education* ruling. Its students were transferred to the formerly all-white Harris Teachers' College, later renamed Harris-Stowe.

17
Sumner High School
National Register: April 19, 1988
4248 West Cottage Avenue

Years of struggle to secure public education for blacks in St. Louis culminated in 1875 with the establishment of the original Charles Sumner High School in a former elementary school building at 11th and Spruce Streets. The first such high school west of the Mississippi, Sumner moved to another old school at 15th and Walnut before pressure from parents spurred the School Board to purchase a site for a new building in the Ville and construct in 1908 a Georgian Revival red brick building designed by nationally acclaimed School Board architect William B. Ittner, St. Louis. Attracting teachers unusually well qualified to teach at the high school level, Sumner enjoyed a fine reputation for both quality education and a full range of extra-curricular activities. Noted graduates include activist Dick Gregory, opera singers Grace Bumbry and Robert McFerrin (the first African-American to sing at the Metropolitan Opera), pop stars Chuck Berry and Tina Turner and tennis great Arthur Ashe.

18
Tandy Community Center
National Register: September 17, 1999
4206 West Kennerly Avenue

Black population had reached more than 11% of the city's 821,960 residents by 1930, but municipal recreation centers throughout the city were open only to whites. In 1934, a group of the Ville's leading citizens organized to lobby city government. As a result a bond issue was passed to finance two community centers; three were eventually built thanks to federal Depression-era assistance. Tandy was one of dozens of building projects in the St. Louis area subsidized by the Public Works Administration. From the time of the PWA's authorization in 1933 until St. Louis area projects were completed in 1940, millions of dollars in building program assistance were disbursed in the form of grants and loans. In the first four years of the program alone, the PWA claimed to have spent about $8.5 million in St. Louis.

At its dedication in 1938, Mayor Dickmann suggested that from Tandy's "splendid gymnasium" might emerge a second Joe Lewis. Instead, Tandy's tennis courts incubated the young Arthur Ashe, the first successful black player in professional men's tennis. The center also sponsored sports leagues covered prominently in the sports pages of the local black press during the 1930s and 1940s. Today, the Art Moderne building designed by Albert Osburg (architect with the Board of Public Service) continues to serve the local community with updated amenities including a computer lab.

19
**Charles Turner Open Air School
(Turner Middle School Branch)**
National Register: September 17, 1999
4235 W. Kennerly Avenue

St. Louis' first school for black children with physical disabilities and illnesses, and reportedly the first of its kind in the nation, Turner School filled an important role when it opened in 1925. Tuberculosis was a critical public health problem said to affect black St. Louisans at a rate five times higher than their white counterparts. Prevention and treatment were attempted, when possible, by isolation and regular exposure to healthful air. In a school setting, this translated to special "open-air" classrooms where full-height windows could be left open year round.

Although the school is best remembered for photographs of teachers and children wearing winter coats (as well as wool leggings, mittens, mufflers and hats furnished by the school), Turner served children with a wide range of disabilities. Ramps rather than stairs provided access for the "crippled children;" special classes were offered for the deaf and speech-impaired. A sight conservation program was offered for those whose "visual energies need to be conserved." Turner School remained open for several years after desegregation. In later years the open-air classroom's enormous window openings were resized to approximate the others. The building now functions as a branch of Turner Middle School located just west in the former **Stowe Teachers' College** (previous page).

Sumner High School
Robert C. Pettus, 1988

Chapter 7

Map of Bellefontaine Cemetery

Pat Hays Baer

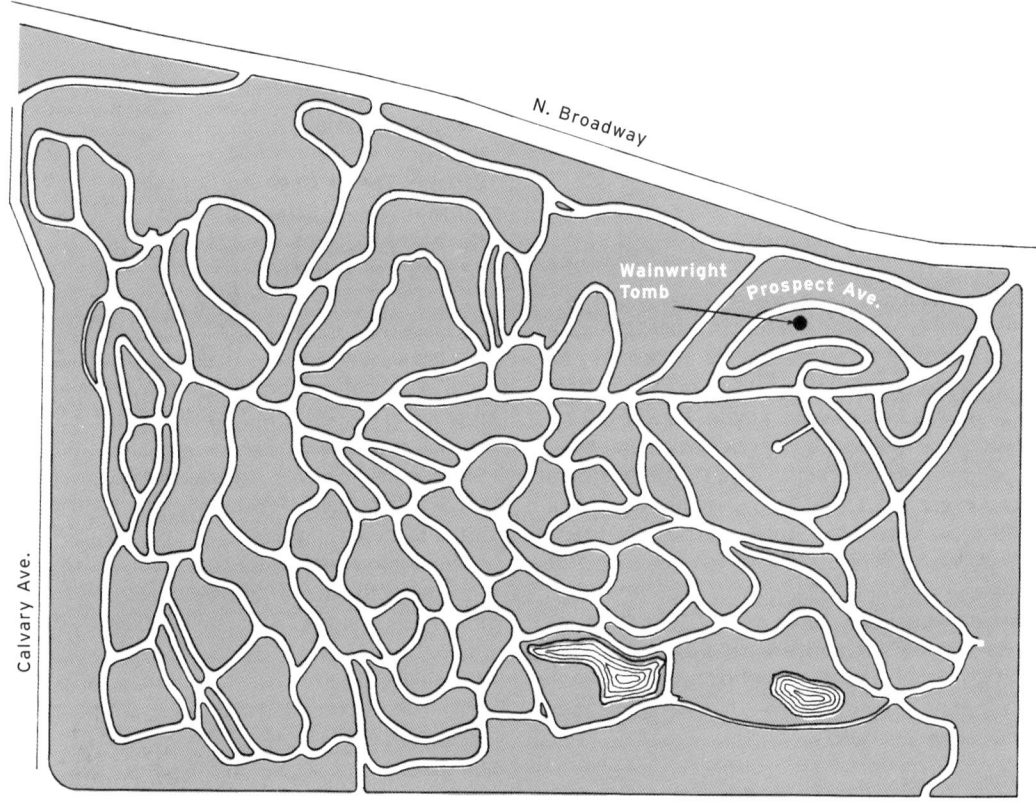

Detail: Wainwright Tomb

Gary R. Tetley, 1989

20
Wainwright Tomb
City Landmark: September 1966
National Register: June 15, 1970
Prospect Avenue in Bellefontaine Cemetery

Commissioned in 1891 by Ellis Wainwright after the death of his beautiful young wife, the tomb by Adler & Sullivan (Chicago) with Charles K. Ramsey (St. Louis) ranks among the most perfect works of architecture in the country. The serene geometry, executed in almost seamless limestone, is decorated with raised panels of delicate ornament now tragically made less precise by weathering and pollution. Above the burial slabs set in a mosaic floor, a single gold star shines in the deep blue mosaic tiles lining the dome. Ellis Wainwright, who also commissioned Adler & Sullivan's office building that bears his name, died in 1924 and is buried next to Charlotte Dickson Wainwright.

The tomb is located near the southeast corner of the picturesque cemetery laid out in 1849 by Almerin Hotchkiss—a civil engineer trained in horticulture. Hotchkiss, who was acquainted with Frederick Law Olmsted, came to Bellefontaine from Greenwood Cemetery in Brooklyn bringing along that aesthetic to the 138 acres of rolling tree-covered hills in St. Louis County. The movement for a new rural cemetery (led by William McPherson, banker and prominent layman in Second Baptist Church, and former Mayor John F. Darby) coincided with the first dramatic decade of growth in St. Louis. Family plots in town had been outlawed; churchyard resting places and small cemeteries were being overrun. This pastoral setting for the deceased with the "soothing murmuring of trees" also became a grand, dignified Victorian park in the sacred landscape genre.

CHAPTER 8 Southeast

2620-30 South 12th Street
Robert C. Pettus, 1973

Chapter 8

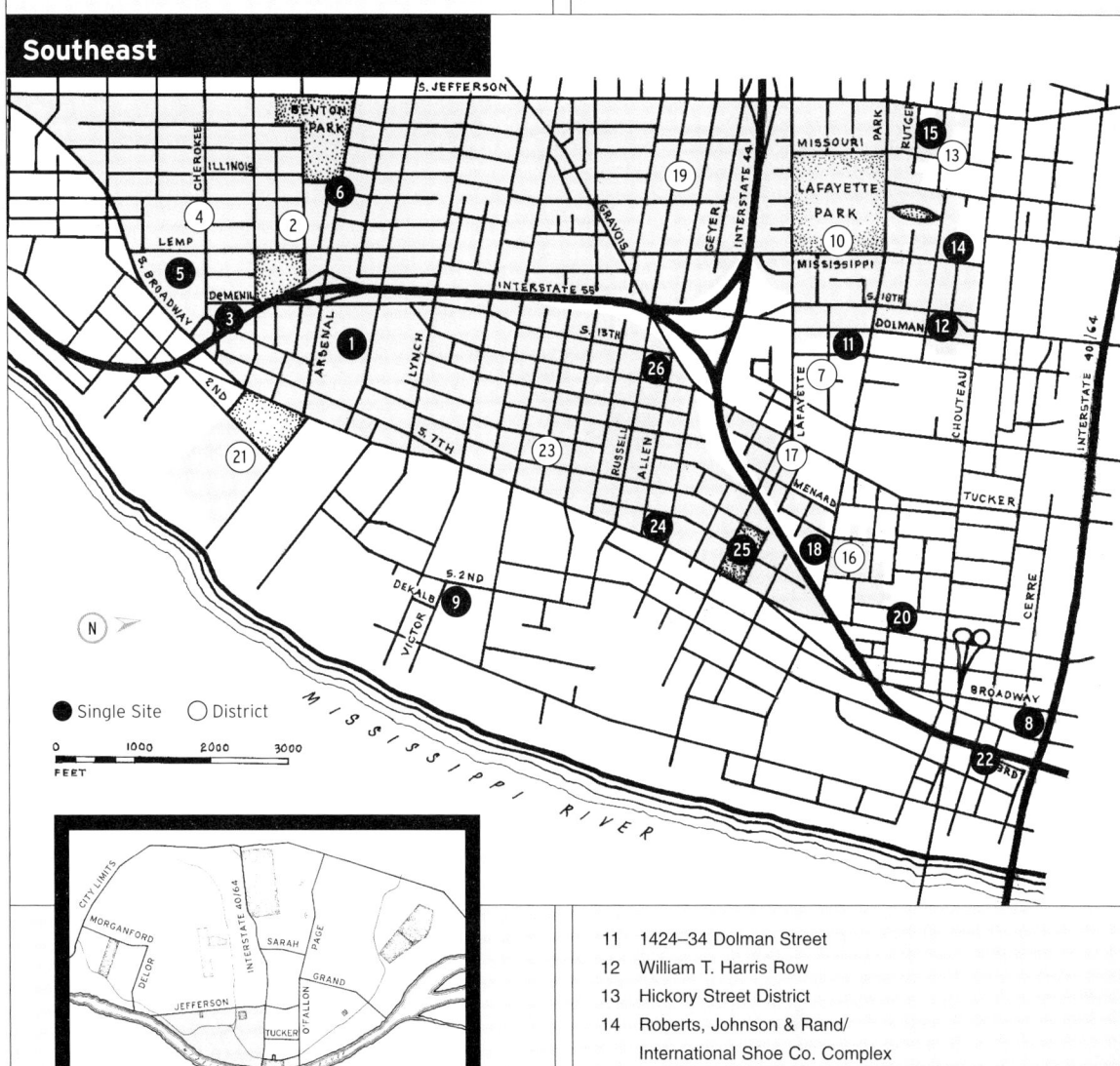

Southeast

1. Anheuser-Busch Brewery
2. Benton Park Neighborhood District
3. Chatillon-DeMenil House
4. Cherokee Street District
5. Lemp Brewery Complex
6. Schollmeyer Building
7. City Hospital District
8. Eugene Field House
9. C. Hager & Sons Hinge Company
10. Lafayette Square District
11. 1424–34 Dolman Street
12. William T. Harris Row
13. Hickory Street District
14. Roberts, Johnson & Rand/ International Shoe Co. Complex
15. 2327–35 Rutger Street
16. LaSalle Park Multiple Resource Area
17. St. John Nepomuk Parish District
18. St. Vincent de Paul Church
19. McKinley Fox District
20. Moloney Electric Company
21. St. Louis Arsenal District
22. St. Mary of Victories Parish Complex
23. Soulard District
24. SS. Peter and Paul Parish Complex
25. Soulard Market
26. Brown Shoe Company's Homes-Take Factory

1
Anheuser-Busch Brewery
City Landmark: September 1966
National Historic Landmark: November 13, 1966
Bounded by Lynch, South Broadway, Arsenal and I-55.

To see a Clydesdale is to think immediately of Anheuser-Busch, the big-time winner in St. Louis' brewing sweepstakes. Indeed, creative marketing had set this company apart even before its eagle trademark was registered in 1877. In 1860, Eberhard Anheuser (a successful soap manufacturer) acquired a small brewery in operation at this site since 1852, then brought son-in-law Adolphus Busch into the business in 1864. Budweiser, introduced in 1876, was an immediate success thanks to Busch's promotional verve and the company's innovative refrigerated railroad cars. Michelob made its debut in 1896. Most of the magnificent historic structures (including the stable from 1885 and the brew house from 1891) date from a turn-of-the-century period of expansion. All were designed by E. Jungenfeld & Co. and successor Widmann, Walsh & Boisselier (St. Louis).

Anheuser-Busch Brewery, Bevo Plant Entrance circa 1919
Landmarks Collection

Anheuser-Busch Brewery in 1902

Anheuser-Busch Brewery, Bevo Plant circa 1917

Anheuser-Busch topped the million-barrel mark by 1901, capturing first place among St. Louis breweries. The 6,000 employees ranged from doctors and lawyers to day laborers, *Bier Meisters,* technicians at the company-owned railroad and six guides trained to take of visitors. In 1916, August Busch (by then a millionaire and friend of U.S. Presidents) correctly gauged the tidal support for Prohibition and launched Bevo—a near beer selling over two million cases in the first year. The massive Bevo bottling and shipping plant (by Widmann, Walsh & Boisselier with Klipstein & Rathmann) constructed the following year contains a marvelous tile interior from the Rookwood Pottery in Cincinnati, Ohio. Few of their local competitors outlasted Prohibition. Anheuser-Busch diversified successfully to emerge as the nation's leader in the production of baker's yeast and, of course, first in the world of beer.

2
Benton Park Neighborhood District
National Register: December 30, 1985
Bounded roughly by Jefferson, South Broadway and Gravois Avenue

The site of what is now Benton Park in the neighborhood of the same name was set aside as a public burial ground in 1842 at the same time the city began selling off the surrounding Common Fields. Most of the district's early houses were small, one-story brick cottages built in the 1850s and 60s by German immigrants attracted by cheap land in an area still dotted with sinkholes, quarries, brickyards and an old earthen fortification. Less common, in the citywide context, was the presence of French-born immigrants (Icarians) who had come to this country to establish a communal colony. The Icarians had first settled in Nauvoo, Illinois in 1848 (occupying homes left by the Mormons) before moving to an estate (now razed) in Cheltenham near the current Hill neighborhood. Dissension in the ranks sent at least twelve families to the expanding Benton Park area in the early 1860s.

By 1865, the neighborhood had grown sufficiently to relocate the cemetery and establish a park named for Thomas Hart Benton. A generation later Benton Park exhibited all the characteristics of a fully developed urban immigrant neighborhood: public and parochial schools, ethnic churches, a Turnverein (razed), numerous beer gardens, corner stores, saloons and the Consumers and **Lemp** *(page 186)* Breweries. Impressive new houses, bedecked with ornamental brick and terra cotta designed in Queen Anne and Romanesque

Revival styles, stood alongside the earlier vernacular, Italianate and Second Empire residences. A neighborhood shopping concentration along Cherokee Street intersected with Jefferson Avenue where larger merchants had formed a businessmen's association in 1900 to compete with downtown shopping and challenge all the public improvement money lavished pre-World's Fair on the Central West End while south side neighborhood streets remained unpaved.

Although the association (renamed the Southwestern Mercantile Association) grew dramatically in number, scope and influence, rhetoric in its "Local Patriotism" article written circa 1909 for *Southwest Saint Louis: Its Mercantile Interests and Prominent Citizens* reveals an organization willing to use any verbal weapon in its losing fight with the downtown commercial palaces: *How many young persons have been ruined by being*

Above:

1943 Utah
Robert C. Pettus, 1988

Left, top to bottom:

2036-18 Sidney
Landmarks, 1984

2900 McNair
Landmarks, 1984

Benton Park in 1917 postcard
Landmarks Collection

Chapter 8   Southeast

Lemp Mansion
Esley Hamilton, 1999

Left to right:

2225-27 Arsenal
Landmarks, 1984

Bridge in Benton Park with new grill designed by Ray Simon
Landmarks, 2000

sent downtown to work? Where do you find all the mashers and 'spider-leg dudes'? Consult your divorce records and find how many divorces are caused by women meeting their paramours downtown. Who pays for all the swell West End residences and the automobiles that the officers and managers of the department stores ride in? It is the 'sucker' who can't buy a paper of pins without running downtown. If you want to bring about the universal brotherhood of man and help your brother and yourself, patronize the community in which you live.

Hyperbole notwithstanding, the first major change in the neighborhood occurred after WW II with demolition at the eastern edge for the Ozark Expressway and the beginning of an influx of rural migrants. By the early 1970s, abandonment and demolition were becoming increasingly common. In 1976, Benton Park was selected as the first St. Louis location for a Neighborhood Housing Services program. Since then, an active arts community and a spirited neighborhood association have organized numerous events to publicize the district's opportunities for rehabilitation while enlisting the financial support of Martie Aboussie, one of the most influential aldermen in the city, to help demonstrate the value of historic preservation. The importance of urban archaeology was underscored in 1999 when demolition of a city-owned property on Lemp Avenue unearthed possible ties to the Underground Railroad. A belated dig including eager high school students is expected to yield valuable artifacts about a portion of local history seldom noted in written sources.

3
Chatillon-DeMenil House
City Landmark: June 1966
National Register: June 9, 1978
3352 DeMenil Place

Henry (fur trader and owner of a profitable tavern on the levee) and Odile Delor Chatillon (granddaughter of the founder of **Carondelet**, Chapter 9) built the first portion of the current house (shaded gray in the drawing below) circa 1849. In 1856, the four-room farmhouse and accompanying five acres brought $16,120 as a summer retreat for the Eugene Miltenberger and Nicholas DeMenil families. Miltenberger sold his interest to the DeMenils in 1861 who engaged English-born Henry Pitcher to incorporate the small 1849 house into a Greek Revival mansion suitable for a family of substance. Dr. Nicholas N. DeMenil had emigrated from France in 1834, married Emily Sophie Chouteau (granddaughter of Mme. Marie Therese Chouteau, the "mother of St. Louis") and opened one of the first successful drug store chains in the city.

Upon Nicholas' death in 1882, the house passed to son Alexander who in turn willed the property to his son George. George DeMenil inherited the mansion in 1928 and lived there until he married. After his caretakers on the premises reported that most of their time was taken up showing the mansion and grounds to sightseers, George gave them permission to rent the entire place, occupying what part of it they needed. Antique furnishing, objects of art, mantelpieces and chandeliers were removed first. In 1945, DeMenil sold the property to an entrepreneur. Scheduled for demolition in the 1950s for the Ozark Expressway (Interstate 55), the house was saved by Landmarks Association with generous support from the Union Electric Company. Restoration work by Gerhardt Kramer (St. Louis) began in 1964; in 1965, Landmarks turned the property over to the Chatillon-DeMenil House Foundation which continues to operate it as a fine house museum. Today, a lovely restaurant in the carriage house offers a view out to the river above the re-routed expressway.

Above:
The Chatillon-DeMenil House before renovation circa 1960
Dr. William G. Swekosky

Left:
The Chatillon-DeMenil House before renovation circa 1964
Landmarks Collection

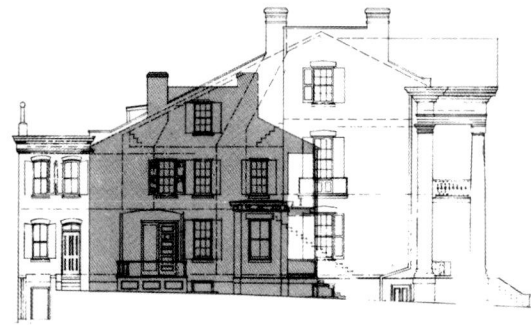

The Chatillon-DeMenil House: south façade
Gerhardt Kramer, 1966

Chapter 8 — Southeast

2018 Cherokee Street
Landmarks, 1984

4
Cherokee Street District
City District: March 19, 1987

In 1915, the four and a half blocks of Cherokee between Indiana and Lemp Streets were bustling with activity. Over sixty shops provided almost everything a family could want: doctors, a dentist, a midwife and drug stores; an electrician, a carpenter, a paint contractor, a sign company and hardware stores; bakeries, confectioneries, butchers and produce; furniture, dry goods, clothing, millinery, shoes, notions, cigars, wine and saloons.

Sixty years later many shops were vacant. Efforts to revive Cherokee Street have sprung from two separate but compatible efforts. West of Jefferson Avenue the street was declared a redevelopment area; the portion to the east in the Benton Park

1953-55 Cherokee Street
Robert C. Pettus, 1988

Lemp Brewery Complex
Esley Hamilton, 1998

National Register district elected to become a city historic district. Most of the small-scale buildings in this section were built in the 1880s and 90s; a few date from the mid 19th century. In a perfect setting for pedestrian-based shopping, antique stores began to establish a lively new identity. West of Jefferson on Cherokee, where later and larger stores are the rule, the situation has been complicated. Low-rent uses became more and more common; a substantial number of buildings remained empty. Recent Mexican immigrants have introduced their language on the street, along with a cuisine sought out by residents from throughout the city.

5
Lemp Brewery Complex
City Landmark: November 1975
Bounded roughly by South Broadway, Cherokee and Lemp Avenue

Lemp's Western Brewery was not the first brewery to locate in the Benton Park neighborhood. At least six firms, attracted by the presence of limestone caves for storage, were established in the area by 1864 when William J. Lemp relocated his father's brewery to Cherokee Street. By the mid 1870s, Lemp had become St. Louis' largest producer of beer. Annual sales totaled $1,250,000; bottled beer was shipped in large quantities to South America, China, Japan and Australia. Some was exported to London, Paris and even cities in Germany. Continued expansion of the William J. Lemp Brewing Co. (as it was called after 1892) eventually covered five city blocks.

The Italian Renaissance style (featuring round arched windows, pilaster strips and corbelled brick

Granary: Lemp Brewery Complex
Ken Konchel, 1996

cornices) employed in the earliest brewery buildings was maintained for major new structures throughout the nearly forty-year building history. Widmann, Walsh & Boisselier, successor firm to E. Jungenfeld & Co. of St. Louis and architects for Anheuser Busch, designed some of the turn-of-the century buildings. The Barnett & Record Construction Company (a Minneapolis firm that held the patents for their distinctive, undulating form) designed the striking group of granary stacks built in 1905. In 1922, the complex was sold at auction to International Shoe Co. for less than $600,000.

An expensive candidate for conversion to another use, the twenty-nine building complex has tantalized would-be entrepreneurs for years. Ad hoc artist studios, storage, architectural model making and light-industrial companies had taken about 30% of the space when the complex was purchased in 1999 by a local partnership, The Lemp Brewery Redevelopment Corporation. After concentrating on acquiring more tenants (one of the newest is a branch of Science Applications International, a Fortune 500 company based in San Diego), the corporation expects soon to resume brewing Lemp products for the first time since Prohibition.

6
Schollmeyer Building
National Register: September 28, 1984
1976–82 Arsenal Street

Built in 1889 for commission merchant Christian Schollmeyer, this late entry into the architectural lexicon of Benton Park combines Second Empire forms with Queen Anne details. The family held on to the two-story corner property as an investment well into the 1930s. Jeff Hicks of Series, Inc. prepared plans for a 1985 renovation.

7
City Hospital District
National Register: February 2, 2001
Bounded by Lafayette Avenue, Grattan, Carroll, Dillon, St. Ange and South 14th Streets.

The first hospital operated by the city of St. Louis (only the third in the city) opened on this site in 1846. Rebuilt after a fire ten years later, the hospital was destroyed again in 1896—this time by the tornado which also claimed several thousand homes. Stalled by legal disputes over funding, the hospital stayed in "temporary" emergency quarters near Union Station for nine years. The long-awaited opening of a new hospital in 1905 was attended by a large crowd of onlookers, the most curious of whom climbed in the windows when the police tried to bar them from the reception room. (All of the 1905 octagonal ward buildings were later demolished as the complex evolved; the only building to survive from this first group is the original Kitchen or "E" building, buried in the middle of the complex.)

By the time the present Commissioner's Building was added in 1907, the hospital was already acknowledged to be far too small to meet the city's medical needs. Floor space doubled when Albert B. Groves'

City Hospital District
Pat Hays Baer

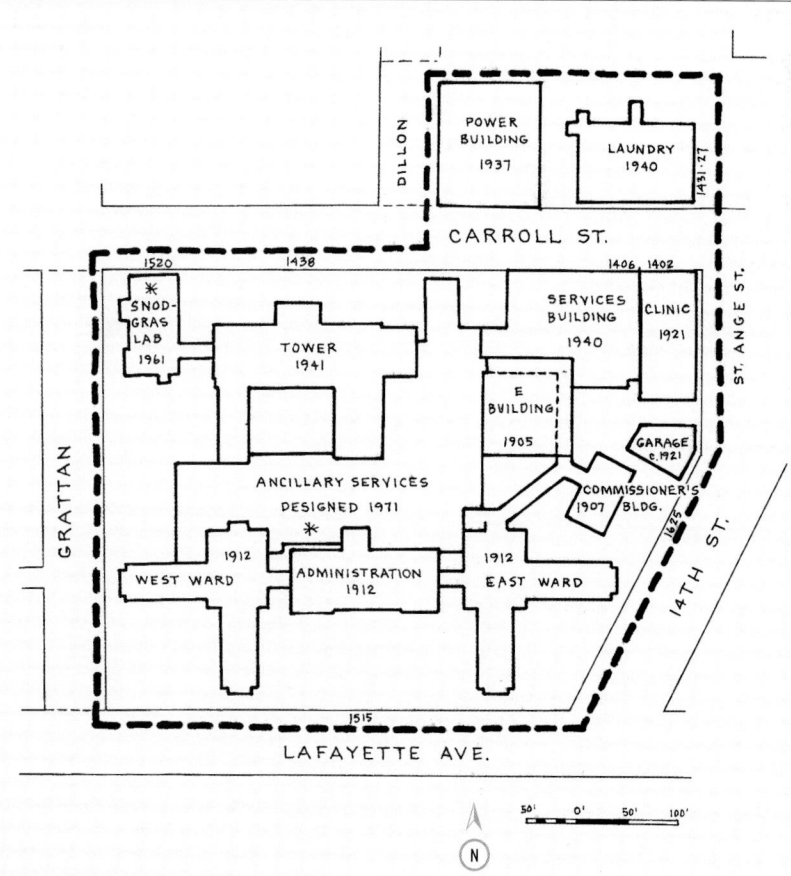

City Hospital District: Administration Building in 1988
Landmarks Collection

City Hospital District: Power Plant
Landmarks, 1999

Administration and Ward Buildings on Lafayette (now recognized as the front elevation of the complex) were opened in 1912, but a growing population insured that the hospital was consistently short on space throughout the first half of the century. New technology also required frequent remodeling, while the public's increasing expectations for medical care placed even more pressure on the facilities. Even as a separate hospital facility was purchased to segregate black patients in 1919 (replaced with **Homer G. Phillips Hospital** in the **Ville**, *page 172*), City Hospital could not keep up with demand. An aggressive building program gave the complex a new clinic (1921), nurses home (1932, demolished) and WPA-era buildings including a laundry, power plant and kitchen. Malcolm Bliss Mental Hospital and the thirteen-story Tower Building replaced the octagonal wards and dwarfed the rest of the complex in 1941. (Two newer buildings, the 1961 Snodgras Laboratory and the 1971 Ancillary Services Building, round out the complex.) By the 1970s, the hospital system was in crisis; reports showed that City Hospital was only 60% occupied. Even the consolidation achieved by closing Homer G. Phillips in 1979 couldn't save the facility. It closed in 1985.

The site has been owned by the city's Land Reutilization Authority (LRA) since 1993, after a redevelopment plan by Pantheon Corporation ran out of steam. During city stewardship fearless vandals climbed to the top of the signature Administration Building to strip copper from the cupola; below, professional scavengers hauled away massive stone stairs. Forlorn, with few champions, the red brick hospital complex continued to deteriorate next to the infamous Darst-Webbe public housing project in similar condition. The decision to demolish the public housing for a Hope VI project (a rebuilt neighborhood with mixed-income housing) put City Hospital in the spotlight. At first, it was assumed that the hospital buildings must go; but in 1999, LRA (to its credit) selected a development proposal based on adaptive reuse.

8
Eugene Field House
City Landmark: June 1966
National Register: August 19, 1975
634 South Broadway

Built as part of a row circa 1845, the house features a large collection of antique toys and dolls as well as furnishings, manuscripts and Eugene Field's personal belongings. Field, remembered for his still-popular children's poems, also had an eventful career as a reporter, critic and popular columnist with newspapers in St. Louis, St. Joseph, Kansas City, Denver and finally Chicago from where his daily column "Sharps and Flats" was reprinted in newspapers throughout the country. After Field's death in 1895, the red brick rowhouse passed to the St. Louis Board of Education.

Admirers from many places, inspired by the crusading efforts of Irving Dillard—an editorial writer at the *Post-Dispatch*—united to help save the house in 1934 when the Board of Education proposed its demolition for a parking lot. Landmarks Association operated the museum house from 1968 to 1981 at which time a separate foundation was formed. Gerhardt Kramer, St. Louis, directed restoration work at the house for many years. More recently, local architect Jeff Brambila was brought in to supervise essential work on the exterior. After eight years of negotiation with five different owners, the foundation acquired land to the north in May 2001. A much-needed expansion will bring an elevator, adequate storage and display space to a singular museum house.

9
C. Hager & Sons Hinge Company
National Register: February 26, 1987
139 Victor Street

Founded in 1849 by German-born Carl Hager, the company grew from a blacksmith shop supplying forged iron wagon furnishings to become the second largest hinge manufacturer in the world. It is also one of the four longest-lived enterprises founded by German immigrants in St. Louis along with Teutenberg Bakeries in 1812, Schaeffer Manufacturing in 1839 and Schuedding Stonecutter's Tool Works in 1849. The three-building part of the Hager Hinge Company complex enclosing a courtyard was renovated by L. J. Torno, Jr. & Associates (St. Louis) in 1984.

Left:
Eugene Field House
Philip Cotton

Lafayette Square District, tornado damage in 1896

Chapter 8   Southeast

Clockwise from top left:

Deutsches Haus built in 1928
Ken Konchel, 1997

2031 Park designed by E. Jungenfeld in 1895 for Ernst Link
Robert C. Pettus, 1973

1827-29 Kennett Place built for John Pullis in 1878
Robert C. Pettus, 1973

Missouri Avenue facing Lafayette Square
Pat Hays Baer

10
Lafayette Square District
City District: June 30, 1972
National Register: June 28, 1972 and July 24, 1986
Roughly bounded by Jefferson, I-44, Grattan and Chouteau Avenue

The expanded (1986) National Register District includes over 550 buildings built between 1860 and 1935. Although excellent examples of terra cotta and decorative brickwork abound, the district's collection of post-Civil War stone front townhouses is unmatched in the Midwest. Many of them face the park, a thirty-acre public square formally designed between 1864 and 1870 by accomplished landscape gardener Maximilian G. Kern. Others are located on Benton Place, laid out in 1868 as an oval private street around a central green.

The district's two earliest churches, both offshoots of prominent congregations from the central corridor, were designed in Gothic Revival styles by Frederick W. Raeder (St. Louis): the former Unitarian Church of the Unity (1869-70) at 1322 Mackey Place and the former St. John's Episcopal (1872) at the northeast corner of Hickory and Dolman. Presbyterians, another indicator

Houses from the late 1870s on Missouri Avenue before renovation
Robert C. Pettus, 1973

of social standing, built a Gothic Revival church in 1883 on a lot overlooking the park at 1505 Missouri from plans by John H. Maurice—district architect/resident who along with George I. Barnett designed many of the contemporary Second Empire townhouses. By the late 1880s, however, Romanesque Revival and Queen Anne brought stylish new forms to Lafayette Square.

Hard hit by the 1896 tornado, the district seemed a bit old-fashioned to some residents who chose to move to **Compton Heights** *(page 218)* or the new private streets in the **Central West End** *(page 99)* rather than rebuild. Although property immediately adjacent to the Square and on many streets leading from it was protected by deed restrictions prohibiting non-residential use, industry began to encroach. The first was American Bed Company, incorporated in 1900, which began construction of a multi-building plant in 1902. Located between South 18th, McNulty and Vail Place, their city-block complex was tucked almost out of sight just east of the park. **Roberts, Johnson & Rand Shoe** *(page 193)* broke ground for a five-story factory at the northern edge in 1903. Boarding houses began to appear around World War I. By 1947, Lafayette Square (like Soulard) was dismissed as obsolete; the Comprehensive City Plan from that year envisioned massive demolition for a watered-down Corbusier townscape of rectangular housing blocks.

The late John Albury Bryan, architect and architectural historian, was one of the first newcomers to move to the district in 1949 and urge its preservation. In 1969, younger pioneers formed the Lafayette Square Restoration Committee and began working for historic district designation. Lafayette Square became the first National Register district in the city and the first local historic district in June 1972. Since that time the district has experienced tremendous revitalization promoted first by individual homeowners, later joined by developers. Decades of debate concerning the North/South Distributor road proposed for the district's eastern edge along Grattan changed the scope of the project from an interstate highway to a parkway. Construction finally got underway in the beginning of the 21st century.

Rehab pioneer John Albury Bryan and his 1870 Benton Place house designed by John Maurice
Landmarks Collection

Chapter 8   Southeast

Hickory Street District: "Park Terrace," 2325-01 Hickory Street built in 1893
Robert C. Pettus, 1973

Below, left to right:

William T. Harris Row
Esley Hamilton, 2001

Hickory Street District: 2221-23 Rutger built by stonecutter George F. Bruce in 1887
Landmarks, 1986

11
1424-34 Dolman Street
National Register: January 19, 1984

More common in **Soulard** *(page 198)* and **Old North St. Louis** *(page 156)* than Lafayette Square, this red brick vernacular building type was constructed in St. Louis from about 1840 until the 1890s with only minor modifications in exterior form. The row of three, two-story double houses on Dolman (then named Curran) was built circa 1876 as income property by realtor Charles H. Franke.

12
William T. Harris Row
City Landmark: January 1972
1100-18 South 18th Street

An unadorned yet stately row of ten, two-story townhouses with stone fronts was built circa 1874 as income property for attorney William S. Pope. The row was later named in honor of Connecticut-born William T. Harris who came to St. Louis in 1857 at age 22, advancing from Assistant Teacher to Superintendent of Public Schools by 1862. Harris lived at 1116 South 18th from 1875 until the early 1880s before a career move took him to Washington D.C. where he served as United States Commissioner of Education from 1889 to 1907.

13
Hickory Street District
National Register: January 18, 1985
Roughly bounded by Jefferson, LaSalle, Missouri and Rutger Avenue

Representatives of St. Louis' two largest 19th century ethnic groups, the German and Irish, built the majority of the forty-eight houses in this district. A number were employed in the building trades; most were working class. Headquarters of the Jefferson Avenue Railway Company at the corner of LaSalle and Jefferson and the company's red brick streetcar barn built in 1895 attracted transit workers to the district. The 1900 Census reported a large number of streetcar conductors and motormen renting flats at 2301-15 Hickory in the Eastlake-detailed "Park Terrace" constructed in 1893 by German-born carpenter Jacob Schenck. Another distinctive building at 2221-23 Rutger displays the craftsmanship of Scottish-born stonecutter George F. Bruce in his own house built in 1887 for $6,500.

14
Roberts, Johnson & Rand/International Shoe Co. (Lofts at Lafayette Square and Mississippi Lofts)
National Register: August 23, 1984
1105-25 Mississippi Street

Between 1890 and 1900, St. Louis evolved from a distribution center for eastern-made shoes to the nation's foremost center of shoe manufacturing with Roberts, Johnson & Rand/International emerging as the single largest company in the country. Constructed between 1903 and 1922 on the site of Schnaider's Garden, a fashionable 19th century summer retreat adjacent to Schnaider's Brewery, the complex is a well-preserved example of early 20th century industrial architecture

featuring functionally efficient design and fine red brick masonry construction. (Theodore Link, St. Louis, designed the 1903-12 portion.) The factory's location at the northern fringe of the Lafayette Square neighborhood overlooking downtown has made it an ideal candidate for adaptive reuse. Its size has made it a challenge. Two different developers (LoftWorks and the Jeffery E. Smith Co.) embarked on adjacent projects with a total of more than 150 new residential lofts opening in 2002-03.

15
2327-35 Rutger Street
National Register: January 19, 1984

This pair of two-story, six-family flats featuring handsome yellow brick fronts is located outside the first boundaries of the Lafayette Square National Register district. Cited as a good example of the late 19th century St. Louis transition from rowhouses to small apartments, the Renaissance Revival-inspired designs (1895 and 1897) by an unknown architect also demonstrate the ascendance of yellow brick at the turn of the century.

16
LaSalle Park Multiple Resource Area
National Register: August 19, 1983
Two districts ("Soulard-Page" and "Speck") east of Tucker between I-44/55 and Hickory Street

Post World War II clearance for industrial expansion, freeways and public housing isolated what is now LaSalle Park from Lafayette Square to the west and Soulard to the southeast. When Ralston Purina immediately to the north made a decision in the late 1960s to keep its corporate headquarters in the city, its expansion program was tailored to fit urban renewal guidelines. Intervention by Landmarks Association of St. Louis in the mid-1970s caused a dramatic redirection in a plan that would have demolished what was left of the residential neighborhood. Instead, Ralston (starting with the donation of the house at 911 Park Avenue to Landmarks Association for a Bicentennial project) made a solid commitment to preservation.

The ethnic mixture of historic LaSalle Park was among the most colorful in the city. Early French and free blacks were replaced by Germans and Czechs who in turn were replaced by rural white migrants and a late

Robert, Johnson & Rand/International Shoe Co. Complex: Sole Leather Plant from Shoe & Leather Gazette, 1909

LaSalle Park: 911 Park
Robert C. Pettus, 1973

LaSalle Park: neighborhood in 1944 before highway demolition
Landmarks Collection

Left to right:

LaSalle Park: Checkerboard Square postcard
Landmarks Collection

St. John Nepomuk Church and Hall circa 1905
Emil Boehl, Missouri Historical Society

home to Obata Design at 1614 Menard Street. The South St. Louis Turnverein at 1529-19 S. 10th Street (built in stages between 1881 and 1943) was recycled in 1981 to loft condominiums from plans by Claybour Architects, St. Louis.

17
St. John Nepomuk Parish District
City Landmark: April 1971
National Register: June 19, 1972
Six buildings clustered around the church at 1631 South 11th Street

In 1854, Czech Catholics built a small frame church on the corner of Soulard (now Lafayette) and Rosati (now 12th Street). This inauspicious structure where Father DeSmet (famous missionary to the Indians) sang the first High Mass was the earliest Bohemian Catholic Church outside the mother country and the nucleus of "Bohemian Hill," a community that eventually numbered 5,000 Czechs. Although many of the

immigration group in St. Louis—the Lebanese, whose political influence in the city has been staggering in relationship to their numbers. Today's residents, save clergy at St. Vincent's and St. John's, are newcomers. Some were attracted to the historic buildings; others have been enticed to the neighborhood by new construction that is still underway.

All of the 130 or so remaining historic buildings (excluding the **St. John Nepomuk District** described below) are residential except for three churches, two parochial schools and a remnant of the "Cordage Mill"—a cotton factory established in 1848 and converted to cordage in 1899. One church, the former First German Presbyterian Church (an 1871 design of Adolphus Druiding at 10th and Rutger Streets) was adapted as a photographer's studio in the 1980s from plans by Thomas H. Cohen, St. Louis. Another, the Markham Memorial Presbyterian Church designed in 1896 by Grable, Weber & Groves, found a new use as

St. John Nepomuk
Landmarks Collection

immigrants were anticlerics happy to have left the state religion imposed in Bohemia by the Hapsburgs, at least half of them stayed with the church in the new country. By 1895, their numbers were sufficient to build another church (St. Wenceslaus) in the 3000 block of Oregon southwest of Bohemian Hill. The following year, a devastating tornado destroyed almost all of St. John's. Rebuilt by late 1897 following plans by Adolphus Druiding, the new church contains many wood statues from Bohemia spared by the tornado. Windows from 1929 by Frei Art Glass of St. Louis were made in Munich.

In spite of out-migration beginning in the 1920s and the clearance of much of what was Bohemian Hill for public housing projects, St. John Nepomuk is still open. Many worshippers come from outlying regions for homecoming and ethnic events; Midnight Mass was still in Czech as late as the mid 1970s. In 1988, the newer of the school buildings was recycled to condos by Mark Conner from plans by J. Bradley Pope, St. Louis. Ten years later the name "Bohemian Hill" was revived to identify a housing project diagonally across from the parish hall. Designed to demonstrate that contemporary design can fit comfortably within a historic setting, the initiative came from collaboration between Landmarks Association, Washington University's School of Architecture and Youth, Health & Education in Soulard.

18
St. Vincent de Paul Church
City Landmark: March 1971
1417 South 9th Street

In contrast to nearby **St. Mary of Victories** (page 197), St. Vincent de Paul was intended to serve English- and German-speaking Catholics in the growing south side neighborhoods. The church was built in two phases: the nave of 1844-45 by London-trained George I. Barnett; the narthex and facade circa 1849 by Franz Saler. The parish has been in the care of the Vincentian Fathers from its founding to the present. Three well-known institutions (St. Ann's Home, the House of Good Shepherd and St. Vincent's Hospital) established within parish boundaries moved on after the 1896 tornado or clearance for the Third Street Highway in the early 1950s.

St. Vincent de Paul Church
Robert C. Pettus, 1975

Chapter 8 Southeast

McKinley Fox District: St. Michael the Archangel Russian Orthodox Church
Landmarks, 1988

The parish complex once boasted an impressive grouping of red brick Classical Revival buildings including Julia and Benjamin A. Soulard's 1837 mansion. Adapted as the diocesan seminary and priests' house, the Soulard mansion was razed in 1952 along with the Vincentian Foreign Mission building and other parish property. Looking out over blocks of rubble, a writer for the *Post-Dispatch* reflected: "Members of the old parish, once one of the most flourishing in the city, wonder what effect the new highway will have on its future. Will there be more industrial and commercial development, and fewer families in residence?" There would be fewer and fewer families. All would have been gone had not the LaSalle Park Urban Renewal project *(page 193)* been redirected to include rehabilitation. Today, the Vincentians provide after-school tutoring and summer camp as part of their mission to the community.

19
McKinley Fox District
National Register: September 7, 1984
Roughly bounded by Jefferson, Gravois, South 18th and I-44

Sharing boundaries with previously described **Lafayette Square** (from which it was severed by the construction of Interstate 44) on the north and **Soulard** *(page 198)* to the east, McKinley Fox has

pockets that resemble those neighboring historic districts. In general, however, its character is early 20th century with orderly, multi-family flats dominating many streetscapes. Some were built by German carpenter/owners who rented to the newly arrived Serbs and Russians in the neighborhood. Both groups gave the district distinctive ecclesiastical buildings that add an exotic note to the vernacular red brick neighborhood: St. Michael the Archangel Russian Orthodox Church from 1928 at 1901 Ann and the Serbian Eastern Orthodox Church, also built in 1928, at 1910 McNair.

The district's best known building is the Jacobethan high school at 2156 Russell designed in 1902 by nationally recognized architect William B. Ittner. (See **Carr School**, *page 54* for background.) The first public high school on the south side, McKinley introduced manual training to the system in a successful attempt by School Board President Calvin Woodward to reverse an alarming dropout rate. The new school, a major destination for visitors from the field of education during the 1904 World's Fair, was adapted for use as the McKinley Classical Junior Academy for middle-school students in 1994.

Left to right:

McKinley Fox District: 2005-07 Geyer
Landmarks, 1998

McKinley Fox District: 2200 block of Charless
Landmarks, 1984

196

20
Moloney Electric Company Building
National Register: March 28, 2002
1141-51 South 7th Street

The reemergence of the original industrial building, hidden under brown paint and blocked-in windows until 2001, stands as a testimony to the power of imagination. Before the concrete blocks came out of the windows and the paint was stripped away, few would have guessed that this site was one of the birthplaces of St. Louis' early 20th century electrical industry. The building was constructed in two sections (the first in 1903-04 and the second in 1916) for brothers-in law and partners Thomas O. Moloney and James Mullen. From this location the duo developed many of their revolutionary designs for transformers, including innovations that would later be adopted as industry standards. By the 1920s, the partners operated two additional factories and a Canadian office, eventually building the business up to the world's largest exclusive manufacturer of electrical transformers.

21
St. Louis Arsenal District
National Register: January 17, 1975
Second at Arsenal Streets

The federal government acquired land for an arsenal in 1827. Within a few years Morton & Laveille (St. Louis) had completed the first of ten extant historic buildings in time to supply ordnance for the Black Hawk and Mexican wars. Three other buildings by George I. Barnett were built in 1856. The arsenal, critically important to the Union during the Civil War, was the principal supplier to federal troops in the Mississippi Valley arena. In 1870, the grateful government granted seven acres to the city for a park centered on a monument in honor of Brigadier General Nathaniel Lyon. Lyon had kept St. Louis and the arsenal from falling into secessionist hands at the battle of Camp Jackson. (An equestrian statue of Lyon finally arrived at the arsenal site after it was displaced from Camp Jackson Park opposite St. Louis University nearly ninety years later.) In 1871, the ordnance function was transferred to the Jefferson Barracks Army Post in St. Louis County. The thirty-seven-acre reservation is now under the jurisdiction of the Defense Department's National Imaging and Mapping Agency (NIMA).

22
St. Mary of Victories Parish Complex
City Landmark: January 1973
National Register: August 28, 1980
744 South 3rd Street

Bishop Peter Richard Kenrick established St. Louis' first national parish in 1843 with the decision to build St. Mary of Victories. For the rest of the century, Catholics in the city would be segregated by language group. This policy fostered ethnic identity and often rivalry. Although the cornerstone for the German-language church was laid on June 25, 1843, only the nave could be completed in 1844 due to the large diocesan debt incurred during construction of the **Old Cathedral** *(page 6)*. The transept-apse and belfry, added in 1859-60 following the original cruciform plan by George I. Barnett (St. Louis), brought total costs to $13,000. An elegant, simple Classical Revival building with monumental doorway (originally marbleized), St. Mary of Victories has been home for St. Stephen's Hungarian parish since 1957. Members have breathed new life into St. Mary's by sponsoring fund-raising concerts and Hungarian meals and pastries. The small complex is difficult to find due to the grossly insensitive path of Interstate 55.

St. Mary of Victories circa 1900
St. Louis Public Library

Chapter 8   Southeast

2631 South 12th Street (designed in 1885 for brewer Louis Obert) circa 1970
Landmarks Collection

23
Soulard District
National Register: December 24, 1972
City District: November 26, 1975

Soulard as it exists today is only a portion of a 19th century collection of subdivisions opened for development beginning in 1836. Within sixty years immigrants (mostly Germans, Central and Eastern Europeans) had built one of the most densely inhabited communities in the world. The neighborhood, like other "stepping-off" concentrations in St. Louis, was a sea of red brick: simple vernacular Federal or Italianate rowhouses built by carpenter/developers; alley houses, often built first and then rented when the immigrant had saved enough money to build a larger house at the street; pre-1860 and later Victorian cottages and "flounders"—houses sporting only half a front-gabled roof. A few residents who gained considerable wealth

Gangway or "mousehole" at 1016 Geyer
Robert C. Pettus, 1973

(especially beer barons) erected showy Second Empire townhouses, Queen Anne and Romanesque mansions in the 1880s and 90s.

Built as a walking neighborhood with churches, halls, corner stores and factories, Soulard remained stable until after the Depression when even the most recent groups of immigrants were assimilated. Feeling little nostalgic identification with Soulard, many (as had those who could before them) moved to the south and west. The 1947 *Comprehensive City Plan* for St. Louis reflected the post World War II biases of the planning profession and the country at large. Soulard (with its mix of single and multi-family housing amidst corner commercial and nearby industrial) was considered a textbook classic of bad land use. Both the Soulard and Lafayette Square neighborhoods were declared obsolete, to be replaced by large-scale housing blocks set in a pattern of suburban cul-de-sacs.

Elevation of South 8th Street punctuated by Trinity (Missouri Synod) Lutheran Church
Michael Emrick, 1975

198

1205-23 Sidney
Robert C. Pettus, 1973

With more expansive boundaries than those drawn for the earlier National Register district, the city designation has been critical in halting unnecessary demolition. Thanks to the Investment Tax Credits for historic renovation, Soulard's multi-family buildings have attracted developers while single-family homes have continued to increase in value as new construction fills vacant lots. Rambunctious crowds from throughout the region descend on the neighborhood each Mardi Gras; the discerning choose to patronize the many restaurants offering jazz and blues on other occasions to savor the historic setting as well as the food.

Left to right:
1019 Shenandoah
Robert C. Pettus, 1973

2517 South 9th
Robert C. Pettus, 1973

The 1950s and 60s brought massive public housing and freeway construction to the near south side. By 1970, abandonment and demolition within the heart of the neighborhood had become a serious problem. Meanwhile, the newest arrivals in Soulard were poor, white rural migrants who arrived in a city on the decline. The first neighborhood organization, the Soulard Neighborhood Improvement Association, was formed in the early 1960s to enable Soulard to qualify for federal funds. By the 1970s, back-to-the-city newcomers began to buy the then-cheap houses for tedious do-it-yourself renovations. The Soulard Restoration Group was formed in 1974 in the midst of an effort to create a local historic district.

Chapter 8   Southeast

Left to right:

SS. Peter and Paul circa 1900
Emil Boehl, Missouri Historical Society

Soulard Market
Landmarks Collection

destroyed by the tornado of 1896; makeshift replacement sheds were torn down in 1928 for a buff brick building derived from Brunelleschi's Foundling Hospital in Florence, Italy. The design was by Albert E. Osburg, architect with the Board of Public Service, who also drew plans for **Homer G. Phillips Hospital** (page 172) and the diminutive Art Deco police stations scattered about the city. (The one in Soulard, now an art gallery, is located just north of the tour entrance to **Anheuser-Busch Brewery**, page 181.)

24
SS. Peter and Paul Parish Complex
City Landmark: March 1972
South 8th at Allen Street

Impressed by his 1870 design for a German Catholic Church in Detroit, Father Francis Goller (pastor 1858-1910 at SS. Peter & Paul) brought German-trained Franz Georg Himpler to St. Louis in 1872 to draw up plans for the parish's third church at the same site. German-language newspapers, in describing the new limestone building based on 14th century models, admired its close adherence to medieval construction methods and praised the stained glass windows imported from Innsbruck, Austria. A 214-foot spire completed in 1890 followed Himpler's original Gothic Revival plans. In 1984, pews seating 3,000 were replaced by a circular seating arrangement near the front of the lofty hall-church design. A large facility in the basement was set up to help provide shelter for the homeless as part of the church's mission to the community.

25
Soulard Market
City Landmark: April 1971
Lafayette at South 8th Street

Soulard Market, certainly the noisiest and most colorful City Landmark, sits on land donated to the city in the 1840s by Julia Soulard, widow of the Surveyor of Upper Louisiana. The first market building was

26
Brown Shoe Company's Homes-Take Factory ("Mexican Hat Factory," now Allen Market Lane Apartments)
National Register: October 20, 1980
1201 Russell Boulevard

Specializing in women and girls' shoes, the four-story red brick factory built in 1904 from plans by Weber & Groves (St. Louis) was acclaimed one of the best lighted and arranged plants in the country. (The company, organized by George Warren Brown in 1878, won a double grand prize for its participation in a model shoe factory exhibit at the 1904 World's Fair.) From 1954 to 1976, the International Hat Co. and its subsidiary, the Mexican-American Hat Co., occupied the building. Recycled as the Allen Market Lane Apartments for the elderly from plans by SRT Architects/Planners in 1980, the building is managed by Youth, Education & Health in Soulard.

Brown Shoe (Mexican Hat Factory)
Robert C. Pettus, 1973

CHAPTER 9 Carondelet

Joseph Otzenberger
House
Landmarks, 1979

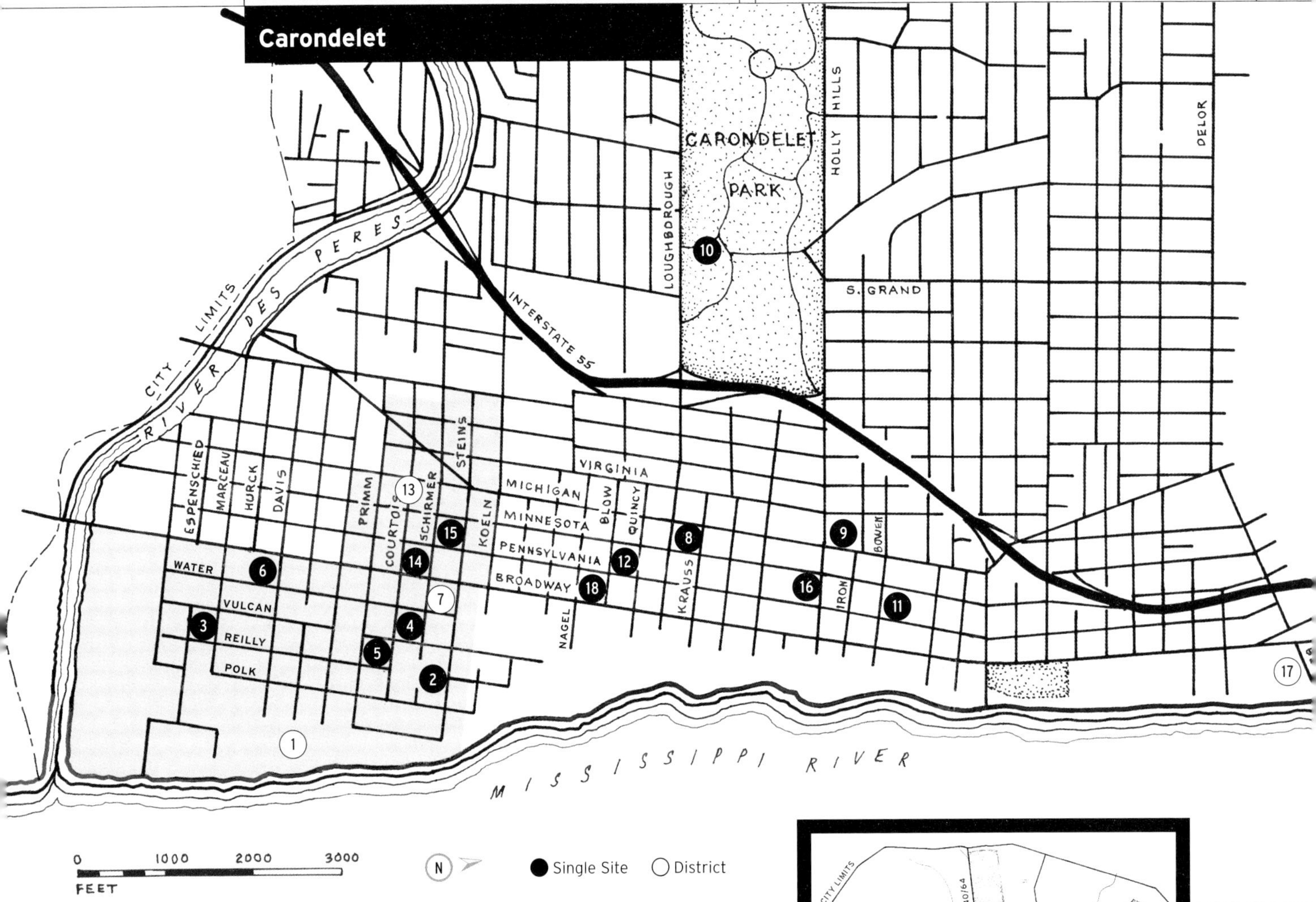

Chapter 9

Carondelet

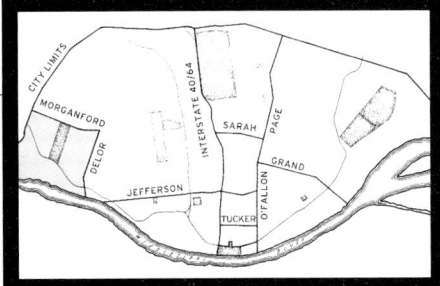

- Single Site ○ District

1. Carondelet/East of Broadway
2. Jacob Steins House
3. Charles Schlichtig House
4. Henry Zeiss Houses
5. Joseph Otzenberger House
6. Carlin/Rathgeber House
7. Steins Street District
8. Carondelet Branch Library
9. Des Peres School
10. Lyle Mansion
11. Quinn Chapel A.M.E. Church
12. "Rock House"
13. St. Boniface District
14. Anton Schmitt House
15. Steins Street Row Houses
16. Sisters of St. Joseph of Carondelet Convent
17. South Broadway Bluff Area
18. Store Buildings at 7121–29 South Broadway

Meier Iron Company in ruins
Landmarks Collection

1
Carondelet/East of Broadway
National Register: May 16, 1980
Multiple Resource Area including one small district and five single sites.

Founded in 1767 and a separate community until 1870, Carondelet was settled by Creoles (colonial people of French or Spanish descent, many from Illinois), French, Canadians and a handful of slaves. Some were farmers and woodcutters. A few were independent trappers, though most "mountain men" conducted their business through the Laclede-Chouteau headquarters in nearby St. Louis. Sleepy Carondelet was not incorporated as a village until 1832 by which time a small but stable German population had drifted there. Substantial German and Irish immigration began in the 1840s. New arrivals found ample supplies of limestone to quarry and clay to make bricks. Both groups worked in the building trades; both contributed other essential skills to the old settlement. By 1850, all four butchers, all three bakers and both shoemakers were German as was the lone cabinetmaker. The Irish claimed many ship carpenters, stonemasons and quarrymen. When the narrow gauge St. Louis & Iron Mountain Railroad came through in 1858, opportunities for industrial development near the river became irresistible.

The outbreak of the Civil War a few years later brought stark divisiveness within the population as well as the opening of James B. Eads' Union Marine Works, employing 900 men in the production of iron clad gunboats. But aggressive spending for post-war public improvements in the face of low property taxes combined to reduce Carondelet to easy prey for the city of St. Louis which quietly included the suburb in expanded boundaries under consideration at the State Legislature. On the eighth of April 1870, Carondelet ceased to exist as an independent political entity.

The industrialization of Carondelet east of Broadway did not place the community on the high road to prosperity that its promoters had imaged. Although the Vulcan and Meier Iron Works companies employed hundreds and produced thousands of tons of steel rails, Missouri furnaces were never terribly efficient and the Ozark iron range could not compete with the newly discovered high-grade ores in Minnesota. By the turn of the 19th century, iron mining in Missouri was moribund. Carondelet slipped into a steady decline. A city zoning ordinance adopted in 1918 (later struck down as unconstitutional) designated the Carondelet riverfront area "industrial and unrestricted." So did the 1947 Comprehensive Plan.

An attempt at a form of preservation made its first appearances in the City Plan Commission's *St. Louis Riverfront Plan* of 1967 and in the 1973 *Development Program*. Both documents proposed moving historic buildings to recreate the spirit of the original Carondelet village. At the end of the decade, however, a far different proposal emerged for Carondelet east of Broadway from the office of new Mayor James

Chapter 9 — Carondelet

Population in 1799 map
Pat Hays Baer

Conway. This plan would have razed about 40% of the housing stock as well as nineteen businesses and inserted a four-lane collector road for heavy truck traffic. Controversy began to mount during preliminary hearings. When the Mayor refused to confine redevelopment to vacant areas, Alderman Albert "Red" Villa (one of the most powerful politicians at City Hall) successfully "called in IOUs from many years back" to block public funds for acquisition. Instead, the weeds of recent history have spread truck parking, random manufacturing and residential disinvestment.

2
Jacob Steins House
City Landmark: September 1976
Southwest corner of Steins and Reilly Streets

One of the most important mid 19th century arrivals to Carondelet was Jacob Steins, a glazier from Cologne who built a large stone house in 1843 and attempted to farm. In 1852, he converted a portion of the house to a tavern. Some of his patrons were probably attracted to Carondelet by Steins' quasi-official role as immigration agent. The building continued to serve as both home and business for succeeding owners including three generations of Fanettis, the name associated with a restaurant in this building and *The Bugle* (a quirky neighborhood newspaper) into the 1980s.

3
Charles Schlichtig House
City Landmark: October 1979
300 Marceau Street

Built of locally quarried limestone in 1852 by German-born stonemason Charles Schlichtig, this two-story house remained in the family for a century. (The side hall plan is the only example left in the area.) All three of Schlichtig's sons were ship carpenters employed by Carondelet's important waterway firms. After donation to Landmarks Association, the property was transferred to a sympathetic owner who recycled it to offices in 1984 from plans by Gerhardt Kramer, St. Louis.

Steins House circa 1890
Landmarks Collection

4
Henry Zeiss Houses
7707-13 Vulcan Street

The growth of mason Henry Zeiss' prosperity and the size of his family can be followed in his move from two side-by-side 1850s stone cottages to the capacious two-story brick house built next door in 1870. The brick house remained in the Zeiss family for three generations. The 19th century firm founded by Henry Zeiss and later owned by the Ruprecht Company exemplifies the long history of stone quarrying in the area as a vital economic base for the immigrants of Carondelet.

5
Joseph Otzenberger House
Northwest corner of Reilly and Primm Streets

Built by Alsatian-born Otzenberger in 1858 on a choice lot overlooking a city square, this cottage is now in a hostile setting of concrete manufacturing. An elevated gallery with stairs leading to a second-story entrance and integration of the back porch with the roof structure were once features that connected this house to Alsatian building traditions with roots reaching back to medieval architecture.

6
Carlin/Rathgeber House
122 Davis Street

Two phases of American architectural taste are encapsulated in the Greek Revival core of this house (built for Delphy Carlin in 1848) and its later roof, porch and subordinate wing added in the 1880s by German-born John Krauss. At his death in 1897, Krauss (head blacksmith for the Iron Mountain Railroad and manager of later enterprises) was considered the wealthiest and most prominent citizen of Carondelet. His daughter, Julia Krauss Rathgeber, was the second of five generations of Krauss-Rathgebers to reside in the Davis Street house where wide vistas of the Mississippi River were possible.

7
Steins Street District
100-128 Steins Street

Approaching the district from the southwest corner of Steins and Water Streets, one moves chronologically from 1850s brick and stone

cottages to the 1898 residence and place of business on Broadway designed by Arthur Zeller for butcher Herman Haag. Sadly, the earliest buildings are now gone. A gas explosion in the 1990s damaged this representative city block illuminating a half-century of settlement and building in Carondelet east of Broadway.

Clockwise from left:

Zeiss Houses
Robert C. Pettus, 1974

Steins Street District circa 1965
Landmarks Collection

Joseph Otzenberger House
Robert C. Pettus, 1974

Chapter 9 Carondelet

The Carondelet Branch library soon after opening in 1908
St. Louis Public Library

The Carondelet Branch library circulation desk in 1911
St. Louis Public Library

8
Carondelet Branch Library
City Landmark: May 1969
6800 Michigan Avenue

Although Prague-born and Vienna-trained Ernst Preisler designed innumerable houses in south St. Louis, this Bedford stone library (opened in 1908 as the third Carnegie branch in the city) may be his only institutional building. The varied collection inside the Classical Revival facade includes abundant material on Carondelet history and south St. Louis institutions. The east wall of the adult reading room features a WPA mural, "Founding of St. Louis," by St. Louis artist Robert Rigsby.

9
Des Peres School
National Register: September 2, 1982
6303 Michigan Avenue

Private play schools based on educational reform espoused in the 1830s by Swiss educator Friedrich Froebel took root in several German-American communities before the pivotal collaboration of Susan Blow and William T. Harris brought the movement to public school education. Susan Blow, a young woman of exceptional background and education, had traveled in Europe and visited with proponents of Froebel's methods in the eastern part of the United States before volunteering her expertise to Harris. Harris' interest in kindergartens began soon after he assumed the position of Superintendent of St. Louis Public Schools in the late 1860s when overcrowding in many of the working class neighborhoods plus roving bands of street children were believed to pose serious threats to the general population. Des Peres' experimental kindergarten class of forty-two students, held the first year the school opened, became a model copied throughout the country

A simple two-story red brick structure built in 1873 from plans by Frederick W. Raeder (architect for the School Board), the building was enlarged in 1897, closed in 1935 and survives today because of its association with educators Blow and Harris. Subsequent uses

Des Peres School in 1876
Emil Boehl, Missouri Historical Society

Albert Jefferson, charter member of the Carondelet Historical Society, in 1975

Landmarks Collection

included a restaurant, Veterans Post and supermarket warehouse. Purchased by the Carondelet Historical Society in 1982, Des Peres school is now the Carondelet Historic Center housing archives, a museum and meeting rooms. An addition to the Center will open in late 2002.

10
Lyle Mansion
City Landmark: May 1969
Carondelet Park

Carondelet Park, offering the most varied topography of any park in the city, can also claim several buildings of great architectural interest. Foremost is the Lyle Mansion, a fitting metaphor for the town's tumultuous early history. Built circa 1850 on a sheltered site by carpenter/oilman Alexander Lacy Lyle, the splendid frame house sheltered a family of sixteen. (Lyle had inherited the 180-acre Spanish land grant from his grandfather.) Little more than a decade later, the Lyle family like many other prominent residents with Southern sympathies fled Carondelet at the outbreak of the Civil War. Ownership of the tract passed to a cousin of poet Eugene Field.

Winning political support for the creation of Forest Park after the Civil War meant balancing that centrally located amenity with retreats on the north and south sides of St. Louis. A citywide vote in 1875 authorized O'Fallon Park in the north and Carondelet Park (almost named Independence Park) on the south. Payment of $143,000 transferred the Lyle family house and its 180-acre tract to the city. Formal dedication ceremonies at the park on July 4, 1876 started at dawn with a thirteen-gun salute in honor of the original colonies; next came a thirty-eight-gun salute for the then-current number of states. A 100-gun salute in honor of the U.S. Centennial occurred at noon. The Lyle Mansion, used for a time as the park keeper's residence, is now underused as a recreation center for senior citizens. Its architectural merit and historical importance warrant a long-range restoration plan.

11
Quinn Chapel A.M.E. Church
National Register: October 16, 1974
227 Bowen Street

This austere red brick building designed in late 1869 as one of three public markets in the soon-to-be-absorbed city of Carondelet was sold by the city of St. Louis to the neighborhood African Methodist Episcopal Church for $600 in 1880. (Another of the market buildings still stands at 7701 South Broadway, see **St. Boniface District,** below.) Named in honor of the first black Methodist bishop, William Paul Quinn, who preached in Missouri and evangelized the West, the church was vital in the lives of early congregants. (The entrance tower was added circa 1900 to house the gift of a church bell allegedly donated by a junk dealer who had bought it for $50.) The U.S. Census of 1870 documented the black population in Carondelet at 345; ten years later the number had risen to 450 and would continue to grow, reaching a peak of 1,063 residents in 1920. Membership at Quinn Chapel declined after the 1920s in correspondence to the rise of **The Ville** *(page 170)* as the citywide center for black institutions, education and social life.

12
"Rock House"
City Landmark: November 1974
7012 Minnesota Avenue

Limestone for this two-story house built circa 1842 came from a nearby quarry located between Reilly and Polk Avenues. One of the largest of the early stone buildings to survive, this twelve-room house originally faced the river. Today, it fronts on South St. Louis Square—land forever reserved for park purposes when this part of Carondelet was laid out in 1832.

13
St. Boniface District
National Register: May 9, 2002
Bounded roughly by Koeln, South Broadway, Tesson and Alabama Streets

Few towns in the Union have increased in population so rapidly as our sister city of Carondelet. In 1853 the total population was 1,580; in 1856, 1,701 and in November of the present year it is 3,102. The census has just been taken, and in the space of one year the population has nearly doubled.

The *Missouri Republican's* story in its November 16, 1858 edition proclaiming booming growth in one of St. Louis' suburbs coincided with the opening of the St. Louis & Iron Mountain Railroad and the influx of German and Irish immigrants into the new John C.

St. Boniface Church circa 1900

Archdiocesan Archives

Ivory subdivision carved from the former Carondelet common fields. In early 1860, German Catholics bought four lots from Ivory, contracted with Irish-born architect Thomas W. Brady (St. Louis) and by the end of the year held the first German-language services in their unfinished Romanesque Revival church of St. Boniface.

Post Civil War prosperity allowed the congregation to reduce debt and complete the south tower in 1868; the twin tower to the north was not added until 1890. Meanwhile, commercial nodes had developed along Ivory (a diagonal slash through the otherwise regular grid) and Broadway. Most of the district's housing was built by the end of the century; many of the working-class residents were employed in the buildings trades or in heavy industry along the riverfront. Interesting 19th century commercial buildings include the former South St. Louis public market completed in 1869 (right before Carondelet was annexed by the city of St. Louis) and Jodd's Hall—an imposing three-story building on Broadway overlooking South City Square Park. A statue of the legendary Alderman "Red" Villa added to the triangular park on Ivory in front of St. Boniface in 1990 marks the other open space within district boundaries.

Chapter 9 Carondelet

Clockwise from top left:

Schmitt House after move to South St. Louis Park
Landmarks, 2000

Schmitt House first floor plan
Pat Hays Baer

Schmitt House at original location
Landmarks, 1991

14
Anton Schmitt House
National Register: April 30, 1992
and January 27, 1999
7727 South Broadway

Schmitt, a laborer of Bavarian birth, began construction of this one-and-a-half-story duplex shortly after purchasing the property in 1859. By 1860, he and his family occupied one side; it appears that relatives lived in the other. Within three decades industrial encroachments at the original Alaska Avenue site stranded the house between railroad tracks and a large chemical plant. The Schmitts sold the house in the late 1880s. It continued to be used as a residence until purchase in 1990 by Monsanto, which by then owned all the surrounding land.

The house itself was of no interest to Monsanto, so the company agreed to donate it to the city. In 1992, Monsanto financed both the National Register listing (the nomination had to be revised after the building was relocated) and the complicated move to its present location in South St. Louis Square Park. The solid stone house survived the eight-block journey east with some non-critical structural damage; after landing, it sat boarded in the park for almost a decade. The Carondelet Historical Society plans to lease the house from the city and open it to the public as a German heritage museum.

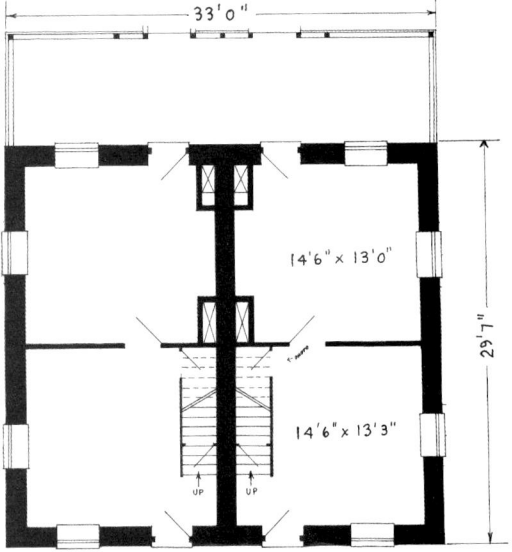

Steins Street Row Houses circa 1988
Ralph Wafer, 1989

15
Steins Street Row Houses
City Landmark: November 1974
National Register: March 27, 1980
200-04 Steins Street

By far the largest concentration of mid 19th century stone houses in the urban area can be found in Carondelet. Fine craftsmanship, clean lines and individual nuances add subtle variety to these vernacular houses built by Irish and German immigrants. This four-house row (the earliest extant building in the St. Boniface district) was built circa 1851 for Ignatz Uhrig, proprietor of the popular cave and brewery located at the southwest corner of Jefferson and Washington in the city of St. Louis. Subjected to abandonment and fire in the late 20th century, the row was rescued from sure demolition by a consortium of interested groups and public agencies.

16
Sisters of St. Joseph of Carondelet Convent
City Landmark: November 1974
National Register: February 28, 1980
6400 Minnesota Avenue

Perched at the crest of a hill overlooking the Mississippi River stands a two-block complex constructed in stages from 1841 into the 20th century for the Sisters of St. Joseph of Carondelet. The convent, built on the site of the first formal school in the town of Carondelet, is the motherhouse to hundreds of religious communities spread throughout all fifty states, Japan and Peru. The first six sisters came from Lyon, France to St. Louis in 1836 at the request of Bishop Rosati; two sisters trained to teach deaf-mutes arrived in 1837. In addition to their special mission to the deaf, the sisters also opened a school for the daughters of free blacks in 1845 and staffed parish schools in St. Louis and other parts of the Archdiocese. Many hospitals and orphanages were also in their charge. Through the sisters' efforts, Fontbonne College in St. Louis County was established in 1924 in order to provide higher education for young women and train teachers to help profoundly deaf children learn how to speak.

Sisters of St. Joseph of Carondelet Convent
Gary R. Tetley, 2002

Still very active in Carondelet community life, the convent provides day care facilities, leadership in community organizations and a strong voice for neighborhood stability. In 1998, a major rehabilitation project focused first on the Holy Family Chapel from 1897 by Aloysius Gillick (St. Louis) who had designed a chapel a year earlier adjoining the former **Clemens House** *(page 148)*. The current multi-year renovation under the direction of Trivers Associates is another testimony to the order's commitment to St. Louis.

Chapter 9 Carondelet

17
South Broadway Bluff Area
City Landmark: September 1971

The significance of this site located on commanding limestone bluffs above the tracks of the old narrow gauge Iron Mountain Railroad has been greatly reduced due to the demolition of several historic structures.

18
Store Buildings at 7121-29 South Broadway
City Landmark: November 1974

This prototypical mid 19th century vernacular brick row trimmed with stone and wrought iron balconies dates to 1879. Best known for the years associated with Southern Commercial and Savings Bank (1891-1904), it is currently intact though underused.

South Broadway Bluff circa 1970
Landmarks Collection

Store Buildings at 7121-29 South Broadway circa 1988
Landmarks Collection

CHAPTER 10 Southwest

Lambskin Temple
Gary R. Tetley, 2002

Chapter 10

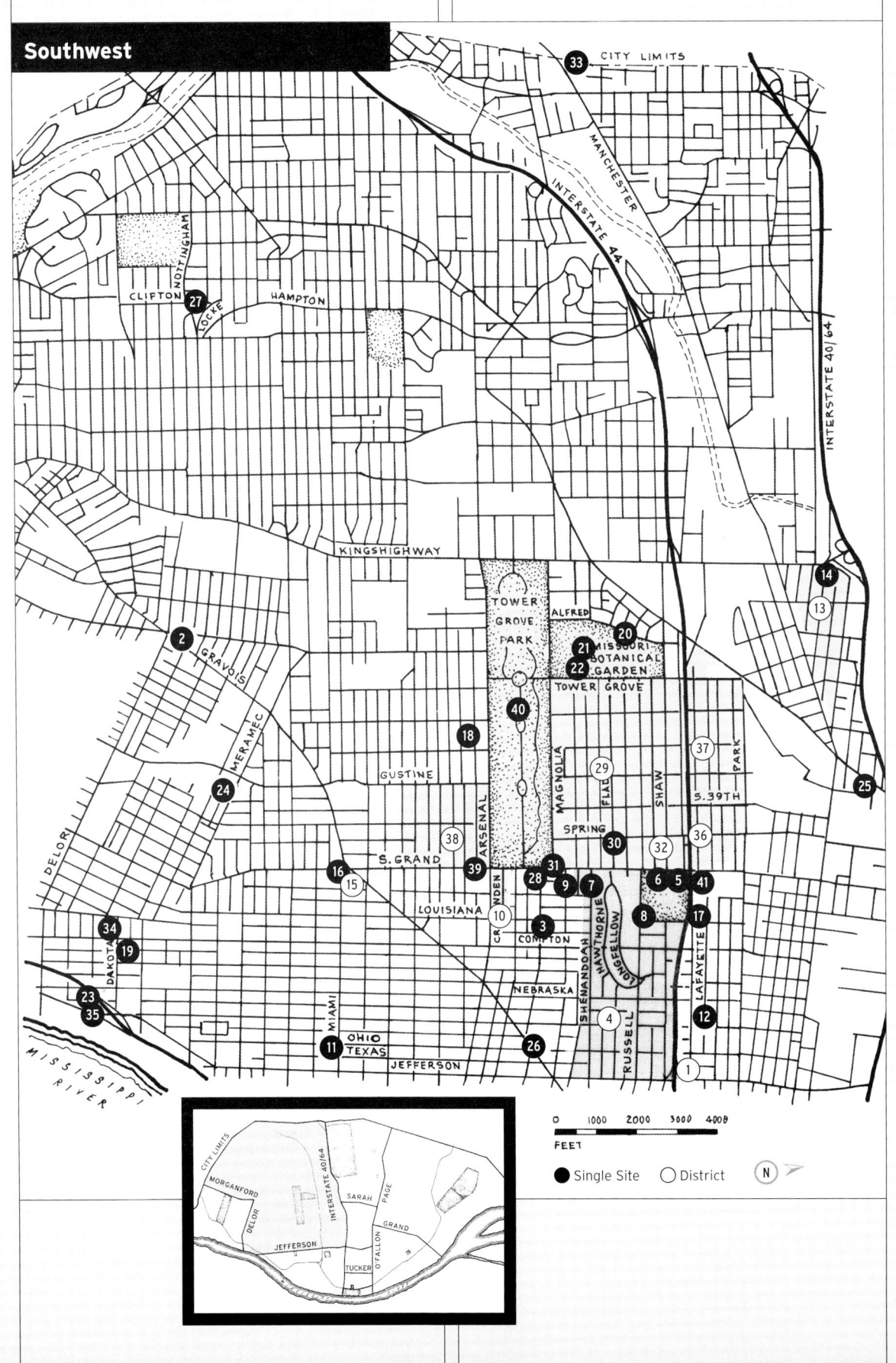

1. Barr Branch Library District
2. Bevo Mill
3. William Buehler House
4. Compton Heights/Fox Park District
5. Compton Hill Water Tower
6. "Naked Truth"
7. Pelican's Restaurant
8. Charles Stockstrom House
9. Strassberger Conservatory
10. Crittenden District
11. Holy Cross Lutheran Church
12. Immaculate Conception School
13. Forest Park Southeast District
14. Lambskin Temple
15. Grand and Gravois Commercial District
16. South Side National Bank
17. Loretto Academy
18. Mann School
19. Eugene and Mary Miltenberger House
20. Missouri Botanical Garden (Shaw's Garden)
21. Henry Shaw's Country House
22. Henry Shaw's Townhouse
23. Mount Pleasant School
24. Resurrection Catholic Church
25. Rock Spring School
26. St. Francis de Sales Parish Complex
27. St. Mark's Episcopal Church
28. Seventh District Police Station
29. Shaw Neighborhood District
30. B'nai El Temple
31. Memorial Home
32. Shaw Place District
33. Shining Light Tabernacle Church
34. Stork Inn
35. Sugarloaf Mound
36. Tiffany Neighborhood District
37. I-44 Neighborhood District
38. Tower Grove Heights District
39. Dickmann Building
40. Tower Grove Park
41. Wyman School

Detail: Dickmann Building

Gary R. Tetley, 2002

Chapter 10 Southwest

**"Barr's Block"
before renovation**
Landmarks, 1981

**Barr Branch
Library**
Esley Hamilton,
2001

1
Barr Branch Library District
National Register: September 2, 1982
Southwest corner of Jefferson and Lafayette and
2618-30 Lafayette Avenue

The *St. Louis Republican* in response to an editorial critical of high rents in St. Louis published an unsigned letter on September 28, 1875: *William Barr, Esq. is just completing a block of seven dwellings in one of the best neighborhoods about St. Louis, viz: one block west of Lafayette Park and thirty-minutes ride from the court house, and has instructed his agents to offer same at $700 per annum, equal to about $58 per month. When it is stated that these houses each occupy twenty-two front feet, have double-parlors, dining room and kitchen on first floor, four bedrooms, bath and washrooms on second floor, and two bedrooms in mansard roof, finished laundry in basement, marble mantels throughout the whole house, closets in every room... it must be conceded that even taking the extra cost of building into consideration cheaper houses are not offered even in Philadelphia.* The 1880 U.S. Census reveals that most of the early tenants in "Barr's Block" on Lafayette were partners or executives in commercial enterprises. All households had at least one servant. (In subsequent moves typical of his business acumen, Barr built a new commercial palace on a full city block downtown, now the site of Famous-Barr, and expanded his real estate holdings throughout the city.)

Mt. Calvary Episcopal Church located at the southwest corner of Lafayette and Jefferson just east of

216

"Barr's Block" was among the many south side churches heavily damaged by the 1896 tornado. When the ailing congregation could not meet its payment schedule, Barr repossessed the land and cleared the site. Less than a decade later, he would donate that parcel for a branch library to meet the challenge grant offered by Andrew Carnegie. The Renaissance Revival library designed by Theodore C. Link in 1905 was the culmination of nearly thirty years of effort by librarian Frederick Crunden to establish free and convenient access to books for all St. Louisans. At the cornerstone-laying ceremony for the first branch library in St. Louis, Barr and Carnegie were praised for their generosity. But the real hero of the day was librarian Crunden who "for long years... fought the good fight almost alone, against public apathy, official stupidity and lack of funds." Barr Branch underwent a major renovation in 1995. Sadly, the branch library (opened in 1909) named for Frederick Crunden now sits defaced and ignored on Cass Avenue.

2
Bevo Mill
City Landmark: April 1971
4749 Gravois Avenue

In the second decade of the 20th century, Anheuser-Busch constructed a series of south side restaurant/taverns designed to replace the popular perception (promoted by Prohibition supporters) of saloons as dens of vice with a wholesome, family-oriented image. The best known of these establishments are the three which laid on the old-world charm with medieval-inspired half timbering and picturesque silhouettes. **The Stork Inn** *(page 238)* designed in 1910 and the Feasting Fox (1913) at Meramec and South Grand were almost razed. Survival of "The Bevo" has never been in doubt. The original wooden windmill blades have been replaced by steel from Stupp Brothers; an outdoor garden, lit by birch-bark lanterns, has been paved over for a parking lot. But the Bevo, remodeled in 1986, remains a symbol of south St. Louis and everyone's favorite piece of fantasy architecture.

3
William Buehler House
National Register: December 28, 2000
2610 Tennessee Avenue

When Herman Lemm designed the house for cooper William Buehler in 1894, expectations were probably high for this neighborhood to develop as a southern extension of the newly opened **Compton Heights** *(next page)* subdivision located just over a block to the north. Lemm's distinctive design dominated by an ogee-roofed tower is comparable in quality to the series of houses on Compton, the next block west, developed by Severin Prag throughout the 1890s. But by the first decade of the new century, it had become clear that the neighborhood's high-end enclave would not expand to include Tennessee Avenue. As a result the Buehler house stands out among its more modest neighbors, a striking example of late 19th century revival style architecture.

Bevo Mill
Robert C. Pettus, 1988

Chapter 10   Southwest

Graced by four acres of landscaped grounds, the Compton Hill house was a retreat prescribed for James B. Eads by his doctors.
Missouri Historical Society

3533 to 3439 Longfellow circa 1898
Missouri Historical Society

4
Compton Heights/Fox Park District
City District: November 1978 and March 1985
Bounded roughly by Grand, I-44, Jefferson and Shenandoah Avenue

In a retrospective feature story in 1905, the *St. Louis Globe Democrat* commented that the "only thing higher in social scale then [post Civil War] than Lucas Place was Compton Hill." Captain James B. Eads, Governor Thomas C. Fletcher, Surveyor Julius Pitzman (who would lay out most of the city's private streets) and an assortment of prosperous capitalists had all moved their families to houses on or near Compton Hill by 1875. Many of them would become investors in the nearby Compton Heights subdivision opened for development in 1890.

Pitzman's ambitious site plan for Compton Heights was a hybrid with roots in the traditional residential squares and crescents of London and romantic landscape parks. St. Louis' first example of the latter was Bellefontaine Cemetery, laid out in intricate loops by Almerin Hotchkiss in 1849. *(See* **Wainwright Tomb**, *page 178.)* Creating Pitzman's curvilinear street pattern in the twelve-block grid vacated by the city put 600 men with 300 mule teams to work for months. By the time the first parcel was put on the market, over $300,000 in improvements had been invested in a tract costing $400,000 to assemble. Meanwhile, more modest town houses and rows in the Italianate/Second Empire tradition had been constructed closer to Jefferson in the eastern portion of the district near George C. Fox's multi-block planing and millwork company. Part of that firm's lumberyard is now the park that bears Fox's name.

The heavily German south side was shattered on May 27, 1896, when a deadly tornado skipped a path from the Liggett & Myers complex under construction on Park Avenue west of Grand (see **Tiffany District**, page 238) and dropped into Compton Heights before roaring through Soulard and Lafayette Square. Exploitation publications rushed into print with pictures of the damaged and destroyed. But by June of 1896, ground was broken for new buildings adjacent to district houses under repair.

The vast majority of the houses of architectural interest on Hawthorne and Longfellow were completed before 1930. Most of the architects, contractors and original residents were first or second generation German-Americans. German-born Ernst C. Janssen designed at least fourteen houses in the Heights; Otto J. Wilhelmi designed twelve. Although both Janssen and Wilhelmi received commissions in the larger historic district, the majority of the buildings in Fox Park were designed and built by

Clockwise from Top Left:

Tornado damage at 3153 Longfellow in 1896
Missouri Historical Society

3009 Hawthorne designed in 1894 by Otto J. Wilhelmi
Robert C. Pettus, 1984

Fox Brothers Manufacturing Company in 1902
Landmarks Collection

3522 Hawthorne designed in 1894 (architect unknown)
Robert C. Pettus, 1984

The resulting high cost of Compton Heights lots, massive auctions with plentiful property available at lower costs in nearby Tyler Place, complaints about the lack of water pressure on the south side during the summer months, aggressive competition from the newly opening private streets in the favored **Central West End** (page 99) plus a severe economic depression in 1893 resulted in only modest early building activity. Worried shareholders, including surveyor Pitzman and Adolphus Busch, bought some of the lots. But by 1894, confidence had been restored. More houses were built that year on Hawthorne and Longfellow Boulevards than in any other save 1905 and 1908.

Chapter 10

3263 Hawthorne designed in 1903 by Ernst Janssen
Robert C. Pettus, 1984

Left to Right:

2854-46 Accomac designed in 1895 by Ernst Janssen
Esley Hamilton, 1998

3249 Longfellow designed in 1908 by William H. Gruen
Robert C. Pettus, 1984

contractors such as John B. Westermayer, Louis G. Hormann and the Remmers brothers. The brothers designed and built the 1892 Bethlehem Methodist Episcopal Church at Jefferson and Accomac; architect/builder Frederick Bonsack (St. Louis) designed the Romanesque Revival stone church at Jefferson and Armand for Emmaus Lutheran in 1901. Rockwell M. Milligan designed the handsome public school at 3412 Shenandoah in 1925.

A small number of houses on Hawthorne and Longfellow were abandoned during the Depression. Rooming houses appeared on neighboring streets; attempts were made to open several in the Heights. Only a few houses were demolished within the Heights, but random demolitions on Grand and Russell began to erode the stability of the neighborhood. A Compton Heights neighborhood association,

formed at the beginning of the century to promote the area and to make sure that deed restrictions were enforced, became active. When it was revealed that **"Naked Truth"** (described at right) sat serenely in the planned path of an on-ramp to Interstate 44, the influence of Mrs. Edward G. Brungard (Director of Parks, Recreation and Forestry and a resident on Hawthorne) guaranteed that the once-controversial statue would be moved. In 1966, Frank T. Hilliker (preservationist, realtor and resident of the Heights) collaborated with resident artist Rodney Winfield on the design and production of new entrance markers placed on the old cast iron standards. From the low point in the early 1970s when $25,000 would buy just about any house to prices well over ten times that amount in 2002, the rise of property values in Compton Heights over the last thirty years parallels that experienced in the Central West End.

5
Compton Hill Water Tower
City Landmark: September 1966
National Register: September 29, 1972
Reservoir Park on South Grand
between Russell and I-44

Land for a Compton Hill reservoir to supply water to fledgling **Tower Grove Park** *(page 242)* was purchased in the 1860s during Mayor James S. Thomas' administration. Not surprisingly, Mayor Thomas (a resident of Compton Hill) was among the original Commissioners selected by park benefactor Henry Shaw to run Tower Grove Park. But the reservoir could not support the vast residential developments of the 1890s without a standpipe to control either surges in or lack of water pressure. Designed by the peripatetic Harvey Ellis for George R. Mann in 1898, this is the last of the three monumental St. Louis water towers. This asymmetrical brick and stone structure rising almost 180 feet is also the most romantic.

6
"Naked Truth"
City Landmark: June 1969
Reservoir Park on South Grand
between Russell and I-44

Adolphus Busch, who in 1893 bought the entrance wedge of land where Longfellow and Hawthorne meet east of Grand, was the biggest contributor ($20,000) to a fund to underwrite a memorial honoring three German-born St. Louis journalists: Emil Preetorius, Carl Schurz and Carl Daenzer. A jury was selected to evaluate the seven entries. Five contestants came from St. Louis, one from New York and one from the Fatherland—Prof. Wilhelm Wandschneider of Berlin. In May of 1913, the jury selected the entry by Wandschneider and cabled him to come to St. Louis. Prof. and Frau Wandschneider set sail for New York. But the memorial committee headed by Busch, appalled at the selection, declared that the jury had overstepped its bounds.

Left to Right:

Compton Hill Water Tower
Robert C. Pettus, 1984

"Naked Truth"
Robert C. Pettus, 1984

Charles Stockstrom House

Robert C. Pettus, 1984

Greeted by news of the dissension when they arrived in New York, the Wandschneiders nonetheless boarded the train for St. Louis. One of the loudest of the losing sculptors charged jury member William K. Bixby with undue influence as a member of the Washington University "art clique." The press was off and running, frolicking in the most splendid local art romp ever. Worries that the winner could sue for damages were reported daily along with charges and countercharges. Wandschneider refused to consider adding drapery to the unadorned female figure; the opposition contended that he had plagiarized the design from a pornographic European cartoon. Both Wandschneiders spoke excellent English: "Why, we were given to understand that you have a very excellent art gallery here.... Can it be that all the subjects in your great gallery are draped?" Besieged, the memorial committee narrowly voted fourteen to twelve to honor the original selection if the figure's nudity were de-emphasized by the choice of a material other than white marble. Executed in bronze, the work was moved to its present location from the path of Interstate 44 in the 1960s.

7
Pelican's Restaurant
City Landmark: October 1976
2256 South Grand Avenue

This turreted corner restaurant was built in 1895 for beer baron Anton Griesedieck. German-born Carl Anschuetz was hired away after fourteen years at the legendary Tony Faust's in downtown to run a "first-class restaurant and liquortorium" complete with elegant terrace and garden dining. Known later for owners James and Catherine Pelican, who ran the restaurant from 1945 to 1978, the once-popular establishment was recycled as offices in 1986 from plans by Rich Friedewald, St. Louis.

8
Charles Stockstrom House
City Landmark: April 1971
3400 Russell Boulevard

German-born Ernst C. Janssen designed the most lavish mansion on the south side for the Charles A. Stockstrom family in 1907. Inside a resplendent French Renaissance Revival exterior executed in buff brick with lavish hemp-colored terra cotta ornament, the first floor plan featured a delicate, airy French-style drawing and music room on one side of the formidably sized, twenty-five foot square reception area. On the other side, in sharp contrast, Janssen produced a robustly German oak-paneled library and dining room. Moving past the smaller dining area and large butler's pantry into the kitchen, one encountered the cooking stove that made this thirty-room $49,500 house possible. Charles Stockstrom was co-owner of the Quick Meal (later Magic Chef) Stove Company.

The house and two-acre grounds boasting a Janssen-designed carriage house from 1908 (which cost an additional $5,800) remained in the family until 1990. Fabulous chandeliers, carved-bear coat trees and original furniture had already been auctioned off when Glynn and Shelley Donaho threw caution to the wind and bought the house. The intrepid couple performed most of the exquisite restoration by themselves, tracked down and bought back many fine furnishings (paying a pretty penny) while raising a toddler during their ten-plus years of work at the house.

9
Strassberger Conservatory
City Landmark: August 1976
National Register: March 27, 1980
2300 South Grand Avenue

Designed in 1904 by St. Louis architect Otto J. Wilhelmi, the conservatory offered lessons in music, deportment and dancing to the large south side German-American population to whom these talents were essential. Although not yet accepted by the snootiest of St. Louis society no matter what their financial circumstances, it appears that the turn-of-the-century Germans might have been having more fun. *The Spectator,* commenting on a masquerade ball at the Liederkranz Club, marveled at the energetic participation by all generations and opined: "A German matron has something to look forward to as long as she lives, while with Americans, as a rule, marriage winds up all interest for them with the world. If they go out at all they are neglected for the maidens... and as for their joining in the dance, that is almost an unheard of possibility." The red brick conservatory adorned with terra cotta busts of famous composers set in arches above third-story windows was recycled to apartments with some first-floor commercial space in 1984 from plans by John Lark & Associates (St. Louis).

10
Crittenden District
National Register: July 7, 1983

The small Crittenden district presents a cohesive streetscape of early 20th century middle-class houses and flats mostly designed and built by second-generation or German-born architects and contractors for their compatriots. From South Grand the block-and-a-half view east is closed by the High Victorian St. Elizabeth Academy—a private high school for girls established by the German-speaking Precious Blood Sisters in 1882. The 1927 gymnasium at the Academy features one of the first Midwest applications of the lamella roof, a system of interlocking transverse arches spanning large spaces without intermediate vertical supports perfected by Gustel Kiewitt. (The Arena, a much larger St. Louis project from 1929 designed and engineered by Kiewitt, was imploded in 1999.)

11
Holy Cross Lutheran Church
City Landmark: April 1971
2650 Miami Street

Five ships left the port of Bremen in northern Germany during the winter of 1838 with 668 men, women and children aboard. Their destination was Perry County, Missouri where they hoped to establish a Lutheran colony free from the religious persecution they had experienced in their native state of Saxony.

One ship was lost at sea; the other four landed safely in New Orleans for the journey up the Mississippi River. The first group arrived in St. Louis in 1839. Some left immediately to establish a colony in Perry County; those who remained in the city established **Trinity Lutheran Church** *(page 198)* in 1842 and Concordia Seminary in 1849. (Concordia continues, now from a location in St. Louis County, to train Missouri Synod ministers for pulpits throughout the country.)

Holy Cross Church located in what would become a neighborhood stronghold of Missouri Synod Lutheranism: Concordia Seminary, Lutheran Hospital and Concordia Publishing House. Organized in 1850 as a school to serve members living southwest of the mother church in Soulard, the congregation selected an out-of-town architectural firm recommended by the pastor at Trinity (Reverend C. F. W. Walther). Budget constraints required a two-phase construction of the

Left to Right:

***Crittenden District:
St. Elizabeth Academy***
Robert C. Pettus, 1988

Holy Cross Lutheran Church
Landmarks, 1990

Chapter 10   Southwest

Detail: Holy Cross Lutheran
Landmarks, 1990

Detail: Former Tower Grove Methodist Episcopal Church, Taylor at Gibson
Landmarks, 2002

red brick Gothic Revival building starting in 1867. The addition of transepts, balconies and chancel in 1889 essentially completed *Die Kirche zum Heiligen Kreuz* as designed by Griese & Weile (Cleveland). After the 1896 tornado destroyed the lofty 160-foot steeple, the congregation replaced it with one less elegant. Transept windows were enlarged to accommodate stained glass in 1908.

12
Immaculate Conception School
National Register: May 8, 1985
2912 Lafayette Avenue

The 1908 dedication sermon for the new church of the Immaculate Conception at Lafayette and Longfellow offered Archbishop Glennon a unique opportunity to express his conservative views on contemporary society. Attributing the "decadence of [early 20th century] standards to women's mad rush to satiate ambition and to indulge in vanities of the world," Glennon conferred a new name on St. Kevin's—an Irish parish christened in 1854 in honor of Dublin's patron saint. This change was very much in keeping with the just-celebrated 50th anniversary of Pope Pius IX's official proclamation of the Immaculate Conception dogma.

An Irish outpost in a German-American part of town, Immaculate Conception still sent its children to St. Kevin's old school at Park and Cardinal until the grandson of John Mullanphy (early Irish immigrant and philanthropist) donated land for a new building in 1924. The Archdiocese quickly selected Henry P. Hess for the commission. St. Louis-born Hess had worked for nearly all the prominent local firms including Isaac Taylor and Eames & Young before joining the staff of School Board architect William B. Ittner. When Ittner resigned in 1915, Hess left too. His first independent commission for a Catholic school at St. Rose's on Goodfellow Boulevard established him as a favorite of Cardinal Glennon. For Immaculate Conception Hess produced a Jacobethan Revival red brick school very much in the Ittner tradition.

Immaculate Conception School staffed by Sisters of Loretto served students from kindergarten to 8th grade for many years. But by the 1950s, parish enrollment began to change in ethnicity and numbers. Clearance of a great swath of land to construct Interstate 44 severed the neighborhood along Lafayette from easy access to **Compton Heights** *(page 218)*. In 1969, the Archdiocese took over the school, named it (ironically) Compton Heights and consolidated it with the remaining students from St. Henry, Holy Guardian Angels, **St. John Nepomuk, SS. Peter & Paul** and **St. Vincent De Paul** *(see Index)*. Total enrollment from all those parishes came to fewer than 100 students. The school closed ten years later after Immaculate Conception parish was merged with St. Henry at California and Rutger.

13
Forest Park Southeast District
National Register: December 20, 2001
Bounded roughly by Chouteau, Manchester, Cadet, Kingshighway and Sarah Avenue

Except for the upper-class private streets, most subdivisions west of Grand were dependent upon the opening of new streetcar lines for development to take place. Gibson Heights had to wait until the 1890s for the Chouteau horsecar line to be electrified. Residential buildings in the neighborhood (known for years as Ranken) built between 1890 and the 1920s reflect the

224

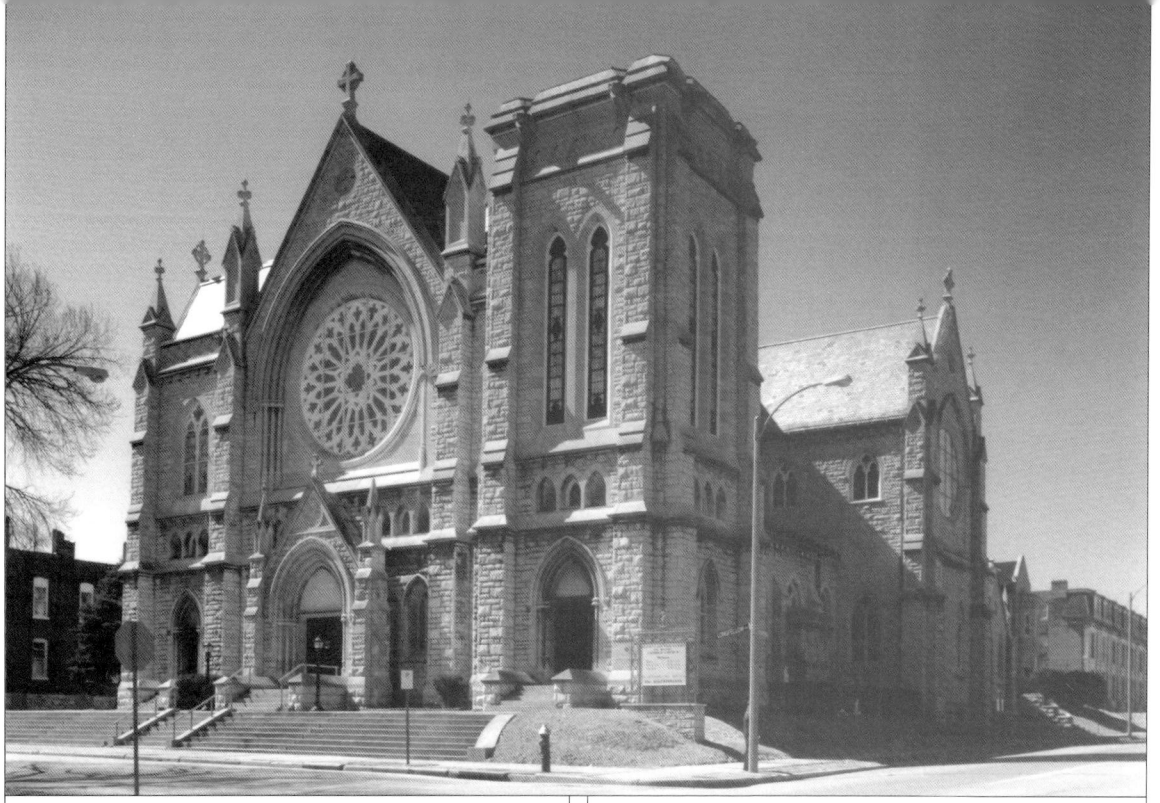

Immaculate Conception Church
Landmarks, 1995

variety of building types and styles common throughout St. Louis' working and middle class neighborhoods. The larger single-family homes are concentrated in the blocks just east of Kingshighway. Developers were responsible for the vast majority of the buildings east of Taylor.

Similar materials and setbacks unify residential architecture; more variety can be found in the churches constructed for various denominations. The pioneer was Tower Grove Methodist Episcopal (1903: James Hal Lynch, architect) followed by St. Paul's English Evangelical Lutheran (1906: Albert B. Groves, architect), Gibson Heights United Presbyterian Church (1910: William Cann, architect) and St. Peter's Lutheran (1925: Theodore Steinmeyer, architect). Also located within district boundaries is one of the city's most distinctive Masonic structures, the **Lambskin Temple**.

14
Lambskin Temple (Temple Apartments)
National Register: August 12, 1987
1052-56 South Kingshighway

The first Masonic lodges in America boasted most of the prominent Revolutionary heroes including George Washington. Seven of the first eleven Governors of Missouri were Masons. Accepting free males from all segments of society and every religion, the Masons espoused the application of moral and religious concepts to everyday life. Atheists were denied membership, should any apply. In May 1872, twelve St. Louis members met to organize a lodge on the south side. The Grand Lodge of Missouri granted the request and Lambskin Lodge #460 was chartered that same year with a membership of 115. By 1913, that number had grown to almost 800 and a building fund was initiated to construct a new lodge.

World War I postponed any action. The site on Kingshighway was not acquired until 1921; by early 1927, sufficient funds had been collected to form a building committee and pick an architect. The choice was Edward F. Nolte, a St. Louis Mason who had just finished his work as consulting architect for the great Masonic Temple on Lindell. With a portfolio of widely divergent but always sure-handed designs, Nolte departed dramatically from the Classical Revival Masonic traditions for Lambskin Temple. Polychromatic, geometric and hard-edged, the Art Deco box was sited high on its

Detail: Gibson Heights Presbyterian Church, Taylor at Arco
Landmarks, 2002

***South Side
National Bank***

Landmarks, 1974

foundation overlooking Forest Park. Local newspapers dubbed it the "Oriental Temple." Top politicians and businessmen came in and out of the doors including former Mayor Henry W. Kiel. But after almost sixty years, the Temple was sold. Dwindling membership, a deteriorating neighborhood and relative isolation occasioned by construction of Highway 40 (I-64) sent members to space rented from another Lodge. In 1988, the Temple reopened as sixteen unique apartments designed by Patricia E. Lloyd.

15
Grand and Gravois Commercial District
City District: December 2001

The four-building group on the southern side of Gravois is a small section of the larger commercial district that grew up around the important intersection. Although businesses (including a saloon, grocery, and blacksmith) were located here by the 1860s, the oldest of the extant buildings was constructed in 1908 at the northeast corner of Grand and Miami. In 1913, the Farmers & Merchants Trust, previously located in rented space on the north side of the intersection, built on the southeast corner. A few years later, the 1,600 seat Melba Theater was constructed on the next block south. The Grandview Arcade Building was erected on Grand in 1925; its Gothic arcade served as a lobby for the theater. (The building works well on its own even after the theater's demolition.) Across Grand, **South Side National Bank** holds down the other southern corner of the intersection.

Grand and Gravois became the city's first new local district in over a decade after local citizens became alarmed at Walgreens' interest in the intersection. A citizen's group sprang to action, backed by Aldermen Marge Vining and Craig Schmid, when a plan was announced to raze South Side National Bank. Walgreens withdrew from the plan after the bank was declared eligible for listing in the National Register; local district designation soon followed to promote development more in keeping with the historic character of the buildings.

***Detail: South Side
National Bank***

Ken Konchel, 1999

16
South Side National Bank
National Register: determined eligible
3606 Gravois Avenue

Designed by the St. Louis Bank Building & Equipment Company (later a national leader in bank construction), South Side National Bank was erected in 1928 after shareholders of the South Side Trust Company and the Farmers & Merchants Trust Company voted to merge. The largest and perhaps the most

significant of the city's neighborhood banks, the ten-story limestone building features fine Art Deco detailing both inside and out. Still remarkably intact is the stunning two-story banking hall complete with coffered ceiling, original teller booths and historic light fixtures suspended from ornamental pendants.

South Side National Bank occupied the facility from the time it was constructed until a 2001 merger with Allegiant Bank. The owners had opposed National Register listing when South Side National Bank planned to demolish the building,

but the new management has shown willingness to work with the community to determine the best use for the building. Neighborhood leaders anticipate that the building will finally be listed in 2002 in order to qualify it for historic tax credits.

17
Loretto Academy (Pillar Place)
National Register: March 5, 1992
3407 Lafayette Avenue

At the beginning of the 20th century, the Sisters of Loretto's school was just one of many religious institutions which cleared out of the "Piety Hill" neighborhood when urban encroachments filtered into the once-fashionable subdivision west of Jefferson Avenue. The Sisters, unlike many houses of worship relocating to the Central West End, chose a location on the south side facing Compton Hill Park. Barnett, Haynes & Barnett produced a design for the new school combining classical and Tudor elements. Far from being an exercise in fanciful eclecticism, however, the 1909 façade is closely based on a 16th-century country house outside London, which was classicized in the 18th century by Robert Adam. Loretto Academy closed in 1952, but the order continued to use the building until 1988. After several years of vacancy, it reopened in 1993 as Pillar Place. Jeffrey Brambila served as architect for the rehabilitation, combining nineteen affordable apartments with support services for low-income families.

18
Horace Mann School
National Register: September 2, 1992
4047 Juniata Street

Horace Mann School (1901) is one in a series of William B. Ittner's early elementary schools illustrating his refinements to the "open plan," the design he pioneered in the United States. (See **Carr School** page 54 for background.) The long spine of the building has two single-room wings on each side: to the south, the kindergarten and a stair tower; to the north, two classroom wings. The division of interior spaces clearly articulated on the exterior is enhanced by a set of minimalistic (for Ittner) Tudor elements.

19
Eugene and Mary Miltenberger House
National Register: May 9, 2002
3218 Osceola Street

Long before the independent town of Carondelet was annexed by St. Louis in 1870, remnants of the old common fields between the two settlements were parceled off to farmers and homebuilders. With a construction date of approximately 1854 or 1855, this is one of the few extant antebellum houses on the south side to predate the established street grid. The slender two-story house,

Eugene and Mary Miltenberger House
Landmarks Collection, 2000

evocative of the Creole buildings already disappearing at the time of its construction, has a full gallery facing east to the Mississippi and a blank brick wall to the west.

Although no documentation relating to the construction of the house has been found, it appears that it was built for Eugene and Mary Miltenberger. Once known as the richest man in Carondelet, Miltenberger profited from a wide-ranging career as an attorney, banker, wholesaler of liquor, railroad entrepreneur, insurance man and real estate investor. In 1999, real estate investor Bob Wood discovered that a century and a half had brought dropped ceilings, aluminum windows, exposed ductwork and other indignities upon the humbled residence. After a sensitive rehabilitation, Wood added the house to his portfolio of rental properties.

Milles sculpture and former Flora Avenue entrance
Robert C. Pettus, 1988

Watercolor portrait of Henry Shaw painted by Emil Hertzinger circa 1862
Missouri Botanical Garden

Linnean House built in 1882
Jack Jennings, Missouri Botanical Garden

20
Missouri Botanical Garden (Shaw's Garden)
National Register: November 19, 1971
Entrance at 4344 Shaw Boulevard

Blessed with extensive European travel, a wide circle of professional botanist friends, a vast personal library on landscape architecture and a singleness of purpose supported by sufficient retirement income, English-born Henry Shaw set out to create an English nobleman's country estate in the 1850s Midwest prairie. An 1858 Act of the State Legislature established the vehicle for Shaw to convey his land (then

outside the city limits) to a Board of Trustees after his death. The next year the fledgling garden opened to the public at no charge. Shaw's favorite architect, George I. Barnett, designed the Museum and Library Building that same year.

Next, Shaw set about providing an endowment for his estate with the construction of **Shaw Place** (page 236). In 1882, Barnett completed plans for the Linnaean House, a brick and glass greenhouse modeled after the Orangerie at Kew Gardens. Barnett also designed Shaw's exquisite mausoleum with the sarcophagus surmounted by a marble likeness of Shaw sculpted by Ferdinand von Miller of Munich. In 1885, four years before his death, Shaw deeded real estate holdings to endow a School of Botany at Washington University and establish a joint professorship and director of the

Garden stipend named for his friend and advisor, Dr. George Engelmann. The Garden was also the recipient of the bulk of Shaw's $3 million estate. St. Louis had been a frontier town of only 4,500 when Shaw arrived in 1819; at his death in 1889, the city numbered over 450,000.

The Garden underwent major changes in 1904 and 1917 when new landscaping plans commissioned by the Board of Trustees called for a redirection in its physical orientation, the relocation of several gardens and the construction of more buildings including a new gatehouse at Flora Avenue in 1921. In 1960, Murphy & Mackey's firm realized a talisman structure derived from the inventive mind of R. Buckminster Fuller: the Climatron—the world's first geodesic dome to be enclosed in rigid Plexiglas panels and the world's first air-conditioned greenhouse. Fanciful sculptures by Carl Milles were added to the reflecting pool approach to the Climatron in 1988. Other recent buildings include the John S. Lehmann Building by Hellmuth, Obata & Kassabaum (St. Louis) from 1973 and the same firm's barrel-vaulted Ridgeway Education and Visitor's Center designed in 1981.

Today, the Missouri Botanical Garden is internationally acclaimed for its beauty and far-ranging research programs under the guidance of Dr. Peter Raven, director since 1971. The lovely Seiwa-En Japanese Garden carved from a marsh in 1977 according to plans by Loichi Kawana (Japan) with Karl Pettit of Mackey & Associates (St. Louis) is a special paradise within the Garden. To its north are extensive grounds developed in the 1990s to demonstrate the many approaches to home gardening. This sprawling section, anchored by a homelike building with small library and meeting space designed by Lou Sauer (St. Louis), is every bit as formal in plan as the more recent labyrinth near Tower Grove House complete with a Victorian-inspired, three-tiered viewing stand.

21
Henry Shaw's Country House
City Landmark: September 1966
Missouri Botanical Garden

Designed and built by George I. Barnett and Charles H. Peck for Henry Shaw in 1849, "Tower Grove House" was named for a stand of native sassafras in the nearly treeless tract of almost 2,000 acres Shaw acquired before 1850. The earliest building in the Botanical Garden, the Italianate villa is a museum house open to visitors.

Shaw's bedroom circa 1965
Landmarks Collection

22
Henry Shaw's Townhouse
City Landmark: May 1969
Missouri Botanical Garden

Henry Shaw's will stipulated that his 1851 George I. Barnett-designed house at the southwest corner of 7th and Locust be dismantled and reconstructed at his country estate. Following those instructions in 1892 cost the Garden's Board of Trustees $33,500. Mauran, Russell & Garden (St. Louis) enlarged the relocated Renaissance Revival townhouse with an addition to the south in 1908.

Left to Right:

Henry Shaw's County House
Jack Jennings, Missouri Botanical Garden

Henry Shaw's Townhouse
Tony Carosella, 2001

23
Mount Pleasant School
National Register: May 2, 1985
4528 Nebraska Avenue

In 1893, after a frustrating four-year experiment hiring different architects for each school, the Board of Education voted to return to a three-year position of staff architect. The salary was set at $5,000. (The Superintendent received only $4,500.) From a number of eager practitioners, the Board selected August H. Kirchner—brother and partner of H. William Kirchner who had held the position in 1881, 1882 and 1886-89. The geography assigned Mount Pleasant was carved out of a larger crowded district in 1895. Seeing no immediate need for a full-size building, Kirchner produced the prototypical four-room expandable grammar school mandated by Board tradition. As such, it was prepared to accept additions of 1913 (William B. Ittner) and 1928 (Rockwell M. Milligan). All of Kirchner's schools conformed to the basic box massing typical throughout the country before the revolutionary concepts introduced by William B. Ittner in the beginning of the 20th century took hold. Mount Pleasant closed in 1980 and was converted to apartments in 1986 by Mark Dotzler, Jr. from plans by Theodore Jockenhoefer, St. Louis.

24
Resurrection Catholic Church
City Landmark: November 1974
3900 Meramec Street

Instructions from the parish called for an open, welcoming church that could comfortably seat 750. In response, the firm of Murphy & Mackey produced a contemporary building of great importance in mid 20th century St. Louis. With an innovative parabolic plan (a mathematical challenge at that juncture) and avant-garde liturgical art, the church is lightly linked to a small openwork stone baptistry reflected in the central glass curtain wall. The stained glass frieze at the sanctuary roofline by Robert Frei, the altar mural by Robert Harmon, sculpture by Hillis Arnold and Stations of the Cross by William Schickel combine to make this 1954 building an exemplar of Modern design.

Resurrection Catholic Church circa 1955

Hedrich Blessing (Chicago)

25
Rock Spring School (Providence Educational Center)
National Register: September 2, 1991
3974 Sarpy Avenue

This relatively small-budget school was built for $40,000 in 1898. It is one of only two St. Louis schools that William B. Ittner designed on a cruciform plan, an experimental effort to break the boxy plan of earlier schools. Good lighting and ventilation are effected with windows on three walls of each classroom, but the interior corridors must have been rather dark in an age before reliable electricity. Low shed dormers, overhanging eaves and exposed rafter tails all reflect the emerging Craftsman aesthetic, while diapered brick work at the top story is the first example of a motif that Ittner would later use in numerous school buildings as well as in the **Missouri Athletic Club** (page 31).

26
St. Francis de Sales Parish Complex
City Landmark: April 1971
National Register: November 2, 1978
2653 Ohio Street

St. Francis de Sales is Gulliver in the Land of the Lilliputians. Sited on a knoll above its small-scale neighborhood, the "Cathedral of the South Side" with towering steeple of 300 feet is a point of reference for much of the city. The parish was organized in 1867 by an offshoot of twenty-eight parishioners from **SS. Peter and Paul** (page 200) in Soulard. In 1894, land at the corner of Iowa and Lynch Streets was acquired and Father Peter Lotz (pastor from 1878-1903) traveled to Berlin to consult with architect Engelbert Seibertz for a new church expected to cost about $135,000. He returned with a project estimated at well over $500,000. In spite of opposition to such an expense, construction began with a cornerstone laying on August 11, 1895. But funds were quickly exhausted and a roof was erected to protect the unfinished basement. Within months the May 1896 tornado destroyed the congregation's original church, leaving worshippers only the new basement for services.

The desire to erect an ethnic symbol drafted in Germany by a German architect modeled after medieval German prototypes is highly significant in a decade that produced the Wainwright Building, a system of boulevards, Union Station, the first automobiles on city streets and the consolidation of most of the competitive transit lines into one citywide company. To the conservative part of the German-American community, the home and parish remained the center of their lives. To some, technology and assimilation were perceived as threats to the faith and the future of their children. To the priest, it was an opportunity to erect "the largest and most beautiful church in St. Louis."

Resurrection Catholic Church and Baptistry
Robert C. Pettus, 1989

St. Francis de Sales Church
Robert C. Pettus, 1995

St. Mark's windows, circa 1940
Mercantile Library

With Father Lotz's death in 1903 came acceptance that the building as designed could not be realized. In 1908, an imposing Gothic Revival church based on the German design but modified by Klutho & Ranft (St. Louis) was completed. Included were stained-glass windows portraying subjects associated with German history: St. Henry, St. Henry II, German emperors, St. Boniface (missionary to Germany) and St. Irmingarde, the granddaughter of Charlemagne. St. Francis de Sales, no longer predominately a German parish, became a leader in community-based neighborhood revitalization efforts during the 1980s. More recently the church has attracted parishioners from one of the newest immigrant groups in St. Louis. In 2001, about 600 people attended the Spanish Mass held each Sunday at noon, prompting this comment from the current pastor: "We were an immigrant parish in the beginning, are now and will be forever."

27
St. Mark's Episcopal Church
City Landmark: September 1973
4712 Clifton Avenue

An austere masterpiece designed by the new partnership of Charles Nagel and Frederick Dunn (St. Louis), St. Mark's was the result of a $75,000 bequest to the Episcopal Diocese of Missouri.

St. Mark's Episcopal Church
Robert C. Pettus, 1988

That small sum covered the land in St. Louis Hills purchased in 1932, architectural fees and all construction costs including interior furnishings and artwork. Dedicated in early 1939 as the city's first contemporary church, the tall, narrow brick building is entered below the single oculus window through a simple doorway accented by an outsize limestone figure of St. Mark by Sheila Burlingame—a St. Louis pupil of renowned sculptor Carl Milles. Other local artistry can be found in the openwork steel lectern and pulpit by Clark Battle Fitzgerald, hand-woven tapestry by Beatrice Root, a crucifix by Sheila Burlingame, hanging metal lamps by architects Nagel and Dunn and the striking figural windows in contemporary stained glass designed by Robert Harmon and executed by Emil Frei Studios. Iconography ranges from a pictorial pun of the architects' names to a cheerful panel illustrating the lessons of men working together in cooperation. At variance are panels depicting the self-destructive lust for money and power with ominous symbolism foreshadowing WWII.

28
Seventh District Police Station (WVP Corporate Headquarters)
National Register: March 22, 1984
2810 South Grand Boulevard

In 1899, through the persistent efforts of Harry B. Hawes, President of the St. Louis Board of Police Commissioners, the State Legislature passed a bill amending the 1861 Act establishing the St. Louis Metropolitan Police Department. Among the significant features of the new statute were provisions for expedient approval of Police Department budgets, a sizable increase of 300 patrolmen and the redistricting of the city from nine to twelve districts, each equipped with a station house. This made possible the creation of a new 7th District with east-west boundaries reaching from Compton to Kingshighway, providing the first police protection west of Grand Avenue on the south side of the city.

A building permit issued in November 1900 for a red brick station (including a gymnasium on the third floor, an innovative feature) and attached stable were the first fruits of the 1899 statute. With its corner location, fortress-like treatment of the attic story recalling 19th-century armory design and fine terra cotta horse's head over the stable, the new station was a proud addition to the rapidly growing neighborhood. The building continued to serve the area until 1960 when the city was redistricted. The next occupant was the National Association of Letter Carriers, a union representing more than 2,000 mailmen in the St. Louis area. In 1985, the property was recycled to office use by WVP Corporation.

29
Shaw Neighborhood District
City District: March 4, 1985

Evidence of Henry Shaw's plan to create a controlled residential area around his country estate first appeared in 1857 when he and Mary L. Tyler, adjacent owners of land extending from Grand to Tower Grove Avenues, agreed by deed "to promote the general salubrity" of their property by opening Shaw, Flora and Tower Grove Avenues. By 1875, all three roadways had been embellished with rows of good-sized trees but only a few houses (see **Memorial Home**, page 236) had been built on South Grand. The rest of the land remained open prairie. Following the completion of **Shaw Place** (page 236) in 1883, more houses were

Seventh District Police Station in 1907
Landmarks Collection

Left to Right:

Detail: Seventh District Police Station
Landmarks Collection, 1983

Gate to Flora Place
Esley Hamilton, 2001

Magnolia Place
Landmarks, 1984

Left to Right:

Hortus Court
Landmarks, 1984

4100 block of Shaw Avenue
Landmarks, 1984

built on Grand (including the still-standing Warner House at 1905 South Grand of 1888 by Theodore C. Link) but extensive development did not occur until the 1890 auction of lots in Tyler Place.

A large subdivision encompassing most of the district south of Shaw Avenue between Tower Grove and Grand Avenues with the exception of a 350-foot strip fronting on Magnolia, Tyler Place imposed deed restrictions establishing a uniform building line and limiting construction to two-story brick buildings. Flora Avenue became Flora Place in 1897, when owners of the south side of the street and the Board of Trustees of Shaw's Garden (title holders to the north side) entered into an optimistic agreement to improve it as a private street in a manner "similar to Vandeventer Place."

Deed restrictions combined with unusually rapid development created a residential architecture of great consistency within most of the Shaw district. About 400 buildings were constructed in the last decade of the 19th century with another 1000 built between 1900 and 1912. Magnolia Place, planned by architect/developer Robert G. Kirsch, opened in 1913 as St. Louis' first subdivision exclusively devoted to the newest rage, the Bungalow. Equally winsome is Kirsch's Hortus Court of 1921 where ten miniature houses with gambrel roofs are approached through a pergola into a central courtyard. A number of low-rise apartment buildings were also constructed in the 1920s as were the district's only high-rise structures—the Saum Hotel (now apartments) at 1919 South Grand and the Hutcheson Arms at 2107 South Grand.

Notable religious buildings in Shaw include the Gothic Revival Tyler Place United Presbyterian Church (designed by Frederick C. Bonsack in 1900) at 3800 Russell; St. Margaret of Scotland Catholic Church (a larger Gothic Revival stone church designed in 1905 by Barnett, Haynes & Barnett) at Spring and Russell; a 1905 synagogue (**B'nai El Temple**) and an overlooked early Modern gem, the 1931 Mount Olive Lutheran Church at 4242 Shaw by Theodore Steinmeyer (St. Louis). Across the street from Mount Olive is the 1914 Bryan Mullanphy grade school with fine brickwork and Tudor Revival detail—the last of almost fifty exceptional buildings designed for the School Board by William B. Ittner (St. Louis).

Until construction of Interstate 44 at its northern boundary, the Shaw neighborhood was a stable mixed-income community. The Shaw Neighborhood Improvement Association was formed in 1958 to counter potential decline and "seek family participation" in reporting housing code violations. A rise in the number of absentee landlords who did not screen tenants or maintain property prompted neighborhood-based redevelopment efforts in the 1980s that included a baffling pattern of street closings. Status as a historic district has brought attention from developers who have acquired and rehabbed a substantial number of the multi-family buildings. Strong leadership evidenced by several of the churches and by the neighborhood association has kept old residents and attracted new ones. But sections of the neighborhood continue to be challenging.

30
B'nai El Temple (Temple Apartments)
National Register: July 21, 1983
3666 Flad Avenue

In 1855, B'nai El (created by a merger of Emanu-El and B'nai B'rith) built the first synagogue in the Mississippi Valley. Located at 6th and Cerre Streets, the octagonal "coffee mill" was a favored subject of local engravers. In 1875, the congregation sold the synagogue to the Episcopalians for use as the Good Samaritan Church for blacks and purchased a Presbyterian church building at 11th and Chouteau. By 1889, approximately 15,000 refugees from the Russian pogroms had settled in St. Louis. Their Orthodox customs and resistance to assimilation provoked an outbreak of overt anti-Semitism.

While all the Reform congregations (B'nai El, United Hebrew, Shaare Emeth and the new and most affluent **Temple Israel** *(pages 81 and 107)* were concerned with the mutual problems of anti-Semitism and the need to help the often ill-educated newcomers, B'nai El with 150 families and 130 children enrolled in religious school was located the farthest east in a changing neighborhood. Many members had already moved west of Grand. In 1904, the rest of the congregation and Rabbi Moritz Spitz (influential editor of *The Jewish Voice*) followed.

The cornerstone for the new Byzantine-Romanesque Revival red brick temple designed by St. Louis architect John Ludwig Wees was laid May 1905. But the congregation would remain at that location for a relatively short time following the death of its long-term rabbi in 1920. Members drifting off to join West End synagogues prompted a decision in 1930 to move the congregation into a church at Delmar and Clara. For the next fifteen years, Compton Heights Christian Church rented the temple on Flad. In 1944, B'nai El sold it to St. Margaret's of Scotland Catholic Church for a short-lived parish school; next, it endured twenty-five years as gym and recreation

B'nai El Temple: Temple Apartments
Barbara E. Martin, 1984

Mount Olive Lutheran Church at 4246 Shaw Boulevard designed in 1931 by Theodore Steinmeyer (St. Louis)
Robert C. Pettus, 1995

235

Chapter 10　　Southwest

Memorial Home circa 1900
Missouri Historical Society

B'nai El Temple: Temple Apartments
Barbara E. Martin, 1984

center for the parish. The Board of Education acquired the property in 1969 for a short-lived Sherman Branch School; developer Mead-McClellan bought the boarded-up building in 1983 for conversion to high-end apartments. That project, designed by Claybour Architects of St. Louis, was one of two in Missouri included in *Remaking America* by Barbaralee Diamonstein, published in 1987.

31
Memorial Home (Beauvais Manor on the Park)
City Landmark: December 1984
South Grand at Magnolia

A distinguished red brick Greek Revival mansion was constructed circa 1866 for Rene Beauvais (a prominent local silversmith and jeweler of French-Canadian descent) and his wife Marie Theresa Odile LeBeau Beauvais. Rene died less than a decade later, leaving his family in acute financial difficulties. In 1882, the Women's Christian Association, a non-denominational Protestant group of women from leading St. Louis families, bought the house for $21,500 and converted it to a home for the aged. Speaking at the dedication, William Greenleaf Eliot remarked on the excellent location and natural beauty of the five-acre site, an "elegant suburban retreat" at the northern edge of Tower Grove Park.

West side of Shaw Place in 1898
Missouri Botanical Garden Archives

The home was the first in the United States to admit couples; its success required the construction of four additions built between 1885 and 1916. Incorporated independent of the Women's Christian Association since the 1950s, Memorial Home built a new facility at the rear of the property in 1984 and the historic facility was closed. Initially, the Board planned to demolish the Beauvais Mansion. Instead, it was persuaded to renovate the historic house. The complex, reopened February 1991 with a capacity of 184 beds, includes residential and nursing care. In 1998, the name was changed to Beauvais Manor on the Park.

32
Shaw Place District
City Landmark: May 1969
National Register: April 12, 1982

A distinctive development in St. Louis architecture and subdivision planning, Shaw Place was built between 1878 and 1883 for Henry Shaw as rental property to provide an endowment for the Missouri Botanical Garden. Building permits from December 1878 estimated that the first four identical houses would cost a total of $10,000. The next four houses are larger, introducing projecting bays, pointed arches and wood porches; the last two are variants. All ten,

Shaw Place
Landmarks, 1980

renting between $50 and $55 per month, were designed by George I. Barnett and Isaac Taylor who quote English Queen Anne details with American suburban imagery on generous lots averaging eighty front feet.

The style selected for the Shaw Place houses is unique in the city today and not easily classified. While the fine ornamental brickwork appearing at the cornices is indigenous to St. Louis vernacular architecture, the sophisticated handling of the chimneys in particular recalls Boston's Panel Brick Style of the 1870s. Yet the design of the place as an architecturally consistent, complete unit maintained as rental property suggests an English prototype. Trustees of the Garden sold Shaw Place in 1915 for $55,000; deed restrictions establishing single-family use and private street status followed in 1916. The "Leda and the Swan" cast iron fountain in the central oval was moved here from Vandeventer Place (razed) in the 1960s.

33
Shining Light Tabernacle Church
City Landmark: September 1978
7121 Manchester Road

Dedicated in early 1891 as the *Deutsches Evangelische Christus Kirche*, a "sister congregation" to St. Mark's Evangelical Church at Jefferson and Potomac, the mission was located in a semi-rural area at the western edge of the city. The original German-born congregation outgrew the "Little White Church" on Manchester and moved to Maplewood in 1919. A Church of the Nazarene congregation later owned the building.

34
Stork Inn
National Register: May 5, 2000
4527 Virginia Avenue

Of all Anheuser-Busch's efforts to appease Prohibitionists with the creation of wholesome, family-friendly restaurant/taverns, the tiny Stork Inn may have gone the farthest. Klipstein & Rathmann,

Stork Inn
Gary R. Tetley, 2002

St. Louis, were commissioned to develop a suitable setting for the promotion of Malt-Nutrine, a non-alcoholic drink marketed to nursing and expectant mothers. Like the later (and larger) Gretchen Inn (1913, now Al Smith's Feasting Fox at Grand and Meramec), the Stork Inn (1910) used brick and half-timbered stucco with prominent corner towers to evoke a romantic Bavarian atmosphere. Despite its creative brick-and-mortar marketing, Anheuser Busch could do little to erase the image of alcohol as a social evil. Even after Prohibition became law, however, the Stork Inn was able to survive through the dry years by continuing as a restaurant and offering A-B's non-alcoholic product lines. Under a series of different owners, the neighborhood tavern stayed open through the mid-1990s. After several years of vacancy, neighbors Dale and Gwyn Preston rehabbed the dilapidated building, then installed Dale's art glass studio, an ice cream shop and an upstairs apartment.

35
Sugarloaf Mound
National Register: February 17, 1984
4400 block of Ohio Avenue

A plaque on North Broadway notes the location of the Great Mound (leveled). Sugarloaf on the city's south side has been built over but was still considered of sufficient interest as an archaeological site to merit National Register listing.

36
Tiffany Neighborhood District (Dundee Place)
National Register: February 10, 1983
and July 26, 1985
Bounded roughly by Grand, Park, 39th and I-44

Opened with great fanfare in 1891 by out-of-town developers, Dundee Place offered one of the city's most promising locations for middle-class homeowners. Eighteen two-story houses had been built as models. The subdivision had just received a big boost with the long-awaited completion of a viaduct over the railroad tracks at Grand Avenue and the arrival of a streetcar line. The promoters, however, had quietly held back a large tract for industry. With the 1895 announcement that Liggett & Myers would construct the world's largest tobacco factory at that location, the early character of Dundee Place shifted from middle- to working-class.

After many years as a stable community, the neighborhood experienced a dramatic downturn in the 1960s as increasing numbers of poor blacks displaced by urban renewal and highway construction brought overcrowding and white flight.

The Midtown Medical Center Redevelopment Corporation (MMCRC) was formed in the late 1970s by a group of nearby hospitals to counter the blight and "redlining" that threatened their institutions. The name Tiffany was chosen for an old streetcar line that ran along 39th Street; a new park with pavilion and fountain was created along with a

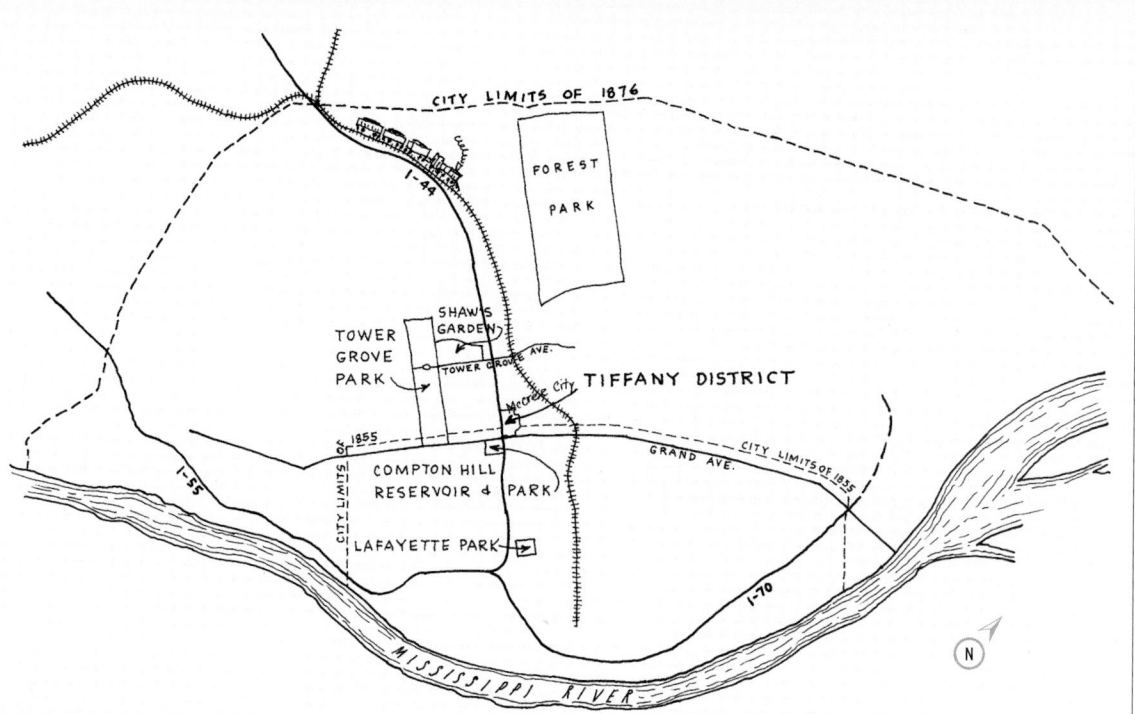

Tiffany Neighborhood District Map

Pat Hays Baer

37
I-44 Neighborhood District (McRee Town)
City District: June 30, 1987
Bounded roughly by Park, 39th, I-44 and Vandeventer Avenue

The **Tiffany District** *(previous page)*, was expanded to the west as a strategy to induce developers to invest in the largely multi-family neighborhood. It failed. Instead, "McRee Town" became known as "a haven for drugs, gangs and despair" (Bill Smith in the August 21, 2001 *Post-Dispatch*). With east/west boundaries stretching from 39th Street to Vandeventer, north/south from Park Avenue to I-44, the 90-acre

Left to right:

3680–64 Blaine
Landmarks, 1982

Southwest corner of Grand and Park Avenue in 1942
Landmarks Collection

Lafayette Avenue 3600 to 3800 blocks after construction of I-44
Landmarks, 1982

community center and marketing office. But in spite of the millions of dollars invested (over $23 million by 1982), Tiffany was merely a small oasis in the larger, very troubled area cut off from the Shaw neighborhood by construction of I-44.

Chapter 10 Southwest

All images (both pages) Tower Grove Heights District

This page, top to bottom:

3637-31 Utah Place
Gary R. Tetley, 2002

3651 Utah Place
Gary R. Tetley, 2002

Opposite page, left to right:

3711 Utah Place
Gary R. Tetley, 2002

3893-91 Utah Place
Gary R. Tetley, 2002

3195-97 South Grand Avenue
Gary R. Tetley, 2002

district is now the subject of the Garden District redevelopment project. The proposal, initiated by leaders from the Missouri Botanical Garden, has been developed within a commission framework including representatives from four surrounding neighborhoods thanks to a $1.5 grant from the Danforth Foundation. Current plans call for the acquisition and demolition of all buildings in the 3900 and 4000 blocks of McRee to make way for a new subdivision with up to 200 single-family homes. Other components under consideration include scattered rehabilitation and the construction of a neighborhood community center.

38
Tower Grove Heights District
National Register: September 6, 2001
Bounded by Grand, Arsenal, Gustine and McDonald

The Connecticut Mutual Life Insurance Company, which opened its St. Louis office in 1848, was not in the business of real estate. No one knows why the company, finding itself in possession of property in 27 blocks that had belonged to an indebted client, made the surprising decision to hold on to the tract and act as developer. Property south of **Tower Grove Park** *(page 242)* was platted in 1881 as the Tower Grove Park and Grand Avenue Addition, renamed Tower Grove Heights in 1897 when additional blocks east of the park were added. *(See* **Crittenden District**, *page 223)*. The company went so far as to pave streets, lay out utility lines and install street lights at its own expense, but most of the addition remained undeveloped when the life insurance company sold it off in 1905.

The first act of the new owners (the Connecticut Realty Company, created specifically for this enterprise by directors of the Mercantile Trust) was to replat the property with restrictions on the size and type of buildings to be constructed, their materials and minimum cost. Within the boundaries of the Tower Grove Heights District (the half of the Tower Grove Heights Addition west of Grand), Utah Place was reserved for single-family dwellings costing a minimum of $4,000.

A heavily advertised auction in June 1905 resulted in sales of most of the remaining lots. Buyers, enticed by the pleasant location and favorable credit terms, were typically prospective homeowners rather than speculators. Within the historic district, about two-thirds of the 770 buildings were constructed between 1905 and 1909. The work of more than 220 different builders is represented, but deed restrictions applied within the contemporary style language resulted in a neighborhood of unusual consistency. Over 70% of the houses follow a simple formula: two stories high, two bays wide and a projecting front porch. Variety is provided by a rich palette of brick colors (often several on the same building), an assortment of different roof configurations and a whole dictionary of decorative details drawn from fashionable revival styles.

Chapter 10   Southwest

Detail: Dickmann Building
Gary R. Tetley, 2002

Tower Grove Park: North (Magnolia Avenue) entrance
Jack Zehrt, 1985

Tower Grove Park: Chinese Pavilion
Jack Zehrt, 1984

39
Dickmann Building
National Register: December 30, 1999
3115 South Grand Boulevard

Constructed by the real estate company of future mayor (1932-41) Bernard Dickmann in 1926, this six-story office building designed by Wedemeyer & Nelson is one of the last additions to the Tower Grove Heights district. A Gothic Revival front elevation of white glazed terra cotta and a height of nearly twice anything else along the Grand commercial strip asserted a bold expression of confidence in the neighborhood's future. In 1999, City Properties undertook a major renovation of the singular structure.

40
Tower Grove Park
National Register: March 17, 1972
National Historic Landmark: December 20, 1989

Not content with transforming part of his country estate into a botanical garden, Henry Shaw created a new city park with the rest of it. His 1856 design, based on extensive reading and travel, was a formal "Gardenesque" landscape developed most probably in consultation with architect Francis Tunica. In 1868, Shaw conveyed land for Tower Grove Park to the city. In return, the city provided $360,000 from a special bond issue for initial improvements to the treeless prairie and to purchase land for the Compton Hill reservoir to supply the park with water. Exclusive control and management of the new park were vested in a small Board of Commissioners with Shaw a life member.

English-born Shaw came to St. Louis in 1819. Twenty years later, profits in hardware and sugar warehousing allowed him to retire with a healthy income from his real estate investments. By the time work began on Tower Grove Park, Shaw had made three trips to Europe and had amassed a large library of books on European landscape architecture. He had also persuaded horticulturist James Gurney to leave London's Regent's Park to become chief gardener for both the **Missouri Botanical Garden** *(page 228)* and Tower Grove Park. Within a few years, Shaw and Gurney had selected and supervised the planting of more than 20,000 trees and shrubs in the park.

The first buildings were simple stone stables built to quarter mules used to construct the meandering roadways. Elaborate carriage entrances to the park and exotic gazebos soon followed. Plans to ring the park with Italianate villas like the one built in 1868 from plans by Francis Tunica (now the director's house at the Magnolia entrance) never were actualized. The bandstand designed by Eugene Greenleaf in 1872

Tower Grove Park: Superintendent's House designed in 1868 by Francis Tunica
Tony Carosella, 2001

Chapter 10 Southwest

Tower Grove Park: East (Grand Avenue) entrance
Jack Zehrt, 1985

Tower Grove Park: Concert at the Bandstand
Jack Zehrt, 1985

inaugurated Sunday summer concerts. Bronze statues of William Shakespeare, Alexander von Humboldt and Christopher Columbus by Ferdinand von Miller were added between 1875-78.

Palm houses designed by George I. Barnett were built in 1877 and 1885. Adaptation of the older of the two (completed in 1999 with the formal opening of Café Madeleine in the renamed Piper Palm House) set the stage for a major conversion of the other into a sophisticated new headquarters for park operations. The 1888 Arsenal Street Gatehouse, the last building completed before Shaw's death, served for decades as the park headquarters and visitors' center. Another use must now be found for the picturesque Arsenal Street building.

Over the years a few new buildings have been added, but the park remains essentially as Shaw had envisioned it: an ornamental pleasure garden of distinctive beauty. Shaw was extremely generous to the park during his lifetime but did not provide an endowment for maintenance. Necessary funds other than a yearly appropriation from the city to conserve this Victorian jewel have been effectively raised by the Friends of Tower Grove Park, an organization established early in the tenure of director John Karel who came to the park in 1987.

41
Wyman School
National Register: September 2, 1992
1547 South Theresa Avenue

One of William B. Ittner's earliest E-shaped school plans, Wyman was under contract late in 1900. It was designed just three years after the architect assumed his job with the Board of Education (see **Carr School** *page 54* for background) and one year after Cope & Stewardson (Philadelphia) presented their first plans for the new Washington University campus. Brookings Hall at the university and Wyman's entrance pavilion are both framed by crenelated octagonal towers.

244

CHAPTER 11 | In Memoriam

(Unitarian) Church of the Messiah
Gary R. Tetley, 1982

Chapter 11   In Memoriam

**Children's Building
August 1994**

Landmarks

1 Ambassador Theatre Building
2 Beaumont Medical Building
3 Blackwell-Wielandy Building
4 De Smet Hall
5 Lincoln Trust (later Title Guaranty) Building
6 Marquette (later Milner) Hotel
7 Negro Masonic Lodge
   (Most Worshipful Prince Hall Grand Lodge #2)
8 Olympia Apartments
9 Olive Street Terra Cotta District
10 Page Boulevard Police Station
11 Rivoli (later Towne) Theatre
12 Sacred Heart Catholic Church
13 SS. Cyril & Methodius District
14 Silk Exchange Building
15 Unitarian Church of the Messiah
16 USS Inaugural
17 Vesper Buick Building
18 Veterans Administration Building
19 Walz House
20 Goldenrod Showboat
21 Mercantile Library Collection

St. Louis Landmarks and Historic Districts

This chapter notes the passing of designated city landmarks or individually listed National Register sites. Not mentioned are landmark buildings worthy of notice, but not formally designated at the time of their destruction (the Children's Building at Clark and 14th Street is an example). Also omitted are key buildings within the boundaries of designated historic districts (such as St. Philomena School and Orphanage at the southwest corner of Cabanne at Union Boulevard in Visitation Park district or the Bronson Hide Building in Laclede's Landing) and scores of background historic buildings in districts north of Delmar.

Two National Register districts have all but disappeared. The Olive Street Terra Cotta district is now reduced to one building; the SS. Cyril & Methodius district is left with only ten of the twenty-two listed buildings. Although both districts are described in the body of the book, each unfortunately has also earned a marker in the graveyard of Chapter 11.

Clockwise from top:

St. Philomena School and Orphanage in 1956
Arteaga Photos

Bronson Hide Building
Robert C. Pettus, 1977

Children's Building March 1996
Landmarks

St. Philomena School and Orphanage
Landmarks, 1996

Chapter 11   In Memoriam

Ambassador Theatre Building
Gary R. Tetley, 1988

1
Ambassador Theatre Building
City Landmark: September 1978
National Register: March 29, 1983
Demolished: 1996
411 North 7th Street

Completed in 1926 from plans by Chicago architects C. W. and George L. Rapp, the Ambassador Building combined an up-to-date eleven-story office tower with an elaborate "Spanish festival" theater. Opening day was promoted as the greatest event in St. Louis since the World's Fair. Ultra-modern mechanical devices (including an intricate lighting system, an eleven-dome atmospheric ceiling and the "world's largest" air conditioning system) helped drive the cost to more than $3.6 million for just the theater space. Also mentioned in Landmarks' National Register nomination was the need for "one of the largest steel trusses in the world" to support the roof of the theater auditorium and the eleven-story office building above. (This fact would become painfully obvious during demolition in 1996.) Financed by the Greek-born Skouras

Ambassador Theatre Building postcard circa 1929
Landmarks Collection

brothers who would go on to national prominence in the film industry, the Ambassador brought the first truly lavish house to the city. The **St. Louis Theatre** *(page 87)* from 1925 was also a creation of architects Rapp & Rapp, but it was comparatively "low budget," according to a 1975 letter from the Chicago area director of the Theatre Historical Society.

The Skouras brothers installed the largest screen in the nation and brought in larger seats to announce Cinerama showings in 1953. Seven years later, Cinerama moved to Lindell Boulevard. Rock concerts and comedy acts were the last to take the stage before the theater closed in 1976. The Loews State Theatre (designed in 1924 by architect Charles Lamb) at 715 Washington Avenue was razed after an attempt to give it City Landmark status failed at a September 1978 meeting of the Landmarks & Urban Design Commission. But in spite of objections, the Ambassador Building was so designated. With a functioning office tower encasing it, the historic corner theater seemed to have a future.

New owners brought in experts from Cleveland and Seattle to discuss converting the theater into a performing arts center. For almost ten years this seemed a real possibility. But in 1988, the owners offered the building with an intact theater for $5 per square foot to the city as part of the Cervantes Convention Center expansion underway a half block to the north. The idea was rejected: "Too far to walk." Next came a $27 million plan from Chicago developers to replace the theater with a five-story mall extending into neighboring Mercantile Bank. Announced in April 1988, the scheme was contingent on the ability of the St. Louis Development Corporation to devise additional public funding as was a later plan to demolish all but two stories and construct a 350-car garage inside the shell.

In 1989, a full-color feature story in the *Post-Dispatch* attracted hundreds of buyers and the curious to an auction stripping the theater interior. The owners were denied a demolition permit for a surface parking lot in 1991. But in July 1992, Mercantile Bank bought the building for $2.6 million, rounded up political support, commissioned architectural renderings and presented the public with a plan to replace the Ambassador Theatre Building with a parking garage. The bank's garage on Washington Avenue at Eighth Street ("structurally unsound, leaks like a sieve") would be demolished for "much-needed green space" across from the nearly completed Convention Center. A demolition permit was unanimously approved at a January 1995 meeting of the Heritage & Urban Design Commission. Testimony from Downtown St. Louis, Inc. predicted that business at St. Louis Centre would improve without the presence of the ugly and intimidating Ambassador. The Mercantile spokesperson agreed that it needed to be taken out like a bad tooth.

But the bank revised its project. Declaring that their crumbling old garage turned out to be usable after all, the bank shifted the "green space" component to the Ambassador. Printed invitations to the July 1997 dedication of Mercantile's unexpectedly expensive corporate plaza began with the words "the dust has settled." The Ambassador's massive steel truss identified in the National Register nomination came as a surprise to Mercantile and Spirtas Wrecking and caused extra shifts at night, a 250-ton crane requiring thirteen tractor-trailers to haul it in and the closure of Locust Street during part of the demolition. The bank and the wrecking company sued each other over the additional cost.

Clockwise from top:

Ambassador Theatre circa 1926
Landmarks Collection

Ambassador Theatre Demolition
Landmarks, 1996

Terra cotta detail: Ambassador Theatre Building
Gary R. Tetley, 1988

Chapter 11 In Memoriam

Detail: Blackwell-Wielandy Building

Gary R. Tetley, 1987

2
Beaumont Medical Building
National Register: January 19, 1984
Demolished: 1997
3714-26 Washington Avenue

The City Center Redevelopment Corporation, a forerunner to Grand Center, purchased the Beaumont Medical building in 1985 with plans to offer the property to a developer as ideal for residential rehabilitation. LaBeaume & Klein (St. Louis) designed the original ten-story buff brick building in 1926. (An annex was built in 1946.) Exterior and interior details reflected LaBeaume's fascination with Spanish medieval and Renaissance architecture. Owned co-operatively by its doctor tenants, the Midtown building was St. Louis' largest and finest medical office building. Among numerous prominent St. Louis physicians important in the field of medicine was principal stockholder Dr. Edwin C. Ernst whose pioneering work in the field of radiology was internationally recognized. The building was dynamited in spring 1997 to vacate land for the Pulitzer Foundation building by Tadao Ando (Japan). Grand Center board chairman Tom Reeves and Mayor Clarence Harmon set off 300 pounds of dynamite before an attentive public invited to witness "this unforgettable event."

Detail: Beaumont Medical Building

Landmarks, 1983

3
Blackwell-Wielandy Building
National Register: July 21, 1983
Demolished: 1988
1601-09 Locust Street

Distinguished by rich terra cotta ornament on both the Locust and St. Charles Street elevations, the Blackwell-Wielandy building was designed in 1907 by Albert B. Groves (St. Louis) for the John L. Boland Book and Stationery Company. The building was acquired in 1910 by an up-and-coming competitor, Blackwell-Wielandy, which would enjoy seven decades at this location as the "largest house of its kind in the country." The company best known for Blue Jay and Big Chief tablets closed in 1982. Out-of-town owners contemplated an adaptive reuse before a disastrous fire in 1984. Demolition commenced September 1988.

4
De Smet Hall
City Landmark: June 1977
Demolished: 1977
3647 West Pine Boulevard

This five-story red brick Gothic Revival classroom building was completed in 1898 as the final piece of St. Louis University's High Victorian quadrangle. By the mid 1970s, De Smet (adapted as a faculty office building) was considered obsolete by administrators whose philosophy was epitomized by Financial Vice President Joseph E. Lynch: "You can't use old buildings; they are not practical." Daniel L. Schlafly, Jr., a history professor at the campus, led the unsuccessful faculty fight to save the building. The cause was joined by Mary C. Means (Regional Director of the National Trust for Historic Preservation) and Landmarks Association. On June 30, 1977 the Landmarks & Urban Design Commission voted unanimously to declare De Smet a City Landmark only to discover that the demolition permit had already been issued.

De Smet Hall
St. Louis
Post-Dispatch, *1977*

5
Lincoln Trust (later Title Guaranty) Building
National Register: March 19, 1982
Demolished: 1983
706 Chestnut Street

Probably the first and arguably the best of Eames & Young's skyscrapers, the twelve-story Lincoln Trust Building was designed in 1898 and built that same year by preeminent contractor George A. Fuller. Only two stories taller than the Wainwright Building across the street, the H-shaped Title Guaranty seemed to soar to a breathtaking cornice crafted by the Winkle Terra Cotta Company of St. Louis. The main entrance on Chestnut was announced by highly polished rose granite columns flanked by piers covered with terra cotta panels of putti and immodest damsels amidst lush Renaissance vegetal patterns.

Early tenants, including architects Eames & Young, reflected the spectacular economic development of turn-of-the-century St. Louis as well as the accompanying corruption and subsequent reform efforts celebrated by Lincoln Steffens. Employees sharing the elevators came from Jay Gould's Wabash Railroad, the American Car and Foundry Company presided over by William K. Bixby and the office of Joseph W. Folk—a crusading young lawyer from Tennessee who would be swept into the Missouri Governor's office on

Lincoln Trust Building circa 1900
Landmarks Collection

a wave of reform in 1904. After the merger of the Lincoln Trust and Missouri Bank in 1904, the building (known as the Title Guaranty) gradually assumed a different character as part of "Real Estate Row" on Chestnut Street.

Although sporadic interest in a City Beautiful mall running east from the Civil Courts Building had surfaced during the 1960s, plans grew dusty on the shelf until the mid 1970s. With the completion of both General American Life and the Centerre (now Bank of America) new corporate offices on the south side of Market Street, powerful new life was breathed into the concept of a Gateway Mall. In the end the choice was either a critically acclaimed scheme to create smaller urban

Title Guaranty terra cotta cornice in 1982
Landmarks Collection

Chapter 11   In Memoriam

Detail: Title Guaranty Building (former Lincoln Trust) Building with Civil Courts Building in the background
Robert C. Pettus, 1983

Left to right:

Detail: Marquette Hotel
Gary R. Tetley, 1987

Marquette Hotel postcard circa 1920
Landmarks Collection

spaces within the context of restored historic buildings or total demolition and the construction of new buildings along half a mall. The forces for demolition prevailed. The much-maligned Gateway One building is the sole return on a very dear investment.

6
Marquette (later Milner) Hotel
National Register: September 26, 1985
Demolished: 1988
1734 Washington Avenue

This ten-story red brick building embellished with lavish terra cotta ornament was built as the premiere hotel for the wholesale trade in 1906 from plans by Barnett, Haynes & Barnett (St. Louis) for a group of local investors headed by the corporate giants of Washington Avenue. Interiors were by Durvea & Potter of New York City. Tony Faust, Jr., manager of his father's legendary St. Louis restaurants and the brilliant Tyrolean Alps dinery at the 1904 World's Fair, ran the kitchen. Ownership passed to the General American Investment Co. during the Depression; in 1940, the Milner chain took over. But by the late 1970s, the property was acquired for back taxes by the city's Land Reutilization Authority, then sold for $100 to an adjacent owner. Concepts for renovation by would-be developers never left the drawing board. The Marquette was razed for a surface parking lot.

7
**Negro Masonic Lodge
(Most Worshipful Prince Hall Grand Lodge #2)**
National Register: April 15, 1993
Demolished: 1998
3615-9 Dr. Martin Luther King Boulevard

Black Freemasonry in the United States was founded by Prince Hall (1735-1807), a soldier during the American Revolution, and had a long history as did its white counterpart. Most of the prominent colonists were Masons including Hall's commander-in-chief George Washington. Seven of the first eleven Governors of Missouri were Masons. Masonic connections were especially important in the African-American community, providing mutual support for education, burial and relief; supporting black military units; assisting migrants; agitating for better public schools and providing an affirmation of identity and status. St. Louis' three African-American lodges at the close of the Civil War had grown to nine when the Negro Masonic Hall Corporation bought a three-story Romanesque Revival building built in 1886 to convert for its members in 1909. (By then over 100 black Masonic groups had been formed statewide.) It appears that all nine St. Louis lodges of that period met in this building, although within a few years some had acquired halls of their own. Masonic headquarters moved to the 4500 block of Olive in 1942.

8
Olympia Apartments
National Register: August 1, 1986
Demolished: 1993
3863 West Pine Boulevard

In 1926, Ida and Max Weinberg of Weinberg Realty bought a corner site, razed an 1888 mansard-roofed house and hired architect David R. Harrison to design a $200,000 seven-story apartment building with notable terra cotta ornament by the Winkle Terra Cotta Company (St. Louis). Harrison, a former New Yorker, also became established in

Clockwise from left:

Mayor Freeman Bosley, Jr. and Alderwoman Velma Bailey; photo of Masonic Hall in its prime is visible on front of speakers' podium
Jan Cameron, 1993

Negro Masonic Lodge boarded and vacant
Jan Cameron, 1993

Olympia Apartments
Esley Hamilton, 1986

St. Louis as a contractor. Other "Harrison quality built" apartments included 4605 and 4615 Lindell in the Central West End. The City's Heritage & Urban Design Commission, apparently unaware that the still-sound buff brick building was listed on the National Register, approved demolition of the Olympia in 1993 at the request of St. Louis University.

Chapter 11

Clockwise from top left:

Olive Street Terra Cotta District: 608 (at left) and 610 Olive
Landmarks, 1984

Olive Street Terra Cotta District: The Gill Building (right of the parking garage) is extant. Everything left of the parking garage is razed: 610 Olive (designed by A. B. Groves in 1915), 608 Olive (designed by Will Levy for Erker Brothers Optical Company in 1912) and 606-00 Olive (designed by A.B. Groves in 1913 with the addition from 1920 by Tom P. Barnett).
Landmarks, 1984

Page Boulevard Police Station
Gary R. Tetley, 1992

9
Olive Street Terra Cotta District
National Register: January 2, 1986
Demolished 1988

The parking lot built at the corner of 6th and Olive Streets on the site of Boyd's clothing store and its two diminutive neighbors to the west won a Cityscape award from Downtown St. Louis Inc. in 1989. Boyd's grew from a small haberdashery opened in 1876 to a thriving locally owned chain with four stores and sales in 1960 of more than $10 million. Prized for conservative business attire for both men and women and the trademark Threadneedle Street shoes, Boyd's was sold to the manufacturer of Arrow shirts in 1961 . (See *page 37* for a description of the surviving **Gill Building**.)

10
Page Boulevard Police Station
City Landmark: September 1976
National Register: September 11, 1980
Demolished: 1995
Northeast corner of Page and Union Boulevards

Designed in 1908 by Building Commissioner James R. Smith for the twelfth, and last, police district established in the city, the three-story station was estimated to cost $35,959. This was not the first design. The initial announcement of the location brought a storm of protest from nearby residents who were partly mollified by Smith's skillful blend of quotations from Philadelphia's Independence Hall and familiar St. Louis residential architecture. Vacant since 1976, the building was badly damaged by one of several fires attributed to 4th of July fireworks in 1993. Plans for an African-American history museum had already garnered a lead grant of $20,000 from the McDonnell Douglas Foundation.

11
Rivoli (later Towne) Theatre
City Landmark: September 1978
Demolished: 1978
210 North 6th Street

Built for Ellis Wainwright from an 1896 design by Charles K. Ramsey (St. Louis associate of Adler & Sullivan), the small-scale building housed Caesar's Cafe from 1899 to 1915. Major alterations in 1915 and 1922 transformed the cafe into the Rivoli Theatre. Above the marquee was the finest Midwest example of sgraffito, a traditional technique of ornamentation that incised decorative patterns into different colored layers of plaster. Sgrafitto panels at the Rivoli featured languid plant forms indebted to the Art Nouveau movement. Several panels were salvaged when the X-rated Towne Theatre was razed for the giant Metropolitan Life Building.

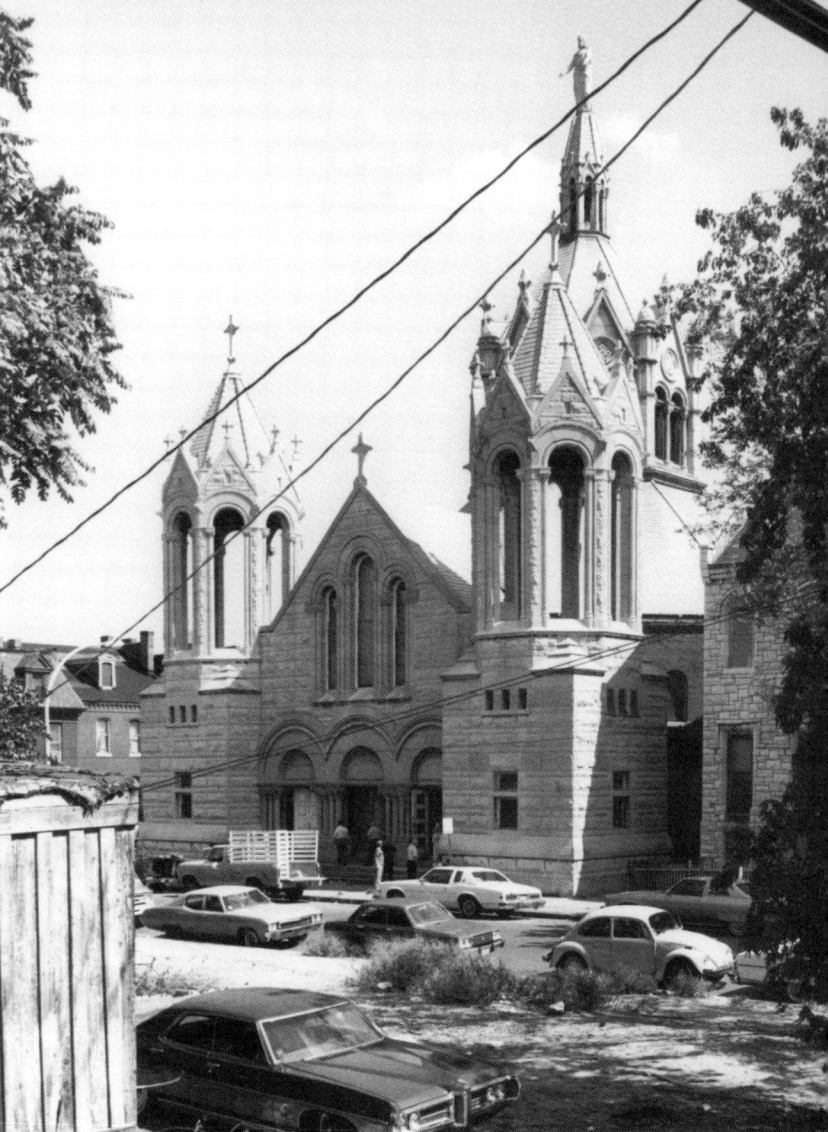

12
Sacred Heart Catholic Church
City Landmark: September 1978
Demolished: 1986
2830 North 25th Street

Designed in 1898 by Barnett, Haynes & Barnett for a north side Irish parish, Sacred Heart was one of the finest examples of the firm's ecclesiastical work. The striking individuality of Sacred Heart was due to its unusual octagonal sanctuary covered with an octagonal copper-clad dome. Exceptionally fine craftsmanship was evident in the Bedford stone facade featuring pierced stone octagonal towers and intricate Byzantine style ornament.

Sacred Heart's location in a in north side neighborhood no longer able to support a solvent parish marked it for demolition by the Archdiocese in 1978. As a prelude captured in embarrassing detail by the media, everything that could be removed from the building (pews, chandeliers, altars, baptismal font, etc.) was auctioned on-site. Demolition was halted as a wrecking crew removed the large statue of Jesus from the central tower. In 1982, the

Clockwise from top right:

Auction at Sacred Heart Church
Landmarks 1978

Sgraffito panels
Pat Hays Baer

Towne (former Rivoli) Theatre
Landmarks, 1983

Chapter 11   In Memoriam

Two photos,
left column:

**Details:
Sacred Heart**
Landmarks, 1986

Right column:

**Sacred Heart
Church, 1944**
Arteaga Photos

**Sacred Heart
Church, 1978**
Bob Voss

Archdiocese transferred ownership to a realtor who attempted to find a workable new use for the battered building. In spite of several fires, Sacred Heart was still structurally sound but open to vagrants when the Archbishop determined in 1986 that its continued presence was "an eyesore to the neighborhood and an insult to the Church of St. Louis." An offer from Landmarks Association to underwrite filling the opening with concrete blocks was rebuffed. The Archbishop enlisted the help of Mayor Vincent C. Schoemehl who appeared before the Heritage & Urban Design Commission to urge that the Shrine of the Sacred Heart be razed. An attempt the next day to file an appeal was futile; the building was already under demolition financed by the city.

Structural remnant: Sacred Heart Church
Landmarks, 1986

13
SS. Cyril & Methodius Historic District
National Register: June 28, 1982
Bounded roughly by North 11th, Tyler, Hadley and Chambers Street
Twelve of the twenty-two buildings demolished since 1982

The double townhouse at 1102-04 Chambers Street, probably the earliest building in the district, was of statewide importance for its association with the accomplished Bernays family. Built in 1859 by John Glassford, a cola merchant originally from Pennsylvania, the property passed briefly to a grocer from Hanover before its sale for $8,250 in 1867 to German-born brothers Dr. George J. and Charles L. Bernays. Journalist Charles left Munich after his revolutionary newspaper was suppressed and joined the senior staff of the *Anzeiger des Westens*, an outspoken and influential St. Louis daily with Republican, pro-Union sympathies. In addition to service as Consul to Zurich and Helsignor for President Lincoln, Charles Bernays was a member of the St. Louis Art Society and instrumental in the introduction of kindergartens into city schools.

George Bernays moved back to Europe long enough to assure his three children a proper education at the University of Heidelberg. Son Augustus became a member of the Royal College of Surgeons in England before returning to St. Louis to set up a practice. In 1882, he was elected Professor of anatomy and clinical surgery in the St. Louis College of Physician and Surgeons. His sister and life-long companion Thekla moved easily in the cultural society of St. Louis and later New York City. A writer, translator and literary critic, Thekla Bernays published essays and criticism in *The Mirror* and served as a foreign correspondent for the *Globe-Democrat* and *Westliche Post*. She was a charter member of the Artists Guild of St. Louis and selected as a member of the jury of arts and crafts for the 1904 World's Fair.

A few members of SS. Cyril & Methodius tried to rescue the forlorn Bernays house in the early 1980s. Lack of funds and continued neighborhood disinvestment doomed the valiant effort.

SS. Cyril & Methodius District: Glassford/Bernays House
Landmarks, 1980

Chapter 11 | In Memoriam

Silk Exchange Building
Landmarks, 1978

Silk Exchange Building
Landmarks, 1995

14
Silk Exchange Building
National Register: September 2, 1982
Demolished: 1995
501-11 North Tucker Boulevard

Built in 1901-02 in a prime location from plans by the office of St. Louis architect Isaac Taylor, the Silk Exchange Building marked the intersection of Washington Avenue's linear march to the west and a City Beautiful vision for 12th Street (later Tucker Boulevard) running north/south. Monochromatic and sparing in the use of ornament, the Silk Exchange Building (named for a ground floor tenant from 1907) was probably designed by Taylor's chief draftsman, Oscar Enders, who signed many of the firm's eloquent renderings. Enders' talents came to Taylor's attention in publications from the Chicago Architectural Sketch Club. By 1895, Enders (enticed to St. Louis by Taylor) had become president of the St. Louis Architectural Club. A photo of the Silk Exchange building under construction was included in the Club's annual exhibition catalogue from 1902.

Small-scale clothing and millinery manufacturers, fabric, button, lace, embroidery and notions merchants and manufacturers' agents sublet the maze of light-filled upper floors at the Silk Exchange for decades. Ironically, those features would attract a very different clientele in the 1990s. After an out-of-town owner decided not to move ahead with renovation plans, the vacant building became a haven for thirty to forty of the city's homeless. Everyone had his own room. The floor was carpeted. "You could sleep there, you could keep your clothes there, and nobody ever bothered anybody else's things," according to a resident forced back on the street by a general alarm fire that started at 1:30 a.m. on June 6, 1995.

(Unitarian) Church of the Messiah
Landmarks, 1982

15
**(Unitarian) Church of the Messiah
(later All Saints Episcopal)**
City Landmark: September 1973
National Register: September 22, 1980
Demolished: 1987
Northeast corner of Locust and Garrison Avenues

This was the third building for the Unitarians and the first St. Louis commission received by the illustrious Boston firm of Peabody & Stearns. An outstanding Gothic Revival stone church designed in 1879 for William Greenleaf Eliot's congregation, the building was owned from 1906 to 1957 by All Saints Episcopal, the only black congregation of the Episcopal Diocese of Missouri. Two Baptist congregations worshiped here before acquisition in 1978 by the First Cathedral Church of the Apostolic Faith. Fires in the mid 1980s presumably set by vagrants caused irreplaceable damage to the dramatic hammer-beamed interior. (Fortunately, the Unitarian congregation had moved most of the exquisite stained-glass windows from the building when it migrated to Union Boulevard—see **Church of the Messiah**, *page 136.*) Although the tower and walls were still sound, a new owner elected to proceed with total demolition in 1987.

Chapter 11   In Memoriam

Veterans Administration Building in the foreground on right, 1912 postcard
Landmarks Collection

16
USS Inaugural
National Historic Landmark: January 14, 1986
Sunk: 1993
300 North Wharf Street

Built by the Winslow Marine Railway & Shipbuilding Co., Winslow, Washington, the USS Inaugural (AM-242) was launched on December 30, 1944. A fleet minesweeper, the Inaugural earned two battle stars in the Pacific and was designated a National Historic Landmark as part of the Theme Study of Warships conducted by the National Park Service.

17
Vesper Buick Building
National Register: October 2, 1986
Demolished: 1995
3900 West Pine Boulevard

General Motors established its supremacy as the largest US auto manufacturer in 1925 with Buick bringing in almost half of their sales revenue. In St. Louis, four different Buick dealers competed in a ferocious, fickle marketplace. The public, by now expecting high style in its autos, had to be lured to the point of sales by "smart showrooms" with unconventional architecture and wide expanses of plate glass. Preston J. Bradshaw's arresting **Plaza Hotel Complex** (page 91) from 1915 included automobile showrooms. His 1927 work for Frederick W. A. Vesper was one of St. Louis' best examples of Spanish Colonial Revival, featuring a stucco exterior, tile parapet, decorative metal grillwork and a display of Churrigueresque terra cotta ornament. The showroom at the corner entrance was capable of displaying sixteen cars. Vesper served as founder and president of the National Automobile Dealers Association and president of the St. Louis Chamber of Commerce. The building was demolished in 1995; the site is now a parking lot for St. Louis University.

Detail: Vesper Buick Building
Landmarks, 1989

18
Veterans Administration Building
City Landmark: March 1977
Demolished: 1977
200 North Broadway

For almost seventy years this building's two-story, copper-clad mansard roof perched high above the financial district was a compass point on the skyline of downtown St. Louis. Completed by 1909 apparently from plans by Mauran, Russell & Garden (St. Louis), the sixteen-story office and bank building was purchased by the Veterans Administration in 1946. It was demolished along with two other early 20th century buildings for a temporary parking lot for the new Boatmen's Bank building before the St. Louis Place office tower was built.

Walz House
St. Louis
Post-Dispatch, *1982*

19
Walz House
City Landmark: November 1971
Demolished: 1982
4708 South Broadway

The earliest part of this frame house that overlooked the Mississippi River was built circa 1849 for Hiram Paddleford, owner of an old shot tower on the river. The property was acquired in 1852 by grain miller Charles L. Tucker, best remembered for the jaunty station he built on the cliffs at Itaska Street next to the Iron Mountain Railroad. Subsequent owners included Alexander H. Smith, Frederick Hoffmann and Mrs. Herman F. Walz. A landmark to riverboat captains, the Walz House sustained considerable fire damage before its owners decided to proceed with demolition in 1982.

20
Goldenrod Showboat
National Historic Landmark: December 24, 1967
City Landmark: February 1972
Moved, but not razed: 1989
Left for other harbors
400 North Wharf Street

Built in 1909 at Parkersburg, West Virginia, "The World's Greatest Showboat" was purchased in 1922 by Captain J. William Menke who toured river towns before tying up in St. Louis in 1937. After repairs from a fire in June of 1962, a succession of St. Louis owners kept the ragtime and melodrama traditions alive. Talk had surfaced off and on about moving the Steamboat Gothic, steel-hulled vessel to another location. It departed for St. Charles in 1989. The first production on the Missouri River (a 1950s musical) was in May 1991; the last one in March 2000 (for a Chinese movie) required a makeover into a gambling casino. After a January 2002 logjam bashed into the hull, the damaged vessel was towed to dock in Frontier Park. It awaits funds for repairs to satisfy Coast Guard standards.

21
Mercantile Library Collection
City Landmark: January 1973
Moved, but not razed: 1997
510 Locust Street

Founded in 1846, Mercantile is the oldest circulating library still in existence west of the Mississippi. Included in the non-circulating collection are rare books, journals and prints. The Association, forced to sell its collection of drawings by George Caleb Bingham due to financial problems in the late 1970s, has benefited recently from increased public support and significant additions to its collection including the Barriger Railroad collection and photographs from the defunct *Globe-Democrat*. After a difficult vote by its membership, the library moved from its downtown location to the campus of the University of Missouri, St. Louis in 1997.

Index

A & P Food Stores Building, 133
Aboussie, Martie, 185
Adams, John Willard, 70
Adams, S. G., Building, 18
Adler & Sullivan, 21, 42-43, 178, 255
Adler, Dankmar, 42-43
Advertising Building (Mary Muffet Lofts), 73
Al Smith's Feasting Fox, 238
All Saints Episcopal Church, 259
Allegiant Bank, 226
Allen Market Lane Apartments, 200
Aloe, Louis, 64
Ambassador Theatre Building, 248-249
American Architect & Building News, 43
American Institute of Architects, 9, 43, 122
American Theatre, 15-16, 30, 41
American Zinc, Lead and Smelting Company Building, 16
Anderson/Miller, 24
Ando, Tadao, 83, 250
Angelic Temple of Deliverance, 107
Anheuser-Busch Brewery, 181, 200
Annan, Thomas B., 32, 62, 83
Annie Malone, 171, 174
Annie Malone Children and Family Service Center, 174
Anschuetz, Carl, 222
Antioch Baptist Church, 170, 172
"Apotheosis of St. Louis," 98
Arcade Building, 16-18, 64, 226
Arcade/Wright Building, 16-18
Architectural Forum, 40
Arena, 223
Arnold, Hillis, 230
Arsenal Street Gatehouse, 244
Ashley Street Powerhouse, 11-12
Aubert Place, 120
Avis, Francis C., 140
Avis, Hall & Proetz, 140
B'nai Amoona Temple, 127
B'nai El Temple, 235-236
Bailey, Velma, 253
Balmer & Weber Music Company Building, 18
Bandel, Hannskarl, 9
Baptist Church of the Good Shepherd, 109
Barnett & Record Construction Company, 187
Barnett, George I., 6, 154, 156, 191, 195, 197, 228-229, 237, 244

Barnett, Haynes & Barnett, 38, 56, 63, 92, 101, 103, 107, 110, 115-116, 120, 124, 140, 227, 235, 252, 255
Barnett, Tom P., 16, 22, 32, 64, 73
Barr Branch Library District, 216
Barr, William, 216
Bartholomew, Harland, & Associates, 5
Basilica of St. Louis, King of France, 6
Baum, Albert H., Jr., 34
Beattie, William John, 57
Beaumont Medical Building, 250
Beauvais Manor on the Park, 236
Becker, William C. E., 123
Bee Hat Building, 47
Beethoven Conservatory, 53, 124
Beinke & Wees, 53
Belcher Sugar, Bath and Water, 11
Bell Telephone Building, 18
Beman, S. S., 69
Benjamin, Brent, 129
Benton College of Law, 85
Benton Park Neighborhood District, 182
Benton Place, 190-191
Benton, Thomas Hart, 8, 183
Bergfeld, George, 133
Bernays, Augustus, Charles L., George J. and Thekla, 257
Bethlehem Lutheran Church, 152
Bethlehem Methodist Episcopal Church, 220
Bevo Mill, 217
Bevo Plant, 181-182
Bissell, Captain Lewis, 153
Bissell Mansion, 153
Bissell Street Water Tower, 152
Bitter, Karl, 122
Bixby, William K., 222, 251
Black, James W., 25
Blackwell-Wielandy Building, 250
Blair School, 148-149
Blind Girls' Home, 165-166
Block Unit #1 District, 98
Blow, Susan, 207
Boatmen's Bank, 19, 31, 260
Boehmer, Otto J., 168
Bofinger, Mary E., Chapel, 57
Bohemian Hill, 194-195
Bond, Governor Kit, 43
Bosley, Mayor Freeman, Jr., 253

Boy Next Door (The), 126
Boyd's, 37, 254
Bradshaw, Preston J., 22, 27, 29, 91, 102, 119, 124, 131, 133, 144, 260
Brady, Thomas W., 209
Brambila, Jeff, 189
Breckenridge, Don, 65
Bremen, 125, 150, 152, 223
Brickbuilder, 45, 135
Bringhurst, Robert P., 91
Bronson Hide Building, 247
Brookings, Robert, 23, 74, 83
Brown, A. D., Building, 47-48
Brown Shoe Company, 71, 200
Brown Shoe Company's Homes-Take Factory, 200
Brown vs. Board of Education, 139, 176
Brownstein Group, 143
Brueggeman, G. F. A., 31
Brunt & Howe, 69
Bruton Stroube Studios, 53
Bryan, John Albury, 8, 53, 191
Buckley, Charles E., 129
Buder Building, 44
Buehler, William, House, 217
Burke, James D., 129
Burks & Landberg, 58
Busch, August A., 32
Busch Stadium, v, 12, 23
Butler Brothers Building, 71
Butler, James Gay, House, 143
Cabanne Branch Library, 138
"Cabanne House," 85, 119
Cameron, Edward A., 69
Camp Derricotte, 93
Camp Jackson, 197
Campbell Design, 91
Campbell, Robert G., House, 53
Cann, William, 225
Carlin/Rathgeber House, 205
Carnegie, Andrew, 56, 217
Carondelet, 149, 172, 185, 201-212, 227
Carondelet Branch Library, 206-207
Carondelet/East of Broadway, 172, 203, 205
Carondelet Historical Society, 208, 210
Carondelet Park, 208
Carr School, 54-55
Carr Square Tenant Management Corporation, 54
Cassilly, Bob and Gail, 73
Castleman/Mackay House, 85
Cathedral Basilica of St. Louis, 101
Catlin Tract, 131-132
Cella, Louis A., 15
Centenary United Methodist Church, 54
Centenary United Methodist Episcopal Church, South, 54
Centennial Christian Church, 120-121
Center for Emerging Technologies, 117-118

Central Public Library, 56
Central West End Bank, 131
Central West End Builders, 125
Central West End District, 99, 143
Century Building, 19-20, 35, 119
Century/Syndicate Trust Building, 19, 39
Chase Park Plaza Hotel, 102
Chatillon-DeMenil House, 185
Chauvenet, William, 3
Cheltenham, 182
Chemical Building, 20-21, 129
Cherokee Street District, 186
Chicago Architectural Sketch Club, 258
Children's Building, 246-247
Chivers, Herbert C., 140
Chopin, Kate, House, 102
Chouteau Apartments/Parkway Dwellings, 116
Chouteau, Auguste, 6, 8-9
Christ Church Cathedral, 57
Christian Peper Building, 10
Christner, Inc., 53
Christopher, E. E., 41
Church of the Messiah, 40, 136-137, 245, 259
Citizens Civil Rights Commission, 20
City Club, 21-22, 31, 108
City Hall, cover, 8, 42, 58, 77, 87, 140, 204, 250
City Hospital District, 187-188
City Museum, 73, 127
City Plan Commission, 60, 91, 99, 203
Civic League, 8, 21, 137
Civil Courts Building, 25, 251-252
Clark Grade School, 138
Claybour Architects, 84, 194, 236
Clemens House/Columbia Brewery District, 147
Clemens, James, Jr., House, 148-149
Clemens, Samuel L., 148
Cloepfil, Brad, 83
Clymer & Drischler, 90
Cobb, Henry Ives, 21
Cohen, Thomas H., 67
Cohn, Kimble, 32, 53
Cohn/Thomson Associates, 10
Compton & Dry, 11
Compton Heights Christian Church, 235
Compton Heights/Fox Park District, 218
Compton Hill Water Tower, 221
Compton, Richard J., 10
Concordia Seminary, 223
Confluence Greenway, 11
Congress of Industrial Organizations (CIO), 59
Conradi, Joseph, 154, 160, 167, 175
Conway, Mayor James, 203-204
Cook, Isaac T., 25
Cooks and Pastry Cooks Local 26, 85
Cope & Stewardson, 244
Cordes Printing Company, 53
Court Square, 50

Index

Crabtree Court Apartments, 117
Crane, C. Howard, 83-84
Craven, T. J., 124
Crawford, D., Drygoods Company, 32
Crittenden District, 223, 240
Crown Candy Company, 156
Crown Loft Apartments, 129
Crunden, Frederick, 217
Culver, Lucius Lewellyn, 63
Cupples, Samuel, 23, 83
Cupples, Samuel, House, 83
Cupples Station Warehouse District, 22
Curtiss, Louis, 37
Daenzer, Carl, 221
Danforth Foundation, 240
Danforth, Senator John C., 58
Darby, Mayor John F., 117, 178
Darst-Webbe Public Housing, 188
Daughters of Charity of St. Vincent de Paul, 166
De Hodiamont House, 117
De Mentureal, J., 101
De Smet Hall, 250-251
Deitering, Charles, 117
Delany Building, 24-25
Delmar Baptist Church, 131
Delmar Loop/Parkview Gardens District, 117
DeMenil Building, 44
DePaul Hospital, 166
Des Peres School, 207-208
Desnoyers Shoe Company, 62
Deutsches Haus, 190
Dickmann Building, 215, 242
Dickmann, Mayor Bernard, 5, 60
Dignity House Christian Art Center, 137
Dillard, Irving, 189
Dinkeloo, John, 9
Dixon, Thomas, 54
Dold, Reverend Louis, 89
Donaho, Glynn and Shelley, 222
Dorr and Zeller Building, 131
Dorris, George Preston, 117
Dorris Lofts, 117-118
Dorris Motor Car Company Building, 117-118
Dorsa Building, 47
Downtown St. Louis, Inc., 249, 254
Druiding, Adolphus, 37, 194-195
Drury, Charles and Shirley, 26
Drury Plaza Hotel, 16, 26
Dry, Camille N., 10
Duncan Architects, 119
Dundee Place, 238
Dunn, Frederick, 58, 232
Durvea & Potter, 252
Dwyer, James, 32
Eads Bridge, 3-4, 10, 16, 23, 25, 32, 35, 45
Eads Bridge Tunnel, 4, 23, 25, 35
Eads, James B., 3, 11, 203, 218

Eagleton, Senator Thomas, 35
Eames, Charles, 139
Eames, William S., 25, 153, 167
Eames & Young, 16, 19, 22, 25, 30, 43, 48, 56, 69, 71, 74, 109, 111-112, 127, 199, 224, 251
EarthWays Home, 82
Eastman-Kodak Building, 25
Eden Publishing Company Building, 34
Edison Brothers Warehouse, 64
Edwards, Joe, 132
Eidlitz, Leopold, 57
Eliot House, 103
Eliot School, 153, 155
Eliot, T. S., 103
Eliot, William Greenleaf, 66, 103, 136-137, 236, 259
Elleardsville, 170-171, 175
Ellis & Mann, 115
Ellis, Harvey, 58, 115, 221
Ely & Walker Dry Goods Company, inside front cover, 71, 169
Emerson Electric Company Building, 59
Emerson School, 166
Emeth, Shaare, 107, 235
Emmaus Lutheran Church, 220
Enders, Oscar, 60, 258
Engelmann, Dr. George, 229
Equal Suffrage League of St. Louis, 20
Erlanger, Joseph, House, 102
Ernst, Dr. Edwin C., 250
Evergreene Painting Studios, 27
Ewald, Lawrence, 88, 137, 142
Farrar, Dr. Bernard G., 150
Fashion Square Building, 73
Faust, Tony, 222, 252
Fendler & Associates, 74
Ferrand, Gabriel, 144
Field, Eugene, House, 189
Field School, 118
First Cathedral Church of the Apostolic Faith, 259
First Church of Christ, Scientist, 108
First German Presbyterian Church, 194
First Unitarian Church of St. Louis, 137
Fischer, Alexander A., 126, 131
Fischer, Francis, 6
Flad, Henry, 3
Fleming Corporation, 173
Fletcher, Governor Thomas C., 218
Flora Place, 233-234
Folk, Joseph W., 251
Fontbonne College, 211
Ford, James L., 5
Ford Motor Car Company Building (Good Will Industries), 90
Forest Park Headquarters Building, 119
Forest Park Hotel, 119
Forest Park Southeast District, 224
Forum for Contemporary Art, 83

Fountain Park District, 120-121, 123
1424-34 Dolman Street, 192
Fox, George C., 218
Fox Theatre, 77, 82-84, 116
Frei, Emil, Art Glass Company, 158
Frei, Robert, 230
French, Daniel Chester, 35
Friedewald, Rich, 222
Friedlander & Dillon, 88
Frisco Building, 24-25
Froebel, Friedrich, 207
Froese, Ewald R., 34
Fuller, George A., 251
Fuller, R. Buckminster, 229
Fullerton, General Joseph Scott, 103
Fullerton's Westminster Place, 103-105, 110
Fulton Bag Company Buildings, 25
Garden, Edward, 135
Gaslight Square, 103, 124
Gast, August, & Company, 62
Gateway Arch, cover, v, 5, 8-9, 98
Gateway Hotel, 27, 40
Gateway Mall, 44, 251
Gerdine, Leigh, 88
German Swedenborgian Church, 156
Gibson Heights United Presbyterian Church, 225
Giedion, Siegfried, 5
Gilbert, Cass, 56-57, 127, 129
Gill Building, 254
Gillick, Aloysius, 149, 211
Glassford/Bernays House, 158, 257
Glassford, John, 257
Glennon, Archbishop John Joseph, 101, 224
Golden, Eugene, 88
Goldenrod Showboat, 261
Goller, Father Francis, 200
Good Samaritan Church, 235
Goodfellow/Julian Concrete Block District, 121
Grace Hill Episcopal Church, 157
Grace Methodist Church, 131
Grand Avenue (Old or White) Water Tower, cover, 154
Grand Center, Inc., 82
Grand and Gravois Commercial District, 226
Grandel Theatre, 79, 82
Gray Design Group, 74
Greenleaf, Eugene L., 158, 242
Gretchen Inn, 238
Grewe Architectural & Engineering Services, Inc., 26
Griese & Weile, 224
Griesedieck, Anton, 222
Groves, Albert B., 29, 59, 63, 71, 73, 85, 108, 115-116, 144, 169, 187, 225, 250
Gruen, William H., 220
Guggenheim, Charles, 9
Gunn, Walter, 88
Gurney, James, 242
Haas, Richard, 64-65

Hadley-Dean Glass Building, 13, 48-49
Hager, C., & Sons Hinge Company, 189
Hall, Ralph Cole, 140
Hamilton-Brown Shoe Company, 47, 60
Hardy, Holzman & Pfeiffer, 129
Harmon, Mayor Clarence, 41, 58, 250
Harmon, Robert, 230, 232
Harris, William T., 192, 207
Harris, William T., Row, 192
Harrison, David R., 73, 253
Hastings & Chivetta, 25, 44
Hatch, Stephen D., 30
Hawes, Harry B., 233
Hawley, Steven, 58
Heiss, Charles, 27, 30, 41
Hellmuth, George W., 26, 129
Hellmuth, Obata & Kassabaum (HOK), 16, 70, 122, 229
Henderson/Gantz, 62
Heritage & Urban Design Commission, 249, 253, 256
Hertzinger, Emil, 228
Hess, Henry, 158, 224
Hickory Street District, 192
Hicks, Jeff, 187
Himpler, Franz Georg, 200
Hirsh, William A., 134
Historic American Buildings Survey, 79-81, 85
Historic Restoration, Inc. (HRI), 41, 50
Historical Christ Baptist Church, 158
HNTB, 129
Hoener, Baum & Froese, 34
Hoener, P. John, 34, 55
Holy Corners District, 107
Holy Cross Lutheran Church, 223
Holy Cross Parish District, 166
Holy Trinity Catholic Church, 154
Homer G. Phillips Hospital, 171-173, 188, 200
Hormann, Louis G., 220
Hortus Court, 234
Hotchkiss, Almerin, 178, 218
Hotel Alverne, 21-22
Hotel DeSoto, 22
Humphrey, O. F., 133
Hutcheson Arms, 234
Hyde Park District, 150
Hydraulic Press Brick Company, 103
I-44 Neighborhood District, 239
Icarians, 156, 182
Immaculate Conception School, 224
Inland Architect, 23
Intake Tower #1 and #2, 167-168
International Fur Exchange Building, 16, 25-26
International Institute, 143
International Shoe Company, 71-74
Isaacs, Henry, 139
Ittner, William B., 31, 34, 54, 56, 77, 118, 131, 135, 138, 153, 155, 157, 166, 169, 172, 174, 176, 196, 224, 227, 230-231, 235, 244

Index

Ives, Halsey Cooley, 127
Jackson School, 153, 155
Jacoby Art Glass, 30
Jamieson & Spearl, 57, 139, 157
Janssen, Ernst C., 219, 222
Jefferson Memorial Building, 122-123
Jefferson National Expansion Memorial Association, 5
Jefferson National Expansion Site, 4-5, 10
Jewel Box, 123
Jockenhoefer, Theodore, 230
Joplin, Scott, House, 90-91
Jungenfeld, E., & Company, 147
Kahn, Albert, 90
Kahn, Julius, 73
Kain, Archbishop John L., 101
Karel, John, 244
Kawana, Loichi, 229
Kennard, J., & Sons Carpet Company, 11, 26
Kenrick, Bishop Peter Richard, 6, 197
Kern, Maximilian G., 190
Kerry Patch, 148, 161
Kessler, George, 98
Kiel, Mayor Henry W., 41, 61, 226
Kiel Opera House, 60-61
Kiewitt, Gustel, 223
King, Martin Luther, Jr., 93, 120
King, Martin Luther, Jr., Bridge, 8, 10
Kingsbury Place, 99, 110
Kirchner, August, 149, 230
Kirchner, H. William, 18, 148, 230
Kirsch, Robert G., 234
Kledus, Louis, 148
Klipstein & Rathmann, 25, 37, 73, 133, 182, 238
Knell, Albert, 143, 147
Knickerbocker Lofts, 74
Koplar, Sam, 102
Kramer, Gerhardt, 53, 185, 189, 204
Kulage House, 168
l'Ecole des Beaux Arts, 15
La Plante & Associates, 40
LaBeaume & Klein, 29, 60, 93, 114, 250
LaBeaume, Louis, 127
Laclede Gas, 11, 27
Laclede's Landing District, 8-9
Laclede's Landing Redevelopment Corporation, 10
Lafayette Park Presbyterian Church, 93
Lafayette Square District, 189-190
Lafayette Square Restoration Committee, 191
Lamb, Charles, 248
Lambert-Deacon-Hull Printing Company Building, 67
Lambert Pharmaceutical Building, 62
Lambskin Temple, 213, 225
Lammert Building, 48
Land Reutilization Authority (LRA), 188
Landberg, Kurt, 86, 114
Landmarks Association, 23, 35, 38, 40, 43, 153, 185, 189, 193, 195, 204, 250, 256

Landmarks & Urban Design Commission, 248, 250
Lansburgh, G. Albert, 15
Lark, John, & Associates, 222
LaSalle Park Multiple Resource Area, 193
Lashly & Baer Law Office, 32
Laveille, Joseph, 6
Lawrence Group Architects, 31
"Leda and the Swan," 237
Ledlie, Charles H., 12
Lee, Francis D., 32
Lee & Rush, 131
Legg, Jerome B., 54
Lemp Brewery Complex, 186-187
Lennox Hotel, 27-28
Lentelli, Leo, 15
Leonardo Apartments, 124
Lesan-Gould Building, 71, 73
Levy, Will, 115, 135-136, 254
Lewis Place District, 124
Liggett, John E., 50, 62
Liggett & Myers Tobacco Company Building, 62
Liguest, Pierre Laclede, 6
Lincoln Trust Building, 251-252
Lindell Real Estate Company Building, 48
Link & Cameron, 69
Link & Rosenheim, 131
Link, Theodore C., 56, 69, 73, 107, 114, 141, 199, 217, 234
Linnaean House, 228
Lionberger House, 18, 84-85
Lippman, Michael, 54
Lister Building, 124-125
Listerine, 62
Lloyd, Patricia E., 226
Loews State Theatre, 248
Loftworks, 29
Loretto Academy, 227
Lotz, Father Peter, 231
Louderman Building, 29
Louisiana Purchase Exposition, 26, 30, 60, 64, 98-99, 109
Lucas Avenue Industrial District, 62
Lucas Park Lofts, 74
Lucas Place, 53, 57, 114, 137, 218
Lucas, J. B., 8
Ludwig-Aeolian Building, 18
Luther, Ely Smith, 5
Luyties Homeopathic Pharmacy Company Building, 125
Lyle Mansion, 208
Lynch, J. Hal, 66, 165
Lyon, Brigadier General Nathaniel, 197
MacDonald, Robert E., 9
Mackey & Associates, 27, 29, 32, 48, 69, 102, 229
Mackey Mitchell Architects, 118
Magic Chef, 64, 222
Magnolia Place, 234
Majestic Hotel, 29

Majestic Manufacturing Company, 62-63
Mallinckrodt Building, 45
Mallinckrodt, Emil, 150
Mann, George G., 58
Mann, John, 136
Mann School, 227
Mardirosian, Aram, 5
Maritz, Raymond E., 88
Maritz, William, 10
Maritz & Young, 18, 132, 144
Mark Twain Hotel, 29
Markham Memorial Presbyterian Church, 194
Marquette Building, 19
Marquette Hotel, 252
Marshall School, 172
Marx & Jones, 116
Maryland Hotel, 29
Mason, David, & Associates, 119
Masonic Temple, 85, 225
Matthews & Clark, 24
Mauran, John, 136-137
Mauran, Russell & Crowell, 27, 39-41, 48, 50, 113
Mauran, Russell, Crowell & Mullgardt, 39
Mauran, Russell & Garden, 11, 21, 48, 55-56, 71, 73, 108-109, 116, 135, 137-139, 229, 260
Maurice, John H., 93, 191
Maybeck, Bernard, 169
Mayer of Munich, 89
Mayfair Hotel, 29
McArdle, Montrose P., 103
McCormack Baron & Associates, 24, 147-148
McCue, George, 64
McElroy-Sloan Shoe Company, 62
McGinnis, Walsh & Sullivan, 101
McGowan Brothers, 74
McKay, Stan, 116
McKinley Classical Junior Academy, 196
McKinley Fox District, 196
McMahon, William P., 133, 175
McNamara, James H., 119
McNamee, Father Maurice B., 83
McPheeters St. Louis Cold Storage Company, 11
McRee Town, 239
Mead-McClellan, 236
Means, Mary C., 250
Medler, Frederick, 92
Meet Me in St. Louis, 126
"Meeting of the Waters," 62, 64, 66
Memorial Home, 165, 233, 236
Memorial Presbyterian Church, 144, 194
Mendelsohn, Erich, 127
Menke, Captain J. William, 261
Mercantile Bank, 151, 249
Mercantile Library Collection, 261
Merchandise Mart, 50
Merchants'-Laclede Building, 30-31
Metropolitan Design & Building, 37

"Mexican Hat Factory', 200
Meyer-Bannerman Building, 32
Midtown District, 77
Midtown Medical Center Redevelopment Corporation, 238
Mill Creek Valley, 25, 174
Miller, H. C., 169
Miller, John F., 64
Miller, L. Cass, 30
Miller, Mayor Victor, 87
Milles, Carl, 62, 64, 229, 232
Milligan, Rockwell M., 131, 220, 230
Mills, William H., 144
Milner Hotel, 252
Miltenberger, Eugene and Mary, House, 227
Minerva Place Apartments, 169
Minor, Mrs. Virginia Louisa, 8
Mississippi Lofts, 193
Mississippi Valley Trust Building, 30
Missouri Athletic Club, 26, 30-32, 39, 231
Missouri Botanical Garden, 228-229, 236, 240, 242
Missouri Historical Society, 144
Mitchell & Giurgola, 44
Mitchell, Robert S., 6
Moloney Electric Company Building, 197
Moohlah Temple, cover, back cover
Moore-Ruble-Yudell, 129
Morgan, Mary Kimball, 169
Morton & Laveille, 197
Morton, George, 6
Most Worshipful Prince Hall Grand Lodge #2, 253
Mount Cabanne/Raymond Place District, 125
Mount Olive Lutheran Church, 235
Mount Pleasant School, 230
Mowbray, F. W., 69
Mullanphy, Bryan, School, 235
Mullanphy District, 156
Mullanphy, Eliza, 149
Mullanphy Emigrant Home, 156
Mullett, Alfred Bult, 35
Municipal Opera ("Muny"), 16, 18
Murphy/Blair, 156-157
Murphy & Mackey, 6, 66, 129, 229-230
Museum of Fine Arts, 40, 137
Museum of Westward Expansion, 5
Mutual Bank Building, 32-33
Myers, George S., 50
Nagel, Charles, 129, 232
Nagel & Dunn, 57, 144, 232
"Naked Truth," 64, 220-221
Nance, Reverend John E., 93
National American Woman Suffrage Association, 20
National Trust for Historic Preservation, 23, 250
Negro Masonic Lodge, 253
Neighborhood Association, 34
Neighborhood Gardens Apartments, 34, 37
New Cathedral, 6, 101

Index

Niehaus, Charles H., 98
1904 World's Fair, 8-9, 12, 58, 63, 69, 89, 98-99, 109, 121-122, 127, 131, 144, 147-148, 167, 196, 200, 252, 257
Nitkiewicz, Walter J., 9
Nolte, Edward F., 121, 127, 133, 225
Nolte & Nauman, 144
Nord St. Louis Bundeschor, 156
Nord St. Louis Turnverein, 151
North Presbyterian Church, 160
North Riverfront Industrial District, 10-11
O'Meara & Hills, 166
Oakherst Place Concrete Block District, 126-127
Obata Design, 194
Old Cathedral, 5-6, 65, 197
Old Courthouse, 1, 5-9, 148
Old May Company Department Store, 31-32
Old North St. Louis District, 156-157
Old Post Office, 16, 20, 35, 37
Old Rock House, 5
Olive Street Terra Cotta District, 37, 247, 254
Olmstead, Frederick Law, 178
Olszewski, Michael, 161
Olympia Apartments, 253
Oppenheimer Properties, 69
Orpheum Circuit, 15, 87
Orpheum Theatre, 30, 41
Osburg, Albert, 157, 173, 177, 200
Otis Elevator, 53
Otzenberger, Joseph, House, 201, 205
Overby, Osmund, 70, 129
Owen Development, 83, 129
Page Boulevard Police Station, 254
Page-Park YMCA Gymnasium, 169
Palace of Fine Arts, 127
Pantheon Corporation, 27, 132, 188
Parkview District, 117, 131, 133-134
Parkview Place, 131, 133
Parrish Temple Christian Methodist Episcopal Church, 136
Patty, Berkebile, Nelson Associates, 35
Peabody & Stearns, 21, 40, 69, 137, 199, 259
Peabody, Stearns & Furber, 40, 69, 199
"Peace & Vigilance," 35
Peck, Charles H., 229
Peckham, Guyton, Albers & Viets, 48
Pegram, George H., 70
Pelican's Restaurant, 222
Pendleton, Louis B., 133
Penney, James Cash, 64
Penney, J. C., Company Warehouse Building, 64
People's Hospital, 66
Perry County, Missouri, 223
Peters Shoe Company, 74
Peterson, Charles E., 9
Pfeifer, Clara, 110
Phipps-Wallace Store Building, 37
Piety Hill, 107, 139, 227

Pilgrim Congregational Church, 139-140
Pillar Place, 227
Piper Palm House, 244
Piquenard, Albert, 156
Pitcher, Henry, 185
Pitzman, Julius, 110, 131, 133, 218
Plaza Commission, 60
Plaza Hotel Complex, 91, 260
Plaza Square Apartments, 55
Pope, J. Bradley, 195
Poro College, 171, 174
Porter, E. F., Jr., 9, 138
Portfolio Gallery & Education Center, 82
Portland Place, 111-113, 125, 199
Post Office Annex: Union Station, 69
Powell, Mary, 32
Powell Symphony Hall, 79, 87
Prag, Severin, 217
Precious Blood Sisters, 223
Preetorius, Emil, 221
Preisler, Ernst, 207
Preston, Dale and Gwyn, 238
Price, Bruce, 69
Principia (The), 169
Proetz, Victor, 140
Providence Education Center, 231
Pruitt-Igoe Public Housing, 161
Public Art in St. Louis, 32
Public Works Administration (PWA), 34, 177
Pulitzer Foundation for the Arts, 83
Purcell, Thomas, 10
Quick Meal Stove Company, 222
Quinn Chapel A. M. E. Church, 208
Racquet Club, 108-109
Raeder, Coffin & Crocker, 19
Raeder, Frederic W., 190, 207
Raeder Place, 10
Railway Exchange Building, 32, 48
Ralston Purina, 73, 193
Ramsey, Charles K., 42-43, 142, 178, 255
Rapp, C. W. and George L., 87, 248
Raven, Dr. Peter, 229
Real Estate Exchange, 98, 170
"Real Estate Row," 251
Recht, Bessie, 47
Red Water Tower, 153
Regional Arts Commission, 10, 133
Reinhardt, Siegfried, 107
Renaissance St. Louis Grand Hotel, 40
Renaissance St. Louis Suites Hotel, 27
Resurrection Catholic Church, 230-231
Rice-Stix Building, 50
Ridington, A. Blair, 121, 127
Rivoli Theatre, 255
Roach, H. E., & Son, 47
Roach, Harry, 19, 29, 39
Roach, Henry E., 62

Roberts, Johnson & Rand Shoe Co., 191, 193
"Rock House," 208
Rock Spring School, 231
Rookwood Pottery, 182
Rollin, J., 115
Rosati, Bishop Joseph, 6
Rosebud Café, 90-91
Rosenheim, Alfred, 37
Ross & Baruzzini, 27
Roth & Study, 133, 168
Rouse Company, 69
Rudman Building, 74
Rüedell & Odenthal, 101, 167
Ruhl, Reverend Matt, 175
Rumbold, William, 6
Saarinen, Eero, 5, 9
Sacred Heart Catholic Church, 255
Saint Louis Ambassadors, 119
Saint Louis Art Museum, 67, 127-129
Saint Louis Brewery and Tap Room, 67
Saint Louis Design Alliance, 133
Saint Louis Design Center, 39-40
SS. Cyril & Methodius Church, 158
SS. Peter & Paul Parish Complex, 200, 224
St. Alphonsus Liguori (Rock Church), 89
St. Augustine's Roman Catholic Church, 158
St. Boniface District, 208, 211
St. Elizabeth Academy, 223
St. Francis de Sales Parish Complex, 231
St. Francis Xavier "College Church," 86
St. John the Apostle & Evangelist Catholic Church, 65
St. John Nepomuk Parish District, 194
St. John's Episcopal Church, 190
St. John's United Methodist Church, 106-107
St. Joseph's Catholic Church, 37-38
St. Liborius Parish District, 160
St. Louis Architectural Club, 258
St. Louis Arsenal District, 197
St. Louis Artists' Guild, 137
St. Louis Bank Building & Equipment Company, 226
St. Louis Black Repertory Company, 82
St. Louis Club, 77, 88
St. Louis Colored Orphans Home, 174
St. Louis Development Corporation, 249
St. Louis Ethical Society, 88
St. Louis & Iron Mountain Railroad, 203, 208
St. Louis Portland Cement Company, 121
St. Louis Post-Dispatch Building, 38
St. Louis Post-Dispatch Printing Building, 39
St. Louis Provident Association Building, 66
St. Louis Provident Society, 136
St. Louis Symphony Orchestra, 53, 61, 87
St. Louis Theatre, 61, 79, 87, 248
St. Louis University, 37, 45, 77, 79, 83, 85-86, 88, 197, 250, 253, 260
St. Louis University Museum of Art, 88
St. Louis Urban League, 98

St. Margaret of Scotland Catholic Church, 235
St. Mark's Episcopal Church, 232
St. Mary of Victories Parish Complex, 197
St. Matthew's Parish Complex, 174
St. Michael the Archangel Russian Orthodox Church, 196
St. Paul's English Evangelical Lutheran Church, 225
St. Peter's Lutheran Church, 225
St. Philomena School and Orphanage, 247
St. Roch's Church, 130-131
St. Stanislaus Kostka Church, 161
St. Stephen's Hungarian Parish, 197
St. Vincent de Paul Church, 195
Saler, Franz, 195
Sanger, George, 176
Sanitol Chemical Company Building, 129
Sauer, Lou, 229
Saum Architects, 133
Saum Hotel, 234
Sayman, T. M., Company, 62
Schickel, William, 160, 230
Schlafly, Daniel L., Jr., 250
Schlafly, Tom, 67
Schlichtig, Charles, House, 204
Schmid, Craig, 226
Schmitt, Anton, House, 210
Schmitt, Conrad Studios, 70
Schoemehl, Mayor Vincent C., 23, 256
Schollmeyer Building, 187
Schopp & Bauman, 102
Schrader & Conradi, 90, 147
Schuchard, Pat, 32
Schurz, Carl, 221
Scientific American, 23
Scott, Anna Lee, 93
Scott, Dred and Harriett, 8
Scruggs-Vandervoort-Barney, 19
Scruggs-Vandervoort-Barney Warehouse, 39
Sculpture City: St. Louis, 64
Second Baptist Church, 109, 178
Second Presbyterian Church, cover, 114
Security Building, 40
Seibertz, Engelbert, 231
Serbian Eastern Orthodox Church, 196
Serra, Richard, 83
"705 Olive" Building, 42
Seventh District Police Station, 233
Shank, Isadore, 100
Shapiro, Benjamin, 107
Shaw, Henry, 221, 228-229, 233, 236, 242
Shaw, Henry, Country House, 229
Shaw, Henry, Townhouse, 229
Shaw Neighborhood District, 233
Shaw Neighborhood Improvement Association, 235
Shaw Place District, 236
Sheldon Memorial, 82, 88
Shelley House, 169-170, 172

Index

Shelley vs. Kraemer, 170
Shepley, George, 18, 84
Shepley, Rutan & Coolidge, 18, 21, 57, 69, 71, 85, 114
Sheraton St. Louis City Center, 64
Sherer, Samuel L., 62, 67
Shining Light Tabernacle Church, 238
Shrine of St. Joseph, 34, 37
Silk Exchange Building, 258
Simmons Colored School, 175
Simmons Hardware Company, 92
Simmons Middle School, 175
Simon, Ray, 184
Singleton, Henry, 6
Sisters of Loretto, 224, 227
Sisters of Notre Dame, 160
Sisters of St. Joseph of Carondelet Convent, 211
SJI Companies, 74
Skinker-DeBaliviere, 131-132
Skinker-DeBaliviere Community Council, 132
Skouras Brothers, 248
Smith Academy & Manual Training School, 139
Smith & Entzeroth, 129
Smith, James R., 254
Soldan High School, 138
Sommer House Restaurant, 66
Soulard District, 198
Soulard, Julia, 200
Soulard Market, 200
South Broadway Bluff Area, 212
South St. Louis Square, 208, 210
South Side National Bank, 226
Southwestern Mercantile Association, 183
Spiering, Louis C., 88, 137
Spirtas Wrecking, 249
Spitz, Rabbi Moritz, 235
Sporting News, 59
SRT Architects/Planners, 109, 200
Stanowski, Father Urban, 161
Starrett Brothers, 64
Statler Hotel, 20, 40
Stauder, Joseph, 155
Steffens, Lincoln, 251
Steinmeyer, Theodore, 225, 235
Steins, Jacob, House, 204
Steins Street District, 205
Steins Street Row Houses, 211
Stephens & Pearson, 133
Stewart, James & Company, 69
Stix, Baer & Fuller, 53
Stockstrom, Charles, House, 222
Stockton, Robert H., House, 92
Stolar, Mary, 99
Store Buildings at 7121-29 South Broadway, 212
Stork Inn, 217, 238
Stowe Teachers' College, 171, 176-177
Strassberger Conservatory, 222
Strauss, Leon and Mary, 83, 84

Struthers, William, 35
Study & Farrar, 144
Stupp Brothers, 217
Sugarloaf Mound, 238
Sullivan, Louis, ii, 42-43, 47
Summers, Meade, Jr., 43
Sumner High School, 170, 176-177
Swasey, W. Albert, 103
Swift Printing, 62
Switzer, Henry, 86
Syndicate Trust Building, 19-20, 39
Tandy Community Center, 171, 177
Tao, Peter, 11
Taxis & Becker, 64
Taxis, Fred C., 16
Taylor, Isaac, 11, 26, 47-48, 50, 60, 62, 74, 122, 224, 237, 258
Team Four Architects, 30
Temple Apartments, 225, 235-236
Temple Israel, 81, 106-107, 235
1015 Washington Building, 48
Terminal Railroad Association, 5, 67, 69
Third Baptist Church, 80, 93
1300 Washington Avenue, 74
Thomas, Mayor James S., 221
Tiffany, Louis Comfort, 83
Tiffany Neighborhood District, 238-239
Title Guaranty Building, 251
Torno, L. J., Jr., & Associates, 189
Torrini, Rudolph, 120
Tower Grove Heights District, 240-242
Tower Grove Methodist Episcopal Church, 224
Tower Grove Park, 221, 236, 240, 242, 244
Tower Village Nursing Care Center, 166
Towne Theatre, 255
Trampe, Steve, 83
Trigen Energy Corporation, 12
Trinity Lutheran Church, 223
Trivers Associates, 24, 29, 50, 83, 147-148, 169, 211
Trova, Ernest, 32
Trueblood, Wilbur, 107
Tuholske, Dr. Herman, 124
Tully & Clark, 57
Tunica, Francis, 242-243
Turner Building, 21, 40
Turner, Charles, Open Air School, 177
Turner Middle School Branch, 177
Turnverein, 150-151, 183, 194
Tuscan Temple, 108
Twain, Mark, 29, 148, 153
2327-35 Rutger Street, 193
Tyler, Mary L., 233
Tyler Place, 219, 234-235
Uhrig, Ignatz, 211
Underground Railroad, 185
Union Avenue Christian Church, 115
Union Electric Light & Power Company, 12